Henry Rogers

The Superhuman Origin of the Bible Inferred from Itself

Henry Rogers

The Superhuman Origin of the Bible Inferred from Itself

ISBN/EAN: 9783744660556

Printed in Europe, USA, Canada, Australia, Japan

Cover: Foto ©Thomas Meinert / pixelio.de

More available books at **www.hansebooks.com**

THE SUPERHUMAN ORIGIN OF THE BIBLE.

THE SUPERHUMAN ORIGIN OF THE BIBLE

INFERRED FROM ITSELF.

THE CONGREGATIONAL UNION LECTURE FOR 1873.

BY

HENRY ROGERS.

SEVENTH EDITION.

𝕷𝖔𝖓𝖉𝖔𝖓:

HODDER AND STOUGHTON,

27, PATERNOSTER ROW.

MDCCCLXXXV.

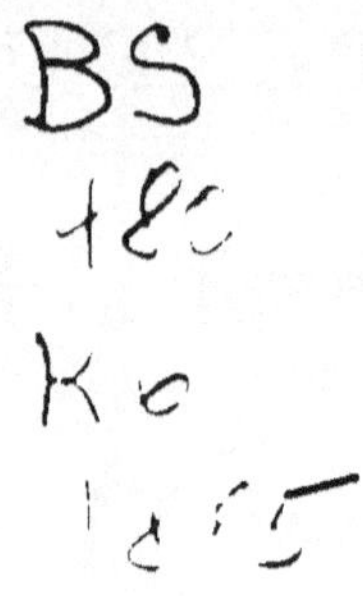

UNWIN BROTHERS, THE GRESHAM PRESS, CHILWORTH AND LONDON.

ADVERTISEMENT

By the Committee of the Congregational Union of England and Wales.

———◆———

THE Congregational Union Lecture has been established with a view to the promotion of Biblical Science and Theological and Ecclesiastical Literature.

It is intended that each Lecture shall consist of a course of Prelections, delivered at the Memorial Hall, but when the convenience of the Lecturer shall so require, the oral delivery will be dispensed with.

The Committee hope that the Lecture will be maintained in an unbroken Annual Series; but they promise to continue it only so long as it seems to be efficiently serving the end for which it has been established, or as they may have the necessary funds at their disposal.

For the opinions advanced in any of the Lectures, the Lecturer alone will be responsible.

18, South Street, Finsbury,
January, 1874.

PREFACE.

I REGRET that so long an interval should have elapsed between the first announcement of these Lectures and their publication ; and I owe my thanks to the Committee of the Union for their patience in waiting for them. But I can hardly charge myself with any fault. The results of a very serious accident, and frequent and prolonged interruptions to health, prevented my touching my task for nearly two years after it was first proposed to me.

These things, together with a feebleness of voice, which made me doubt whether it would not be scant courtesy to the public to allow an audience to be invited to hear what might, in great part, be inaudible, led me to shrink from all thought of oral delivery. This deviation from the usual course, however, is perhaps greater in appearance than reality ; since it rarely happens that more than portions of a series of Lectures of this kind can be given in the time to which the speaker must necessarily restrict himself. They are in general largely supplemented and expanded before publication.

As the Lectures were not to be delivered, I naturally paid less attention than I should have done to those minute proprieties which, I am well aware, ordinarily distinguish spoken from written composition. I have also taken advantage of the same circumstance to determine the length of each Lecture, rather by the nature of the subject than by the Lecturer's hour-glass.

It is often a valuable and interesting feature of volumes of this class (at least it is so in my estimation), that they contain a large supplement of references and citations, for the illustration or corroboration of the Lecturer's positions. In conformity with this time-honoured practice, I also had designed a compilation of passages for the same purpose; but I soon found that the extent of my subject would leave me little space for them, and I have contented myself with throwing a few of my materials into the form of foot-notes. The Appendix to the present volume is simply intended to elucidate some of the points which I could not fully treat in the Lectures themselves.

It may be proper to inform the reader that, in some few places, I have extracted two or three sentences, and in one case several paragraphs, from anonymous and fugitive articles which I wrote some years ago, and which I have no intention to republish. Should the reader recognise any such passages, he will be kind enough to absolve me from the charge of plagiarism.

In the seventh Lecture there are one or two thoughts so like one or two in Professor Leathes' little volume "On the Structure of the Old Testament," that if his book had been published some years ago, and I had read it then, I should surmise that in these cases my memory had unconsciously suggested what it could no longer trace to its source. But as my manuscript was finished many months before the publication of his volume, and was even in the printer's hands before I saw it, I hope that any coincidence (which is purely accidental) may be regarded as some presumption that our views, so far as they agree, are founded on truth.

PENNAL TOWER, MACHYNLLETH,
 December 8th, 1874.

ADVERTISEMENT TO THE SECOND EDITION.

IN this edition, some few verbal errors which had escaped my pen have been carefully corrected. I may also take the opportunity of saying that an intelligent and courteous correspondent, who conceals his name, reminds me that the passage attributed in Lecture VIII. to Sir Thomas Browne, though extracted from Wilkin's accurate edition of his Works (vol. iv. p. 276), where it is given as part of an " unpublished paper" found in the British Museum, is not genuine, the "fragment" having been composed by a very skilful mimic of Sir Thomas Browne's style and manner. The imitation is, indeed, so perfect, that except for the confession of its author it would have continued to impose, as it has often imposed, on the most discerning readers. If *not* Sir Thomas Browne's those who are familiar with his writings would say it deserves to be.

I see that one of my friendly critics has expressed surprise that greater prominence has not been given to the argument derived from the spiritual and moral influence the Scriptures exert, and which, to *Christians in general*, is so principal a reason for believing them to be of superhuman origin. I do indeed believe with him, that to Christians this is, as I have said in the book itself, "the evidence of evidences." But it implies, if admitted, that he who admits it already concedes the conclusion which these Lectures are designed to establish ; while to those who do not, it can only partially, and within certain limits, be insisted on. But in Appendix No. VII. (which may possibly have escaped the notice of my critic) I have touched on the argument itself, its value to those who accept the Bible as of superhuman origin, and the mode and degree in which alone it can be logically valid with those who doubt or deny it. For the reasons just stated, I have purposely treated this matter briefly, and thrown it into the Appendix.

May 13th, 1874.

ADVERTISEMENT TO THE FIFTH EDITION.

THE only difference between this and the previous edition in octavo, consists in a few verbal corrections and alterations, and to or three slight additions.

April 20th, 1877.

CONTENTS.

LECTURE I.

LECTURE VI.

LECTURE VII.

LECTURE VIII.

LECTURE IX.

LECTURE I.

CERTAIN TRAITS OF THE BIBLE VIEWED IN RELATION TO HUMAN NATURE

LECTURE I.

AN argument, of no mean force, for the superhuman origin
of the Bible, may, I conceive, be fairly founded on the
difficulty of accounting for such a phenomenon by referring it
to purely human forces. Human nature in general, as exhibited
in the course of the world's religious history, or again, as
specially conditioned in that people who composed the Bible
and transmitted it to us, seems to me, in many respects, equally
incapable of producing such a book, and unlikely to attempt it.

There will of course be certain generic resemblances among
the professed Revelations which have met with any notable
acceptance among mankind, and for this it is not difficult to
account. They *must* appeal with more or less precision to
those religious principles and instincts which an experience, far
too uniform to be the result of accident, proves to be ineradic-
ably implanted in human nature. That uniformity has prevailed
long and far enough to show, if there be any force in induction
at all, that even if there be no God, men will yet have One, or
even many—rather than be destitute of a God altogether. If,
therefore, professed Revelations successfully appeal to men's
religious nature, it may be expected that there will be points in
which they will *osculate.* Otherwise, it is hard to see how any
one of them, wholly destitute of such points, should have any
chance of success at all. The counterfeit must have some resemblance to the genuine, else it would impose on nobody: it is
precisely this element which makes it dangerous, and it is dan-

gerous in proportion as it possesses it. As Bishop Hampden well observes in his " Essay on the Philosophical Evidence of Christianity :" " Without some conformity with experience, it seems impossible that any religion could obtain even a temporary currency in the world. A system of unmixed absurdity, which recoiled from all contact with the reality of human life, would carry too palpable a refutation of itself on its own front, to be received and embraced to any extent among mankind. . . . Thus we find, even in those superstitions which are most revolting to common sense, some countervailing truths which have both softened and recommended the associated mass of error, otherwise too grossly repulsive for the heart of man ever to have admitted." [1]

Whatever analogies, therefore, may be detected in diverse systems of professed Revelation, we cannot from these alone justly determine the pretensions of any ; for the true, granting for argument's sake one of them to be so, will have analogies with the false, and the false with it. As little can it be hence inferred (though it too often has been) that all Revelations having such analogies are equal, or nearly equal, in their claims on human adoption and respect. To determine this, it is necessary, not only to examine the points of analogy between different Revelations, but to note the points of contrast — the points which are exclusively characteristic of each.

Reading the Bible with this view, I seem to see, unless it be a strange delusion, a multitude of traits, which prevent my accounting for it, as I can for other professed sacred books, by a reference to the known properties and forces which exist in our nature. There are many points in which it seems altogether *out* of analogy with that nature in general, and contradictory to all its prevailing tendencies as exhibited in human history ; and many other traits which could never have been anticipated from the condition of those who composed the book. On the other hand, if in many points it appears at variance with what man

[1] Pp. 132, 133. London, 1827.

would or could have projected, it seems, in many of these very points, in unison with the works and ways of God, as disclosed in " the constitution and course of nature." Again ; if the indications of *unity* about the book, in spite of its being the work of so many writers, separated by such wide intervals of time and space, be not mere fancy, it is impossible to refer them to human contrivance, and almost as impossible to refer them to chance. Further, the manifold unique peculiarities of structure, matter, and style, which, whatever its general resemblance to other books, palpably discriminate the Bible from them all, and the altogether exceptional position and influence which these peculiarities have given it, and still give it in the world, make one at least suspect that more than the hand of man has had to do with its origination. These and many other arguments, the force of which must, of course, depend on the details and illustrations given in the subsequent lectures, have long compelled me to feel the truth of both parts of the following thesis :—*That the Bible is not such a book as man would have made, if he could; or could have made, if he would.*

Nor would it be a sufficient reply, that there may be isolated facts in the doctrine or history of other religious systems, which seem eccentric deviations from the *ordinary* course of human experience, though not absolutely incompatible with it. This is doubtless true ; but it is on the degree, the startling character, and the number of such deviations, that the present argument is founded. It is on the *tout ensemble*, rather than any one or even several of its elements, that its force depends.

One thing more in justice to my theme. I do not pretend to have exhausted it ; I have but touched a few topics under each head, and have no doubt that minds of greater compass and knowledge than mine may indefinitely enlarge them. Nor, whether the argument is strong or otherwise, does it in any way interfere with those other, and doubtless more weighty and direct arguments, on which the claims of the Bible have been usually vindicated.

This, in justice to my theme. In justice to myself, I would say that these lectures are not controversial. I simply speak of the impression which certain features of the Bible have made upon me, and state the reasons of it. If any think it a delusion, I have no right to complain that he does not see with my eyes; but I shall feel amply rewarded for any trouble in writing these lectures, if they should originate or confirm a similar impression in any who may peruse them.

Without further preface, I proceed to enumerate some few of the many traits of Scripture which human nature in general, as known to us by consciousness and experience, would hardly warrant us in expecting, if it be a book of purely human authorship.

1. The inveterate proneness of mankind to idolatry is attested by the nearly universal condition of the world at the earliest dawn of authentic history, through all ages since, and even to the present day. The founders and progenitors of the Jewish nation originally practised it, like the rest of mankind, — as might have been concluded, even if their history had said nothing about it. The facility and obstinacy with which this nation relapsed into it, age after age, in spite of instruction and chastisement, bear witness in like manner to the same proclivity of human nature; while that sure, though gradual process, by which Christianity was at length transformed into something very like the paganism it had supplanted, tells the same tale. One wonders, therefore, by what strange fortuity it is that the Bible, though more varied in its contents than any other book, and composed by different writers living in far distant ages, utters from beginning to end a solitary, but persistent and clamorous protest, against this practice, and everywhere maintains the doctrine of a sublime, elevated, uncompromising *monotheism.* Nor is it an insignificant proof of the tendencies which it opposes, that even these writers for many ages iterated warning and instruction on "ears that would not hear," and

"hearts that would not understand." It is not easy to see how all this came to pass. The tendencies of human nature would seem to be all on one side; the decisive voice of the book,— and of this book alone,—on the other.[1]

Of the lofty character of this monotheism, and the magnificent language and imagery in which the attributes of the One God are expressed, I need say little, because to transcribe the passages which proclaim them, would be to copy many pages of the Bible. The substance of a few will suffice:—" He is God in heaven above, and in earth beneath, there is none else." " His is the greatness, and the power, and the glory, and the victory, and the majesty; for all that is in the heaven and in the earth is His; and He reigneth over all." " He is the high and lofty One, inhabiting eternity, whose name is holy." " Heaven is His throne and earth is His footstool; where is the house" that man " will build for Him, and where the place of His rest?" " The heaven and the heaven of heavens cannot circumscribe Him." " Whither can I go from Thy spirit, or whither shall I flee from Thy presence? If I ascend up to heaven, Thou art there; if I descend to hades, Thou art there; if I take the wings of the morning and dwell in the uttermost parts of the sea, there also Thy hand shall lead me and Thy right hand shall hold me." " The darkness and the light are both alike to Thee." " The heavens shall perish, but Thou shalt endure; they all shall wax old like a garment; as a vesture shalt Thou change them, and they shall be changed; but Thou art the same, and Thy years shall not fail." He is " the King eternal, immortal, invisible, the only wise." He is " infinite in understanding;" He is " able to do

---

[1] It is not necessary to advert to the case of Mahomet. He comes too *late.* He did not *originate* monotheism. His was avowedly an attempt to recall his countrymen to that monotheism of their ancestors from which they had apostatized. That the nation once enlightened in this doctrine had lapsed into idolatry, is (like the similar lapses of the Israelites) a stronger indication of the genuine tendencies of human nature than Mahomet's solitary recovery of the forgotten truth can be of the contrary.

all things;" He knows all things; He foresees all things, "even the end from the beginning;" He "is righteous in all His ways and holy in all His doings."   Though He exercises a dominion absolute and universal, still it is in consonance with infinite beneficence, for "His tender mercies are over all His works;" and though most holy and just, He is "merciful and gracious, slow to anger, and abundant in goodness and truth."   Finally, all the manifestations of Him in His works are yet but inexpressive images of His essential excellence.   However luminous with His glory, they are still but a faint reflection of Himself. They are but a "whisper of Him," according to the strong figure of Job;[1] "but the thunder of His might, who can comprehend?"

Many pages might be filled with a mere enumeration of the passages in which the essential unity and the unlimited perfections of Deity are described with similar unexampled force. Taking them together, there is nothing in the same line with them in the whole range of human literature; nothing as regards grandeur of thought or power of imagery that can be compared with them in any of the casual expressions found in the greatest of heathen poets or philosophers, when they caught momentary glimpses, through the haze of the polytheistic atmosphere about them, of some supreme power which presided over the universe.   We shall in vain search even Homer or Plato for expressions of this nature which will vie in force and sublimity, far less in frequency, copiousness, and *consistency*, with the Scripture representations. They stand alone.[2]

---

[1] Inadequately translated in our version—"These are parts of His ways: but how *little* a portion is heard of him?"

[2] The contrast between the *manner* of ancient philosophy when it lights on anything approaching just conceptions of the Deity, and that of the Scriptures, is as striking as the usual contrast in *matter*.   In the one case, language is cold as philosophic abstraction can make it; that of the Bible is steeped in emotion.   As if to soften and temper that oppressive awe which the needful assertion of the Infinite Majesty must create in us, it everywhere represents Him in vivid sympathy with us, and to enforce this conviction, resorts without scruple to the most familiar images drawn from

Now, considering what human nature had always been, and is still, and not least that *Jewish* human nature which showed so intense a sympathy with the general tendency to idolatry, as to cast a liquorish eye on every wandering form of it that came near them,—it is hard to understand how the Jews came by this curious monopoly of unadulterated monotheism; conserved indeed, not *by* them, but *in spite* of them, by an uninterrupted succession of writers, living in distant ages, one of whose chief functions was perpetually to remind them of what they were perpetually willing to forget!

2. One of the most characteristic and prominent features of the Bible, considered as a whole,—that which runs through it from beginning to end, and which distinguishes it at once from all other books, is that it subordinates everything to the idea of —God. It is not without reason called the Book of God; and *would* be so, in a very intelligible sense, even if it were wholly false, or if there were no God at all. From the first sentence to the last He is the great theme of it, the Alpha and Omega. Infinitely various as are its contents, this is the keynote which runs through the whole. This, considering that it is a book of fragments, written by many different authors in far distant ages, could hardly be expected from *human nature*, whether monotheistic or not. It was not to be expected from human nature, whether the appeal be made to the consciousness of individual man, or to the facts of the religious history of the world. God is here exhibited as exercising an all-pervading moral government over the universe—over the invisible thoughts as well as over the actions of men—and directing

whatever is touching and winning in our own nature. It feels secure (as, I think, Coleridge somewhere expresses it), that though the character and attributes of God are often depicted in Scripture not merely in the sublimest, but the most anthropopathic imagery, the expressions of the spirituality of God are so numerous, perspicuous, and emphatic, that no mind of any candour can for a moment doubt about their meaning. But this is a subject to which I shall return when I come to speak of certain peculiarities of Scripture style.

the whole course of events to the manifestation of His glory and that which is inseparable from it (or, rather, which is identical with it), the felicity of His creatures as involved in the ultimate triumph of a purely moral and spiritual empire. Is man in such sympathy with such objects, judging from human consciousness or from history, as to make this uniform assertion of the paramount claims of God other than a paradox?

We find this exclusive reference to God in the series of Biblical writers; and it is not found elsewhere, not only not among other nations, but not even among the Jews themselves apart from their sacred writers. The Jews, like the rest of the world, had little sympathy with such views, and the iteration of them from age to age in so long a succession of documents was no more than necessary to preserve them from oblivion. The perpetual relapses of the children of Abraham into idolatry, and rebellion against the One God they confessed, show that this tone was no more natural to them than to the rest of the world. They were like the kine that bore back the " Ark " from the land of the Philistines, and who went against their instincts and their inclinations up to Bethshemesh, " lowing as they went," after their calves that had been shut up at home.[1]

[1] This peculiarity of Scripture seems to have particularly struck the mind of the earliest modern Apologist for Christianity, Philip de Mornay, whose work was partly translated into English by Sir Philip Sidney, and at his request completed by Arthur Golding. (London, 1604.) The author has a long and striking section (pp. 393-7) entitled, "The Bible tendeth altogether to the glory of God." It is *unique* among books in this respect, "that it aims at none other mark than the honour of God,—contrary to man's nature." And so impressed was Werenfels with this characteristic of Scripture, and so little able to imagine it the product of human nature, that in his "Meditatio de zelo in Sacrâ Scripturâ ubique conspicuo pro unâ Dei gloriâ," he avows that if there were no other proof of the super-human origin of the Bible, this would convince him. " Subsiste hic, lector, et considera num hæc doctrina quam hic liber ubique urget, quæ animum tuum ab omnibus creaturis abstractum ad Deum dirigit, a creatura sit, an a creatore tuo? Illud si credere potes, monstra si potes, in toto hoc universo, unum tantum ex omnibus omnium gentium et seculorum libris, huic similem: monstra librum cujus unicus ubique scopus sit, tibi ostendere, Deum solum summum esse tuum bonum: de quo tot sapientissimi homines, qui tam

A peculiarity of this book, consequent on its thus subordi-
nating everything, whether in the history of the Jews or of other
nations, to this dominant idea of God, and the claims of His
universal and spiritual government, deserves to be mentioned
here.   There is not only an *unique*, but (looking upon it as the
work of men) an *unnatural* sublimity about it.   The relative
importance of events s eems often inverted.   The book passes
by, or casually notices, most of the things which men regard as
supremely momentous—the rise and fall of empires, the changes
and revolutions which fill great nations with terror or triumph.
These events, which fill the page of ordinary history, it leaves to
be chronicled in other books, or to drop into oblivion.   Touching on an infinity of subjects, dealing with the minutest as well
as most important facts, with the smallest details of private life,
with the fortunes of vast communities; everything, great or
little, is viewed in relation to the government of the Supreme
Ruler, or rather *is* great or little only as it has a bearing on the
development and issues of that invisible spiritual empire which
He is intent on founding and rearing in the world.   In all this
there is something most strange, and, looking at what might be
expected from man, *unnatural*.   The way in which the Bible
treats those themes of history which, in man's estimate, in the
estimate, at least, of each generation that witnesses them, are of
such supreme importance (for though the "Ruins of Empires"
in a measure correct the illusion with respect to the remote
past, they cannot disenchant us of the like illusion in relation
to our own time), is not indeed inhuman, but assuredly *un*-
human.   Of the great political changes which passed over the
ancient world, the Bible is almost as silent and unconcerned as

multa de hoc argumento scripserunt, vix unquam cogitarunt : neque tantum
intellectui tuo hoc ostendere, sed omni nisu cor tuum ad hoc bonum unice
quærendum impellere." (*Opuscula.* 4to, tom. i. p. 107.) In contrasting
the manner of the Bible with that of all other books, and the tone of its
writers with that of all other writers, he has some admirable remarks.
Though there is no proof that he had seen De Mornay's work, he probably
had done so. At all events, the thoughts are often singularly coincident.

sun and stars when they look down upon the tumult and noise of man's battle-fields.   We hear as it were the sound, but it is as the ocean on a distant shore.   The intrigues of courts, the career and achievements of great conquerors, the thrilling events which marked the extinction or transfer of political power and civilization, the great battles which shook the world; in a word, all those things over which the imagination of the ordinary historian lingers with such intense emotion, are touched only as they happen to traverse the religious history of the strange community whose destinies the Bible is tracing, or those ulterior designs of which this people were to be the unconscious instruments to the world.   In brief, all is viewed in relation and subordination to the *religious* ideas which permeate the book.   The fortunes of the nations which surrounded Judæa, as well as those of the Assyrian and Babylonian empires, are cursorily referred to just so far as this ; otherwise the Bible does not deign to notice them at all.   Though the world might be ringing with the achievements of their great captains, and the ground shaking under the tread of their innumerable legions, the writers of this strange book are deaf to it all—all passes before them " silent as a picture ; " or if the Bible condescends to give a transient glance at such things (as it sometimes does, and now and then with touches of surpassing sublimity), it is still only within the limits above mentioned.   As Butler says, " The common affairs of the world, and what is going on in it," are in the estimate of Scripture " a mere scene of distraction."

There are two ways in which an objector might attempt to account for this singular elevation of tone, or this stolid incuriosity, whichever the reader may be pleased to consider it.   A very few words will suffice for each.

It has sometimes been said that those who wrote thus, regarded the Jehovah of the Hebrews as one who did not concern Himself with the fortunes of the world.   The answer is, that they have a thousand times asserted the *contrary*, in the most vivid and emphatic terms.   It can be from no thought of limiting His prerogatives that they have thus spoken. He is, they tell us, " the Judge of all the earth ; " that " He removeth kings and setteth up kings ; " that " His is the greatness, and the power and the glory, and the victory and the majesty ; " and that " His dominion is over all things." The language they put into His mouth, when the course of Bible narrative brings it into contact with pagan nations, is in harmony with all this. He is made to say to Pharaoh, " In very deed, for this cause I have set thee up, to show in thee My power, and that My name may be declared through all the earth." " I know," He says to Sennacherib, " thy abode, and thy going out, and thy coming in, and thy rage against Me. I will put My hook in thy nose, and My bridle in thy lips, and I will turn thee back by the way by which thou camest." He says to Cyrus, " I have surnamed thee, though thou hast not known Me ; " and to Nebuchadnezzar, that he is to be chastised till he shall know " that the Most High ruleth in the kingdom of men, and giveth it to whomsoever He will." If any one say, " We do not believe such words were ever thus actually applied, they are fragments of ' myths,' " be it so : it does not concern my present argument to show the contrary. They prove at all events incontestably what were the sentiments of those who wrote them, and that it was not because they thought that Jehovah had abdicated the throne of universal dominion, that they were so incurious about events which in general stir the hearts of men to their very depths, or that they are so frigid where others are all animation.

Others may perhaps suspect that Jewish vanity led the writers thus to ignore or treat lightly the affairs of all nations *except their own.* The answer is concise, but conclusive. Let Jewish vanity in general be what the reader pleases, these writers would seem to have had none of it. If they have passed by the glorious achievements of secular history, they have recorded all the infamies of their own nation ; and, indeed, their principal references to *other* nations are as " scourges " of their own—scourges justly sent, they confess and aver, for apostacies which had wearied out the patience of heaven !

But the same egregious incuriosity or sublime indifference about the *great* events of the world (except in the one point of view already referred to) characterises the writers of the New Testament just as much as those of the Old. They have frequent occasion in the Gospels and the Acts to refer to such events, as traversing or intersecting the plane of their record ; but their allusions are all similarly incidental, and the events of the Roman empire seem to interest them no more than those of Assyria or Babylon did their predecessors.

In point of *philosophy*, indeed, the Scripture writers, however unnatural their seeming lack of sympathy with what the world thinks so supremely important, might plead some apology for their reticence. For the greater part of these "great events" are at last covered, in spite of either secular or sacred chronicle, with ignominious oblivion. As we wander among the "ruins of empires," and in the "desolate places" of history, we are compelled to feel for the most part how evanescent is what is called "immortal glory," and how little worthy or capable of a durable record. As we look on the mounds of mouldering rubbish which were once mighty cities, and see how soon kindly mother earth covers the red battle-fields of her foolish children with her green mantle, we feel that the Bible may be excused for telling us so little (even if it had not other and far higher objects to attend to) about these problematical glories. Yet we must not be ungrateful to the Bible even in this point. Little as it tells us of that more ancient world which preceded Greece and Rome, that little is at present almost all we know about it. Some nations and empires are not forgotten only because it has occasion to mention them.

Thus, in truth, everything is paradoxical about this singular book. It omits much which human historians could not but have dilated upon ; but what it has said is immortal, and has outlived more voluminous records. Of many of the nations—

the Moabites and Ammonites, for example—which were in contact with the Jews, we know almost nothing, except as their fortunes were involved with those of the Jews; and of even Nineveh and Babylon, almost all that was known for many ages was from the same Jewish source. So completely had "their memorials perished with them," that it is only now we are just beginning to reclaim and decipher them. For centuries they were chiefly remembered by the scanty notices in the book which inscribed their epitaph, and which has preserved their name better than their own annals; though its declaration was also true, that they should lie in "utter and perpetual desolation;" that the "wild beast of the desert" and every "doleful creature" should make his abode there; "the cormorant and the bittern lodge in the lintels, and their voice cry in the windows;" that "dragons and owls should dwell in their pleasant palaces," and their very site be a controversy for ages.

On the whole, this peculiar reserve or indifference of the Bible respecting events in the world's history to which man inevitably attaches such moment, is well worthy of note. It is *natural* to us to exaggerate their importance; to think that revolutions which have shaken the world, the rise and fall of empires, are things on which the eyes of the universe ought to be fixed. So notorious is this tendency, that even those who might have learned better from this very book, and from the tone it has everywhere maintained, will often dream that each stirring event which happens in their own time is of sufficient importance to be chronicled in the volume of its prophecies; and all of us are apt to attach to them a permanent importance, altogether disproportionate to what we see to be, for the most part, their effect upon the world,—or even on a small part of it. A few years, and men are compelled to say of the contests of men as of the contests of bees :—

"Hi motus animorum, atque hæc certamina tanta,
  Pulveris exigui jactu, compressa quiescent."

But the Bible writers and these alone seem to have purged their minds from all such sympathies or prejudices: they view the history of the world, so to. speak, from a heliocentric position. They hardly speak "as men;" they are either above us or below us. To them, the greatest events—events which thrill ordinary humanity with hopes and fears—seem, in the presence of the yet greater things with which they are concerned, as little worthy of exciting vivid emotion as the ordinary pomps and gauds of this world will be thought in that day, when, to use the language of a great divine, "crowns and sceptres shall lie about, as neglected things." [1]

3. Another peculiarity in the Bible, which makes the system of religion it propounds unique among the many propounded by men, is the strict subordination of ethics to theology. Its foundations are laid in the idea of God and our relations to Him; its sanctions are derived from His will. This is a peculiarity of the Hebrew system long ago observed by Josephus in his treatise against Apion.

The great commands of the " Second Table," the duties we owe to ourselves or our fellow-men, are here ultimately based on the relations in which all creatures stand to Him who demands our homage in the " First Table." Not that they are represented as the mere expression of arbitrary Will; on the contrary, they are represented as emanating from a Will itself determined by supreme rectitude, wisdom, and goodness; which knows what is "*good*," and enjoins what it enjoins from a perfect knowledge of our nature, and the necessary conditions of our well-being. How much this draft of morality, consistently articulated as it is with the idea of God, differs from that of the heathen nations in general, is obvious enough to any one who has attentively considered their history.

That this *ought* to be the relation of morality and religion, if there be indeed such a God as the Scripture affirms, probably no rational creature would deny. If there be a God who

<hr>

[1] Howe's "Vanity of man, as mortal."

exercises absolute dominion, but with perfect rectitude and goodness—who is cognizant of thoughts as well as actions—who will make equitable allowance for all infirmity, and whom no cunning can blind and no power can resist,—it is fit that all morality should be thus traced to man's relations to Him. If there be no such Being in the universe, even an intelligent atheist might well say, So much the worse for the universe: if there be, then the supremacy assigned to Him is His right. Every loyal subject of such a King will offer implicit homage at His throne; and to every dutiful child of such a Father, every thought of Him will be welcome as a sunbeam to the soul.

It is on this principle that the whole code of Biblical ethics is constructed. On the other hand, that nothing like the strict conjunction and articulation of morality with religion which is found in the sacred volume, is to be found in any other ancient book, much less in a long succession of books of one and the same nation, will hardly be denied. Among the most advanced and polished nations of antiquity, we see not merely defective views of the principles and obligations of morality, but, what is worse, the almost entire isolation of religion from it; not to say that the very religion itself was too often the grand obstacle to all morality! If we look into the most systematic treatises on ethics bequeathed to us by ancient philosophy, those of Aristotle, we find this great genius taking man to pieces, anatomizing his moral nature and principles of action, with the hope thence to find out what course of conduct will best promote his "happiness," secure the "summum bonum,"—that εὐδαιμονία which, truly understood, is indeed the end of life,—and yet forgetting to take God into account at all! On the other hand, the religion of the Greeks and Romans had a very precarious connection with morals, if indeed it can be said in strictness to have had any. The priest who stood at the altar, and the augur who interpreted omens, addressed themselves almost exclusively to the ear and eye of superstition,—to the credulity of a weak, and the terrors of a guilty being. They prophesied good or evil, after groping in the entrails of the sacrifices, or watching the flight of birds, or the direction of the thunder; they instructed their votaries how they might avert the Nemesis of offended invisible powers, or cleanse the conscience of guilt, by sacrificial offerings or ceremonial lustrations; but they did little more. They forgot the indissoluble connection between religion and morality—that complete subordination of the one to the other, of which Josephus justly boasts as found in the code of his own nation. It has been truly said that with Greeks and Romans religion and morality formed two different spheres of duty, and were taught by totally different masters; the latter by philosophers, who for the most part did not care to radicate it in religion; the former by the priests, who did not care to connect it with morality. In the one case, the tree was severed from its principal root, and no wonder that leaves and blossoms alike languished; in the other, the root itself was rotten, and no wonder that it yielded no fruit at all.

The contrast, then, between the views of the world in general and those of the Bible, in relation to this subject, as seen in this and the last section, being so palpable and undeniable, to what shall we attribute the all-pervading characteristic of the latter, as compared with other books and other systems? I imagine, if we look into ourselves—into human nature, and the current of the world's history as illustrating it—we should not *expect* to find, in any human system, such exclusive and paramount deference to the claims of God, or any similar strait alliance, or rather incorporation, of religion and morality. Whatever modified views may be taken of human depravity,—however the graver facts which Scripture seems to affirm may be denied, or whatever abatement may be made from them,—yet the general *facts* of the world's history show that the whole tendency of mankind (that of the Jews themselves quite as much as of the rest of the race) is in revolt against that view of God's supreme and all-controlling authority, and that perpetual obtrusion of His claims, which characterise the Bible. If the conscience of the natural man speak sincerely, I fancy it will echo this; and if it remain dumb, the *history* of mankind will speak only too eloquently to the same effect. The actions of men, and the general transactions of the world, show that the Bible says truly—that man "does not like to retain God in his thoughts;" much less to give Him the supreme place which the Bible assigns Him.

Some in these days may say, perhaps, that it is fanaticism to do so. Be it even so; the fact is all I am now intent upon. I still ask, How is it that we find it the perpetual characteristic of this book alone,—to inculcate doctrines universally distasteful to mankind? We cannot say that the Jews, of themselves, had any more proclivity to this unwelcome fanaticism than any other people. This their history proves but too plainly. Their perverse indocility, and proneness to every form of revolt; their constant apostacies from that very God whose claims and authority they acknowledged to be paramount, seem to demonstrate that, had only human nature spoken in them, it would have spoken to the same effect as human nature everywhere else in the world. The features of the book in this respect are not in *analogy* with human systems, nor with the human nature which dictated them.

4. There are, as appears to me, certain *characteristics* in the morality of the New Testament in violent contrast with what might be expected from human nature, whether we judge by the systems which are its undoubted product, or,—which is perhaps still more significant of its tendencies,—by the nature and direction of the innovations by which it has, from time to time, corrupted the Christian code of morals. The deflection, purely the effect of human nature, shows how little likely was that nature to construct such a morality.

That the morality of the Scriptures generally, but especially of the New Testament, will bear comparison with that of any other moral system ever propounded, probably few will deny. In the truth, justness, and comprehensiveness of its moral principles and precepts, it is at least equal to any other. In one point it is far superior, if, as I have contended, morality ought to be strictly co-ordinated with religion. Again, in the variety and perspicuity of its moral statements; in the weight and compactness with which moral maxims are expressed; in the earnestness and impressiveness with which they are enforced; in the examples and apophthegms by which they are illustrated; above all, in the vivid, emotional character which pervades it, as contrasted with the cold abstractions of mere philosophy, the New Testament will certainly suffer nothing if compared with the best ethical treatises of pagan antiquity.

But it is not my intention to insist upon this, however strange it may seem that *Jews* should have at least rivalled, not to say outdone, the wisest sages and philosophers of Greece and Rome; nor even to inquire how it is that these same Jews, in the New Testament, should have risen above all their national prepossessions, and revised and transcended the ethical spirit of the Old Testament. Both facts might be added to the paradoxes of the Bible I am now considering; but I pass to a greater.

There are some features of that morality, not only "original," as Soame Jenyns and Paley observe, but so palpably in the face of human nature, as to make it difficult to believe (if we appeal to our own consciousness or the testimony of history) that they were the native utterances of human nature at all. *This*, not the "originality" of these features of New Testament morality ("original," though I think them to be), is the point I would now lay stress upon. "Originality" may, or may not, reflect glory on the authors, or convict them of folly or absurdity; their system may be better or worse than other systems, in the points on which it differs from them. This

it is not necessary to my argument to decide, though I have no
doubt about it.   But I am considering whether man—such a
creature as we know him to be generally, or that variety of the
species known as the *Jew*—would ever have propounded a
moral system containing such features at all.   The points more
particularly referred to are those which Soame Jenyns, in his
little book on the "Internal Evidences of Christianity," first
clearly and comprehensively stated, though, of course, some of
them had often attracted notice before.   Paley has given prominence to them in his work on "The Evidences;" and by
referring to them with such emphasis, shows how deeply his
acute mind was impressed with them.   They are chiefly these:
that Christianity canonizes, and takes under its special patronage, some reputed virtues, of which a heathen moralist, and
perhaps many a modern one, would doubt whether they are
virtues at all; or, if virtues, whether, as practised to the extent
and in the spirit which Christianity enjoins, they would not
cease to be such, or even be transformed into vices;—such,
for example, as humility, and the patient endurance and unlimited forgiveness of injuries.   On these, and kindred moral
qualities, which the world never either admired or practised,
it bestows its special benediction.

Again; as little can the world in general sympathise with the
sternness with which the Gospel so absolutely gauges and determines moral turpitude by thought and feeling.   It pronounces
unresisted evil inclinations to be equally guilty with evil actions;
—not so pernicious in their influence on moral habit, it may
be; not so pernicious to others, certainly; nor so deplorable
in their effects on society; but as equally constituting moral
guilt: consequently, that covetousness indulged is "theft;"
lascivious looks, with no attempt to repress them, "adultery;"
malignant hatred, which would fain go forth in act, "murder."
I specify the limitations, because the context in which they
occur—"out of the *heart* proceed evil thoughts"—requires
them; and because, if the incursion of such thoughts and

feelings be met by a resisting will, their moral quality is visibly changed, and the turpitude of the agent with it.

That, in the *first* of these views, there is much "originality," if we compare the Gospel morality with the systems of the generality of ethical speculators, is pretty plain ; and probably few will deny that, in the *second*, the extent and uncompromising thoroughness with which the principle is asserted and the consequences accepted, also constitute originality. But, as already said, this is not the point I wish at present to press ; but rather, are these ("original," or not) the principles and maxims which human nature, whether Jewish or pagan, would have chosen to consecrate? Are the virtues which Christianity specially regards as worthy of all veneration and imitation ; are the *passive* virtues—those of patience, humility, meekness, forgiveness of injuries — the moral excellences which have secured the admiration of the world? Setting aside those virtues in the inculcation of which all systems of ethics, Christian or otherwise, coincide—such as truthfulness and honesty—and to which, however *base* to be without them, no great merit for that very reason is attached, is it not true (as Paley says) that the more brilliant and enterprising qualities—an emulous love of distinction, a quick sense of honour, dauntless courage, promptness to assert our rights and to resent or repel injuries—are not these, and such as are congenial with these—generosity, public spirit, patriotism—the qualities of human nature, which in the world's estimate are the most worthy of applause, and the constituents of that "heroic character" for which it reserves its highest homage? And are not the qualities which Christianity fondly takes under its wing, pitiful or ignoble things— fit only for a man who has "no spirit"?—the attributes of the worm that crawls, not of the soaring eagle? Whether human nature left to itself, whether any individual man left to himself, would ever have propounded such features of a moral system, far less given them such prominence, the pages of moralists and the facts of history must decide. The model heroes of antiquity—those who got statues in the Pantheon, and inspired eloquence and poetry to celebrate them—were of very different clay ; they were of such material as constitutes the μεγαλοψυχία, the "magnanimity," of Aristotle, and breathed the spirit and maxims which animate the world's " codes of honour."

Probably it will be said, " Well ; and has it not often been contended that the degree in which the maxims concerning humility and meekness are pressed in the New Testament is excessive ; that even if deductions be made for the rhetorical language in which they are clothed, they still seem extravagant ; that they have frequently been condemned on that very ground, as inconsistent with the principles of human nature, and therefore impracticable ? "   If this be said, it is the very thing on which I am insisting as certain to be instinctively felt by human nature ; and I *therefore* wonder that, if the system be of human parentage, humanity should thus have belied itself.

" To turn the left cheek to him who hath smitten us on the right, and to let him who hath taken our coat take our cloak also," even when not interpreted with strict literality, but understood to mean that we are to cherish an unresentful spirit even towards those who have most egregiously injured us, are yet expressions so *unnaturally* rhetorical, that it is a puzzle to me that mere human nature should have ever so expressed itself ; or, if it did, how it could hope to be attended to.

Similarly, the *degree* in which moral conduct is determined from the motive, so as to make the guilt complete, though the corresponding action be not performed, is not " after the manner of men " in general.   People very properly make a great *difference* in social morality between a criminal purpose and its execution, even though no internal arrest of conscience, but merely an outward barrier, has prevented it.   But, *in foro conscientiæ*, and in respect of the actual moral condition of the man himself (supposing nothing but an external obstacle has interposed between his purpose and the action), no doubt the principle laid down in Scripture is unassailable.   It is not a principle, however, which human nature would be likely to propound so absolutely or in so marked a form. It would not be *natural*, considering how generally men have been content to speculate on morals in isolation from religion,—which alone can take adequate cognisance of the interior life of man. They have been busied in constructing a *social* morality, such as society may be contented with, and which will work. Man cannot go beyond the *outside* of his fellow-man : and as he *must* leave, so he is willing to leave, the domain of invisible thought and feeling uninvaded. The principle in question would be likely to be uncompromisingly stated and enforced, only in a system propounded under an engrossing sense of the claims of God ; as a Judge cognisant not only of the visible, but of the invisible actions of His moral and accountable creatures, and determining the true position of man to be virtuous or vicious, not as he *appears*, but as he *is*. To that Judge " the darkness and the light are both alike." He sees all that transpires behind the curtain which conceals each man's interior life, as well as the actions which faintly express it to his fellows. This characteristic of Christian morality is therefore in harmony with what has been already said of the Bible, as alone everywhere asserting the pre-eminent claims of God, and of that spiritual empire which He is represented as administering amidst all the apparent confusion and discordance of the moral world. It is in harmony also with such a morality, that Christ lays such infinite stress on the regulation of the thoughts, and enjoins, consequently, a jealous, watchful inspection of the heart. There, on that invisible stage, the moral life of the man is really transacted. If the thoughts and emotions which well up from that hidden fountain be not pure, exact outward rectitude is impossible ; and if it were possible, being only outward, would be of no worth.

As men in general, if we may judge by their ordinary sentiments, or by the treatises of morality which have given expression to them, would not have propounded a system of ethics marked by the peculiar features of the morality of the Gospel, so certainly the *Jews*, but especially the Jews at that epoch, were as little likely to propound it as any. They showed, indeed, distinctly throughout their whole history that they chafed even under the less spiritual yoke of the Mosaic code, and, as time went on, continually corrupted it; till, when the Gospel morality was proclaimed, they are declared to have made the " law of God of none effect by their traditions.' Thus they exaggerated what was ceremonial at the expense of what was moral, or rather substituted the one for the other. So far from dreaming of such a spirit of boundless forgiveness as that inculcated by Christ, they added a gloss to the words, " Thou shalt love thy neighbour," in a clause, unknown to the Pentateuch, "Thou shalt hate thine enemy." They even, in some cases, made the *pretended* service of God a reason for evading the most sacred obligations—as, for example, of filial piety. They reduced the standard of virtue by measuring it too often by external actions ; sometimes went further still, and commuted its appropriate acts for ceremonial observances. All this they did according to the tendencies of *human nature*, which spoke unequivocally in them, and which so little accounts for such a system of morals as that which the Scripture present· whether in the Old Testament or the New, that when it had got it, it immediately proceeded to adulterate it.

Precisely the same thing was done by the Christian world with the New Testament morality. When Christianity was corrupted, human nature proceeded to mould it into the forms most congenial with itself. All the alterations effected in it were accommodations in one and the same direction, and gradually assimilated it to the more compliant schemes of this world's morality. By so acting, by so *uniformly* acting, human nature testifies how little likely it was to originate a system of ethics so much against the grain as that of the Gospel. The current of resisting tendencies was so strong, it seems, that so far from being likely to propound such a system, man could

only corrupt it.   And the cycle of change was ever the same.
Christians, like the Jews, relaxed the claims of conscience ;
abated the supremacy of motive ; thought more of material
acts than of the springs of action ; too often commuted moral
duties for ritual observances or penances of no moral value at
all ; at last discovered strange methods, not only of absolving
from guilt, but of creating merit, if men could but pay for it ;
leased " sin " out to the wealthy bidder, and sold virtue and
heaven by the penny-weight ! '

5. When we consider the entire character of Christ, as the
Founder and Exemplar of this peculiar system of morality—
so foreign from what had issued, or was likely to issue, from
man—we perceive that the difficulty just touched is only one
of a knot of difficulties of the same kind.   What was a single
paradox, in contemplating the morality alone, becomes, as we
contemplate the history and character of Him who propounded
it, a bundle of paradoxes.   The problem is a very complex
one, moral, intellectual, and literary all at once ; and I, for
one, look in vain for the properties of human nature in any
class of mortals which will enable us to solve it.

Taking the *ensemble* of qualities which make up the character of Christ, together with the originality and wonderful
peculiarities of the form in which it is presented, the entire
phenomenon would seem out of the plane of human nature.
Neither in Greek, nor Roman, nor *Jewish* human nature, can
we discover the elements which could have evolved so peculiar
a creation, whether supposed to be real or fictitious ; and in
the Jews, to which the problem historically limits us, as little
as anywhere.   These had none of the conditions under which
such a character, if *real,* could have spontaneously risen among
them as a simple growth of the national genius, culture, or
institutions, or, if *not* real, could have been ideally conceived
as a deliberate fiction, or developed as a gradual aggregation
of myth or legend.   The first is clearly proved by the shock
which such a Messiah gave to all their prejudices, and the

' See Appendix No. I.

vivid indignation He evoked; by their persecution and cruci-fixion of Him; by their incessant hostility to those who espoused His cause; and by their bitter and immovable hatred of Him from that day to this! Eighteen hundred years have not exhausted, or even sensibly abated their pre-judice; and its inveteracy and constancy bear evidence how little such a character was likely to be generated as an actual phenomenon, or conceived as an ideal creation, in a nation thus conditioned.

On the latter hypothesis, that is, that Christ Himself is a mere fiction or myth, the argument is rather strengthened than otherwise. For how should Jews be either able or willing to paint such a portrait, or embody such a myth, the mere exhibition of which has roused the undying animosity of their nation for eighteen hundred years?

Whether the Gospels present to us a *real* or *imaginary* portrait of Christ (and one of the two suppositions must be true), it seems to me, I confess — if regarded simply as a phenomenon which human nature might have produced or human nature could have invented—crowded with the most startling incongruities.

On the *first* supposition—that Jesus Christ was a real per-sonage, but simply a *man*—not a man in the Unitarian sense, preternaturally endowed with Divine gifts, such as made Him a unique ambassador of God to us, and indefinitely higher than any who had exercised any similar function—but a man in the sense which the theory of a purely human origin of Christianity requires; born under those ordinary conditions of humanity which might have given the world many Christs before Him, or may give us many after Him—a man who, whatever His natural endowments (which must, at any rate, have been great, if we only look at the effects He has produced in the world), was still no more; let us examine how, on that hypothesis, such a person is conceivable, or whether the at-tributes hang together.

But the reader perhaps will say, " How about the miracles imputed to Him?"—I presume, of course, if He was a mere man, that they were never wrought.   On the principles on which I am now arguing, as to whether the Bible can be accounted for by simple human forces, I, for argument's sake, reject them.   The theory which attempts to account for their belief on mythical principles, will be briefly considered when we come to look at this wonderful character as a *fancy portrait*. At present, I will suppose the miracles as unreal as any rationalist can desire.[1]

Let us then, for a moment, put the question of the miracles aside, and confine ourselves to the traits in Christ's character which in a certain degree, and taken separately, might be purely human.   But then, as a question of human nature, what shall we say of their heterogeneousness ; and that, heterogeneous as they are, they exist in Him without limit?   It is impossible not to see that in this light, and viewed as a mere man, instead of deserving the homage generally accorded to Him, the character of Christ is a mere bundle of inconsistencies, and tumbles to pieces the moment we analyse it, by the mere force of incongruity.   How shall we reconcile the humility, the modesty, the self-denial, the gentleness, the unresisting submission to wrong, which are so liberally ascribed to Him, or the *prudence*, no less than humility, which made Him decline all opportunities of aggrandisement and all proffers of greatness, with that impious ambition or more than mid-summer madness (in either case insupportable arrogance) which made Him claim to be the vicegerent of God, the arbiter of human destinies, the " Judge of quick and dead ;" to be "invested with all power in heaven and upon earth," and entitled to the absolute homage and implicit obedience of

[1] At the same time, if we suppose the miracles imputed to the *historic* Christ, and with His acquiescence, as M. Rénan and many others imagine, and as seems most certain to have been the case, some additional and very difficult paradoxes disclose themselves.   For a few observations on this subject, see Appendix No. II.

every human creature?   How shall we reconcile that beautiful humility which pointed to a "little child" as the symbol of the simplicity and docility demanded of all who would "enter the kingdom of heaven," and took occasion thence to administer a severe rebuke to the disciples for contending "which should be the greatest;"—how shall we reconcile it, I say, with that enormous egotism which in the very same breath arrogated an immeasurable superiority over them?—which made Him forbid them to call any man "Master," but only because *He* was their Master, and all His followers brethren?—which thus told them that though there might be differences between *them*— some teachers and others scholars—yet all these differences were of no account, and vanished in comparison with that exclusive superiority which *He* claimed?   Again; what mere man can be imagined perfectly to exemplify (as He is represented to have done) his own system of morals, and that, too, a system so peculiar?   Or what man could challenge exemption from all infirmity, and ask, "Which of you convinceth me of sin?" or rather, what other man would not have "sinned" by his presumption in imagining that he could rightfully challenge such immunity?   How, if He were a mere man, shall we reconcile such traits as these with the moral rectitude, the practical wisdom, the self-abnegation, the intellectual greatness, which have fixed the admiring gaze of mankind for near two thousand years?

M. Rénan, indeed, observes that we must not judge of Christ as of other men; "that what would be an insufferable pride in others, ought not in His case to surprise us."   But, as I have elsewhere said, "If Christ be nothing more than a man, we must try Him by the rules of men.   If He indulged in these fantastical claims to universal power, and fantastical demands of unlimited love and self-sacrifice on the part of the whole species; if He insisted on all the world's bowing down to Him in absolute self-abnegation, and all only in virtue of a '*rêve sublime*,' I think there would be very good reason for not only demurring to His claims, but for treating His pretensions with as sovereign scorn or indifference as we should the pretensions of any straw-crowned monarch of Bedlam." [1]

Perhaps it will be said, " True ; no such incongruities as these could exist in human nature,—least of all in such various combination and such sharp contrasts as we find them in Christ ; *therefore* it must be inferred that no such personage ever existed." If He is to be regarded simply as a *man*, like other men, I concede it. This is precisely what I am contending for. His character is, on such conditions, opposed to all the principles of human nature -- an *ensemble* of heterogeneous and impossible attributes.

Let us, then, look at the other alternative. Whether Christ ever existed or not, His professed *portrait* exists ; there can be no doubt about that. Now, if *not* a portrait, it is, in the first place, a curious paradox, that a painting has to a large extent changed the great facts of the world's history ; or (which comes to the same thing, only more difficult to be believed), if it be the embodiment of myth, then the casual illusions of a multitude of imaginations have issued in a painting of such exquisite skill as to produce the same effects. We are told of an ancient painter, who, finding that he could not depict to his mind the foam about a fiery steed's mouth, dashed his brush against the canvas in a paroxysm of despair; and lo! what skill could not do, chance did for him. It is much the same with the mythical hypothesis, as applied to account for such a transcendent creation as that of Christ.

On the supposition that it is an *ideal* creation, we are no longer met, it is true, by the conflict of heterogeneous qualities such as would make the reality, if a mere man, simply a monster ; for on this supposition, the incongruous attributes

---

[1] Critique on Rénan's " Vie de Jésus." " Reason and Faith," with other Essays, p. 236. The language is no doubt strong, but I use it deliberately. The same alternatives were subsequently put with admirable power in Dr. Liddon's Bampton Lectures. See Lectures III. and IV. (1867.)

must be supposed to form part of the ideal, and we are left only to wonder at the marvellous art which has blended them, however incongruous, in such exquisite union and harmony, that the most heterogeneous qualities do not instantly give the *impression* of incongruity. But we are still met with an equal paradox in human nature; namely, that the very qualities which should have warned the world that it *was* a mere ideal on which it was gazing, have not prevented its mistaking it for a reality; the painter has so overdone his part, that the stupid world has vehemently contended and generally believed that the painting is no painting at all; nay, rather than believe it such, has been willing to receive all those supernatural traits with which it is fraught, as also copied from reality !

But this is not the only or chief thing which runs counter to all probability. It is a still greater paradox in human nature that the artists to whom this painting must be ascribed,—who *actually* painted it, whatever rude materials fancy or myth may have supplied,—were, so far as we can judge, as utterly incapable of imagining or executing such a portrait, as the merest dauber of emulating the divinest performances of a Raphael or a Michael Angelo. In the ordinary Jew of those days, in the class of men to which this problem limits us, there was not one single attribute, moral or intellectual, to account for this *chef-d'œuvre*. It is often and justly said, that it is impossible for men to rise far above the spirit and prejudices of their age. It is so favourite a maxim in modern times, that it is sometimes unreasonably strained into an apology for the most egregious follies or the most atrocious crimes. But it is at least equally true in relation to extraordinary excellence. Now, in contemplating the Jews of that age, it is impossible to imagine men more destitute, whether of the moral or the intellectual elements, essential to equip them for the creation of such an ideal as Christ. The whole stress of their national predilections, which had been fondly cherished for ages, tended in a totally different direction. How came the men who wrote the Gospels to emancipate themselves from the prejudices of their nation, which gloried in exclusive privileges, was steeped in religious bigotry, and consoled itself amidst its calamities with the dream of a conquering Messiah, who should restore and augment the glories of ancient Israel? How came any of them to unswathe themselves from all these lifelong notions, and conceive a Messiah whose whole life is depicted as one series of humiliation and ignominy, whose glories were all to be in the future and invisible world, who shrank from every attempt to coax or force Him to a practical assertion of His sovereignty, and who at last died the death of a common malefactor? His career of obloquy and suffering is only relieved by glimpses of a species of moral greatness, which their education and associations disqualified them from fully appreciating, — and they themselves, so far from being able to invent it, confess their "slowness of heart" to perceive and apprehend it? How came they to originate a " Messiah " who, in direct opposition to their national narrowness and intense bigotry, inculcated universal brotherhood and a world-wide charity; who proclaimed the approaching abolition of all those darling privileges on which a Jew prided himself, in favour of a religion which should no longer know the badge of Jew or Gentile? How was it possible for human nature, conditioned as were the Jews of that age, to rise to a conception like this? [1]

But the moral transformation thus implied in some plebeian Jews of that age, involves no greater anomaly in human nature than to suppose them endowed with the extraordinary *intellectual* qualities which so unique and so wonderful a portrait demands; a portrait which it is inconceivable that even one should successfully execute, and yet which no less than four have dared to essay, and with similar success ; a portrait in which even the combination of the human elements, and their mode of presen-

---

[1] It has been well observed that in the character of Christ we not only do not see the generic qualities of the Jew, but not a trace of any of the prevailing sects,—of the Pharisees, the Sadducees, the Essenes.

tation, are of the most singular originality; in which obscurity, poverty, and suffering are covered with a halo of glory which belongs to no hero of history or romance; in which a boundless sympathy with human frailty is conciliated with a holiness which knows no frailty; in which virtue, perfect as it is, is untinctured with that austerity which is almost always its shadow, and which so often detracts from its loveliness; in which patience and meekness which can bear all wrongs and forgive them, are united with a courage on behalf of truth which the frowns of an opposing world cannot daunt; a gentleness which will not " break the bruised reed or quench the smoking flax," with an indignation which launched at incurable hypocrisy more bitter and burning invectives than ever before fell from human lips. All these, and many traits more, equally unlikely to be combined in human nature, are conjoined with supernatural qualities which, far from betraying discordance with the human elements, are so artfully wrought into the picture, that, as already said, instead of at once convincing the world (as they should have done) that Christ was a mere ideal, have beguiled it into accepting Him as an historic reality! Whence came these four obscure painters to possess this power? to dip their pencils in " colours of the rainbow," and handle them with such skill as to cheat the world into the notion that incredibilities were true, and chimeras realities?

But the marvels of this unnatural achievement do not end here. Not only did this wonderful creation proceed from men whose whole moral and intellectual characteristics would seem to have made it impossible; not only was the task successfully essayed four several times, with variations of incident indeed, yet all in the same unique style; but one and all dared it in the same most difficult of all forms,—that of dramatic exhibition. They undertook to make this ideal personage, whose mere human qualities exist in a combination which would seem to lift it out of the sphere of our sympathy, and are conjoined with preternatural attributes, which would seem to do this yet more effectually, speak and act and live before us !   Utterly hopeless task, one would say.   Yet they have done it, and with such success that the majority of readers not only believe the character *natural*, but believe it *historic*, and have had their sympathies far more deeply moved by it than by all other dramatic personations put together !

Of their *own* peculiarities, we know next to nothing.   They are lost in their subject.   But of this trait, as forming an *unnatural* feature, not of them only, but of the sacred writers in general, I shall take a future opportunity of speaking.

Nothing of a literary character that the contemporaries of their nation, or those who succeeded them, have left, affords the faintest indication that any of them could have originated such a character, or so exhibited it.[1]   Their moral, and for the most part also their intellectual qualifications for such a task, may be measured by the Talmud ; and the " *Talmudic* " tone and spirit are, in general, perfectly true to that form of human nature which, as I have said, might be expected under the given conditions.

And that the Christians were as little capable as the Jews of originating such books as the Gospels, or rather such pamphlets —for all, put together, make less than one hundred quarto pages, though they have made such a prodigious noise in the world—is very distinctly seen in the Apocryphal Gospels.   All that the Christians of after time could do with the original delineation of Christ was to spoil it.

The authors of these seem to have had the original Gospels before them as a model, and yet, in the second and third century, could do no better !   The bulk of these apocryphal writings seem to have been composed with no ill design, though with execrable want of taste and judgment ; but they are things which the world can hardly be prevailed upon to look

---

[1] This point is well argued in the " Essay on Mythical Theories of Christianity," by Rev. Chas. Row, M.A., inserted in the course of lectures against " Modern Scepticism," pp. 305-360.

into. It has been well said: "What strikes every one, whatever be his opinion of the origin and merits of these writings, is their immeasurable inferiority to the Canonical Gospels. Immeasurable, indeed, is a word which faintly expresses the extent of the difference between them. They belong to another sphere. It was short-sighted policy in the scoffing unbelievers of Voltaire's school to bring the two things into contact, in the hope of discrediting the Gospel. And the somewhat similar attempt of Strauss suggests the best refutation of his own theory. No more striking proof could be desired by Christians of the unique character of the Evangelic narrative, nor can any fair-minded sceptic fail to perceive the force of it. An impassable line separates the simple majesty, the lofty moral tone, the profound wisdom and significance of the Canonical Gospels from the qualities which we forbear further to particularise in the writings that claim to be their complement. We feel, as we turn from one region to the other, that the difference must be due to something more than lapse of years, or defect of reliable information. If the contrast between the writings of the Epistles and the apostolic fathers is so great that we are reminded perforce of the doctrine of inspiration, how much more when we turn from the sacred volume to the best of the writings before us? . . . In a word, if these are the legendary records preserved by the simple faith and unassisted powers of early Christian disciples, to what power are we to ascribe the authorship of the New Testament?"[1]

The sentiment, therefore, which Rousseau has put into the mouth of his Savoyard apologist,[2]—and which seems to have been his own, at least *for the moment*,—is profoundly true.

On the whole, the ideal origination of the character of

---

[1] "Edinburgh Review," July, 1868, pp. 105–109.

[2] "Il seroit plus inconcevable que plusieurs hommes d'accord eussent fabriqué ce livre qu'il ne l'est qu'un seul en ait fourni le sujet."—*Rousseau,* "Emile," Liv. IV. tom. iii. pp. 128, 129. *Genève,* 1784.

Christ, and the world's stolid reception of it, notwithstanding, as historic, would seem one continued violation of all laws of human probability; whether we consider the antecedents, moral, intellectual, and literary, of those who produced it, or compare it with any contemporary relics of Jewish, or any subsequent performances of Christian minds : or reflect that this *shadow* has clothed itself with substance, and made the world think that a painting lives !—As it gazes transfixed, it exclaims, like the rapt Leontes before the supposed statue of Hermione, when Pauline proposes to draw the curtain,—

> "Let be, let be :
> What was he that did make it ? See, my lord,
> Would you not dream it breathed, and that those veins
> Did verily bear blood ?"

That we cannot well exaggerate the wonders of this unique creation, whether substance or shadow, real or mythical, is proved alike by the intense veneration and the intense opposition it has evoked. Indeed, it is hard to say whether the boundless admiration, or the vehement hostility to the name and claims of Christ, be the more signal tribute to His power. Is it conceivable that a bundle of myths or fictions should thus permanently stir the heart of humanity? We shovel out of the way, age after age, whole cartloads of this traditional lumber, in every other case but this one ! No man, especially in enlightened and civilized ages like ours, ever thinks of standing up for any forms of mythology, least of all if they be of foreign growth and origin. If there be anything striking in them, we read about them with otiose curiosity, just as we should a nursery tale or a romance. But we should as soon think of believing that the lions and asses in Æsop's fables really talked, as attach the smallest serious value to any mythology, Greek or Roman, Egyptian or Hindoo, ancient or modern. Jupiter in this respect is as Brahma, and Serapis as Vishnu. All are consigned to universal contempt or oblivion; and if any man were to undertake either to claim for them any religious significance to *us*, or elaborately maintain they had none, he would equally be regarded as out of his senses.   But while all cultivated and civilized nations survey all mythologies with the same contempt, and even all superstitious nations look scornfully askance on all mythologies *except* their own, this Christian mythology (if it be mythology), and this alone, is inexhaustibly fascinating.   Amidst the greatest diversities of race, nationality, tradition, culture, in modern as in more ancient times, in regions far remote from its native seat, and ages far distant from the epoch of its birth, it is still capable of exerting such an influence, that the loftiest minds, endowed with all that nature and all that culture can bestow, are not ashamed, in never-ceasing and most animated controversy, to engage in impugning or defending it.   Its truth or falsehood, its historical or mythological origin, is the perpetual battle-field from age to age.   Those who challenge it are as eager as its champions.   Yet if the former really believe it what they profess to believe it, they would (one would imagine) be as reluctant to submit to such lifelong labour to prove it vanity and delusion, as to prove the like of the many other systems, in refutation of which not a soul of them could prevail upon himself to waste a syllable ; they would be as languid about it as about the Mahometan or Hindoo superstition.   But with regard to Christ and His claims, the conflict even becomes more keen in that very region of light which kills all ordinary superstitions.   Strauss, Rénan, Neander, Pressensé, and scores of doughty champions more, are in our day straining every nerve to prove Christianity either true or false, amidst the universal contempt or neglect of so many other systems.[1]

[1] The " Lives " of Christ which this generation alone has produced would make a hundred times the amount of the original " Memoirs " put together. If it be said that all this controversy shows the difficulty of establishing the claims of Christianity to all the world, it certainly does so ; but, *first*, that may be owing to other causes than the difficulties of its evidence ; *secondly*, the strife shows most conclusively the perpetual interest it inspires. That all this trouble should be necessary to *confute* it, if false (as false as other systems about which unbelief does not trouble itself at all), is the

At all events, it is a significant proof that, be the character of Christ real or imaginary, history or myth, it is a wonderful phenomenon. But if it be the latter, its fabrication by the Jewish mind, and its reception by the world as history, are equally paradoxical, and in defiance of human nature.

6. Another paradox strikes me, I confess, in the desperate tenacity and boundless veneration with which the Jews have ever clung to their Scriptures. I feel this, let them be ever so ancient; but far more, if they are, as so many modern critics affirm, of comparatively recent date, and in great part of fictitious origin ; facts which it was far more the interest of the Jew to find out than that of any of the modern critics, who have kindly made the discovery for him, and yet cannot convince him of it ! If fabulous (whether wicked forgeries or crafty fictions), it is difficult to imagine they *could* have been palmed on the nation as its genuine history at either an earlier or later date ; but certainly at neither, without exciting vehement suspicion or protest. Yet this is supposed to have been managed without one syllable or one murmur coming down to us ! Now, when we reflect on their contents, that they constitute (if false) one long libel on the Jewish nation, is it credible they should have been received with one voice, not only as true, but as no less than "sacred and inspired," treasured as the most precious deposit, and transmitted to posterity with the most solicitous care ? One can understand how fables tending *simply* to glorify a nation, may be willingly accepted, be they ever so foolish,—though we do not find nations thus cheating themselves at *late* periods of their history. But when

really wonderful thing ; that it should excite much controversy is not wonderful, for, as Christianity declared from the beginning, that it would be "everywhere spoken against" (and time has verified at least *that* much truth concerning it), so I only wonder, considering what its doctrines are, and what human nature is, that it has not "been spoken against" still more. But that, if it be no more than a contrivance of fiction, or a fardel of myths, it should not have been long since confuted and done with, is, as Bishop Butler says, marvellous indeed.

the pretended records bear witness to little but their shame, are filled with reproaches and denunciations, tax them with the most tremendous guilt, and menace them with terrible punishment; upbraid them with the most egregious folly and the most odious ingratitude; remind them that their fathers had a glorious heritage, and had forfeited it; a noble lineage, and disgraced it; a Divine King, against whom they had been perpetually plotting treason;—when this is the constant burden of these documents, is it conceivable that, if they be in a great measure fictitious, every nerve should not have been strained to prove it; that they should have been received as authentic history, nay, as inspired truth, without *one* effort—such as a score of disinterested critics in our day have gratuitously made on the Jews' behalf—to prove the contrary? If so, it is certainly not after the " manner of men." Age after age, and with one voice, they confess the heavy indictment against them to be just; yea, though these books not only told them that they had been a " perverse and stiffnecked generation," but predict that they would continue so,—would refuse to be warned or reformed, and at last become a " hissing and a by-word among the nations ! " ᵉ

If not true, these documents are little better than what they have been well called, "archives of libel," so dark are the colours in which they paint the nation, and so incessant and vehement the reproaches which they shower upon it. Instead of guarding and transmitting them with such profound veneration, instead of jealously counting each word and syllable, as if loth to be robbed of one iota of their shame, one would have imagined that patriotic Jews would have hunted down these documents for destruction, since, in fact, they are but an enlarged commentary on that pregnant text of Stephen, which he declares to be an epitome of their history—" Ye uncircumcised in heart and ears, ye do *always* resist the Holy Ghost. *As your fathers* did, *so do ye.*" If it be said that the record flatters

them with being the chosen people of God, it as constantly
taxes them with a forfeiture of this privilege; and threatens,
and at length pronounces, their rejection, for their unutterable
apostacies, perverseness, and ingratitude. Were these the
documents which national vanity would so eagerly fasten upon,
and transmit with scrupulous fidelity to posterity? No; had
they been untrue, the mood of the profane Jehoiakim, sitting by
his winter fire, cutting to pieces with his penknife the ominous
roll of the prophet, and tossing the fragments into the flames,
would have been natural enough, and as naturally imitated by
the whole Jewish nation. Each man would have emulously
sought out these infamous libels with more than the zeal of a
Diocletian in his crusade against the copies of the New Testament.[1]

[1] If it be thought that some of the above remarks bear hard on the Jews,
I can only reply that I simply take the statements of their own Scriptures,
which themselves account inspired; but their case would certainly be little
improved by supposing that they tamely acquiesced in such severe condemnation, though unjust. Lest it should seem, however, that I think their
case worse than that of mankind at large, I have no hesitation in saying that
such is my conviction of the indocility of man in relation to God's teaching,
so slow to learn, and so apt to forget, His lessons, that I heartily subscribe
the declaration of Paul, "What then? Are *we* better than they? No; in
no wise." Nor can we forget that the Jews have given unexampled proofs
of heroic constancy and sincerity in their veneration for books which so
reproach them. "Cependant," says Pascal, "ce livre qui les deshonore
en tant de façons, ils le conservent aux dépens de leur vie. C'est une sincé-
rité qui n'a point d'exemple dans le monde, *ni sa racine dans la nature.*"
(Pascal, *Pensées,* tom. ii. p. 189. Ed. Faugère.)

LECTURE II.

THE SAME SUBJECT CONTINUED.

LECTURE II.

IN the present lecture, I propose to resume the subject of the last. Without further preface, I remark :—

7. That it has always seemed to me an incomprehensible anomaly that Jews should by any *natural* process have originated such a book as the New Testament, and such a religion as it contains. If they originated it (as they certainly did), it would seem to be in diametrical contradiction to all the principles and tendencies of *their* nature, as well as of human nature in general. The point has been partly anticipated in discussing the difficulty of accounting for such a " Messiah " as Jewish evangelists have painted ; but the reasoning equally applies to all the writers of the New Testament, and to the origin of Christianity in general. There is hardly a feature of the religion which the Jew might not naturally be supposed the last man in the world to tolerate. The entire system of institutions under which his nature had been formed made him recoil from it, and especially from its cosmopolitan character. That the Jewish nation was the chosen of Heaven ; that to them " were com·mitted the oracles of God," of which they had a monopoly—these were first principles to the Jew ; and everything in his education, habits, prepossessions, made him clutch them passionately to his heart. The Gospel abruptly broke in upon these, and, as with volcanic force, fractured and upturned these solid strata of his belief. It went avowedly on the principle that all the Jew's privileges were transient, and subordinate to higher ends than his glory or welfare ; that they were abrogated by the

Gospel; that under it there was to be "neither Jew nor Greek;" that Christ came to throw down the "middle wall of partition" between them. One of the first lessons taught to Peter when he entered on his apostolic mission (and, like every Jew, he was astonished at it), was that God had abolished this distinction, and that he was henceforth to regard the Gentiles as on a level with himself. That all this should be most repugnant to the ordinary Jew, was natural, and the inevitable effect of the abuse of those privileges on which he had plumed himself for ages. He was of the highest caste, and the Jewish Brahmin looked down on the Gentile Pariah with all the contempt with which the Pharisee regarded the publican. We are not left to conjecture as to the degree of revulsion which his mind experienced; we see how it manifested itself, and may thence exactly measure the improbability of any such religion as that of the Gospel having *naturally* originated with him. It was his grand quarrel with Christ and His apostles that they proposed to ignore the religious prerogatives of the Jews, and their exceptional religious position among the nations of the earth. So slow, indeed, were even the immediate disciples of Christ to entertain any such notion, that the expectation that their Messiah would found a temporal kingdom, of which the Jews should form as it were the aristocracy, and in which they were to cast off the Roman yoke, was a besetting hallucination. We see, again, the same principle at work in the natural reluctance even of many of those Jews who *did* become converts, to part with any tatters of their ancient law that they could retain, and in the infinite trouble which their "Judaising" tendencies gave to the Apostle Paul and the Churches which he had founded. We see it still more strongly in the national hostility to Christ Himself; in the persecutions, which in the first age of the Gospel the Jews almost always originated, and always fomented, against the hated sect of the Nazarenes; and in the persistent abhorrence with which they have recoiled from this religion for near nineteen centuries. How came Jews, then, to fabricate a religion so diametrically opposed to all their native prejudices ? How came they to rise to this grand conception of a universal religion, in which all mankind were to be of equal value in the eyes of God, and equally entitled to a participation in His favour? How came incarnate bigotry to go forth as the spontaneous apostle and herald of universal love ? The narrowness of the Jew had been a proverb among the nations ; he is here, all at once, and of his own accord, the champion of all mankind against himself; strips himself of all in which he had gloried, as the special donative of God ; renounces his own heritage, and gives it to strangers ! It is this Jew, exclusive *par excellence*, who conceives the thought,—of which far less bigoted nations had never dared to dream,—of a universal religion and an unlimited charity. " He who had no dealings with the Samaritans" preaches a religion which not only permits, but commands him, to account "all men his brethren."

Another principle, equally unaccountable, if Jewish human nature alone prompted it, is that intense spirit of proselytism to the new religion by which its founders were from the first animated. It is in violent contrast with all the previous habits of the Jews. Their sullen isolation, their exclusive peculiarities, were notorious. They were not, indeed, forbidden to receive proselytes ; and in truth, their Law enjoined a spirit of frank kindness to the "stranger," which, had it been complied with, might have made many more proselytes, but which their exaggeration of their exceptional privileges too often led them to disregard. But if they unreluctantly received such as spontaneously sought their communion, they were certainly animated in general by no active spirit of proselytism : whereas the " missionary spirit " is the spirit of the early Church, and of Christianity everywhere ; it is the reflex of that universality of dominion to which it aspires, and that universality of privilege which it concedes ; just as the comparative inertness of the Jew was the reflex of his religious monopoly, and consequent isolation. But how came the Jew, self-prompted, to "cast his skin"? to throw off all the ingrained habits of his nature, and to become cosmopolitan?

But the strongest proof of the point now argued has been already alluded to. The very conception of such a Messiah as Christ, implies in itself a *bouleversement* of the deepest principles of the Jewish mind. The idea of a "triumphant" Messiah, who, while swaying His sceptre over the subject nations, should confirm and enhance the privileges of the favoured people, and reflect upon them the lustre of His reign, had been their day-dream for centuries; and so strong had been the illusion, as to blind them to the many professedly prophetic passages of their ancient books, which spake as plainly of the sufferings and humiliation of their promised Deliverer, as of his ultimate victory and glory. In this respect as in others, but in this emphatically, they fulfilled the ancient declaration: "They had eyes but saw not," and "ears but heard not." Yet by them, and against the whole stream of their convictions, interests, and passions, was proclaimed a Messiah, whose humble origin and condition, whose character and teaching, and whose ignominious death, made Him the object of the most intense aversion to the bulk of the nation, and has made Him so from that day to this. That repugnance is not sensibly abated even yet; and as Christ Himself said that the "publicans and harlots" would enter "the kingdom of heaven" before the "Scribes and Pharisees," so, for similar reasons, it would seem that every nation of the world,—civilized or savage, Greek or Roman, "barbarian, Scythian, bond or free," Gaul, Saxon, Indian, Hottentot, Otaheitan, Malagasy,—in spite of infinite prejudices and immemorial superstitions, is more easily persuaded to listen to the Gospel, and with less difficulty proselyted to it, than the "children of Abraham." This, of itself, gives us a measure of the improbability of their having spontaneously projected *such* a Messiah as Christ: and, justly viewed, subverts the foundation of the theory of Strauss, who endeavours to show how such a "myth" as Christ might have grown out of the Jewish interpretations of Messianic prophecy. The intense opposition of the Jew to the Gospel is itself a proof that there was nothing in his preconceptions, his habits, his institutions, which could have led him to *such* a conception, or to tolerate it, had it been presented to him. The very moment it *was* presented, he averted his eyes from it, as from a spectacle that filled him with mingled shame, anger, and horror, which he has retained to this day.

Another anomaly in connection with this last topic deserves notice. If it is wonderful that such a religion as that of the New Testament should have come from a *Jewish* source, it is not less wonderful that, being from such a source, its authors should have prognosticated its rejection by the Jews, and its acceptance, though not without vehement opposition, by the Gentiles, —among whom the New Testament proceeds to narrate its rapid progress. For the former allegation, *if* such a religion could naturally spring up in the mind of Jews at all, there would be plausible ground; for assuredly it was more likely that Jews would reject it than that Jews should invent it. It was also plausible to suspect that such a religion—considering how distasteful are many of its doctrines—would meet with opposition from the heathen world ; but what reason its authors could have—if the religion was a purely human projection of Jewish minds, and its authors spoke from conjecture—so confidently to affirm that it would prosper in spite of that opposition, it is hard to say. True though it turned out to be, it was a most unlikely thing for any men, but especially Jews, to reckon upon.[1]

<hr>

[1] I do not further prosecute this subject, because its full illustration would require me to go beyond Scripture (to which I restrict myself), and enter on the history of the propagation of Christianity in the face of all the obstacles opposed to it. The argument derived from this topic has always been insisted upon as of great force by Christian apologists ; and, I think, most justly. That the religion was vehemently and everywhere opposed is a fact abundantly proved by the history of the first three centuries ; the storm of obloquy and persecution beat upon it incessantly, during which its votaries

It might have been supposed that, looking to the condition of the Jews, their relations to other nations, their unsocial isolation, and the contemptuous estimate formed of them, that as the Pharisees thought no "good thing could come out of Nazareth," so the Gentile would think "that nothing good could come out of Judea," and that the antipathy to any religion emanating thence would be invincible. As there was no element in Judaism, especially as moulded by its misinterpreted prophecies and corrupt traditions, that would be likely to originate Christianity, so when it *was* originated, the very fact that its cradle was Judea could not but operate as an immense obstacle to its reception beyond the pale. If the Jew (as the facts show) was intensely opposed to any *such* Messiah as the New Testament exhibits, the Gentiles were intensely opposed to any Jewish Messiah whatsoever. And in this point of view, again, Strauss's theory completely breaks down: it utterly fails to account for the success of the Gospel, even if it accounted at all for its origination. For even if it were conceded that Jewish *prepossessions* were in favour (as all facts prove they could not be) of any such conception as that of the Messiah of the New Testament, there was not a thought, a sentiment, a prejudice of the Gentiles, which could recommend it.[1]

---

were a "sect everywhere spoken against" and everywhere defenceless, though everywhere growing. As we might conjecture from its character, that this religion *would* excite, so historic fact shows that it *did* excite, the vehement enmity of men when first propounded—of the vulgar and the learned, of rulers and the populace, of priests and philosophers. And it may be argued, as it often has been ably argued, that its propagation and reception, in spite of all that was arrayed against it, and in utter destitution of all that could make for it, is (if it was a purely human phenomenon) not easily accounted for.

[1] "Consider," says Davison, "the *difference* in aptitude and qualification for spreading any system of doctrine, between Jewish and some other teachers. Had it been foretold, for instance, that a novel and prevalent religion should one day appear and take a lasting possession of a considerable part of the civilized world, emanating from *Athens* or from *Rome*, the

In truth, the origin and reception of Christianity in the world bristle with paradoxes. The Jews, though most unlikely to originate that religion which the bulk of them constantly rejected, and still reject, *did* originate it; and that heathen world, which any one would have thought would certainly reject it, did in vast numbers receive it. These are curious facts, which, like so many more on which I am insisting in these pages, it is not easy to account for on any principle of human nature or historic probability.

8. Another paradox—or rather a double paradox—I find in this: that the New Testament dares to propound a religion which aspires to *universal dominion*, and that too to be achieved without violence, and by moral force alone. I am now speaking simply of what the New Testament *says*. I know full well that men have in many cases been so little capable of comprehending it, that they have unwisely and wickedly departed from its programme, and attempted the propagation of this religion by resorting to methods which itself sternly condemns. This is notorious; but what the book propounds is plain enough, and absolves it from all participation in the crime. No system of morals is ever made responsible for the violation of its precepts, and no code of laws for the crimes it expressly prohibits. The command of the Founder of Christianity was " to preach the Gospel to every creature," to proclaim it "to all nations under heaven;" but it is equally incontrovertible that He renounced for Himself, and that His apostles renounced for Him, all employment of *force* in the establishment of His novel

popular philosophy and literature of the one, which had a certain freedom of access to the world at large, or the growing empire of the other, might have furnished some pledge for the accomplishment of the prediction. But *Jewish* doctrine could look to no such auxiliaries in civil or intellectual empire to favour its introduction, or recommend its pretensions. Prophecy, therefore, we may say, when it predicted the reception of a Law of Religion, which was to have Jews for its teachers, and kings and nations for its converts, had nothing to build upon, nothing either in present appearances, or the ordinary calculation of things."—Davison on Prophecy, p. 282.

kingdom. The same thing necessarily follows from the very nature of that kingdom. Its sovereign did not content Himself, as other monarchs, with demanding the homage of lip and knee,—which a man may pay and still be a rebel in heart; but an inward homage which, unless sincere, would make all outward service perfectly worthless. His was an empire over Mind and Will. The only allegiance this strange King would condescend to accept, was a voluntary allegiance, founded on the love of TRUTH, and itself the symbol of submission to it. If the whole world bent the knee and cried "Hosanna!" Christ would regard it as empty form, or rather as hypocrisy added to disloyalty, unless the heart went with it. It is a glorious characteristic of that only true royalty which is ascribed to Him, and "worthy of the King of kings and Lord of lords." Though the symbols of all-various dominion be expressed in the diadem "of many crowns," with which the apocalyptic vision invests Him, no jewel in it sparkles more resplendently than this. The very nature, therefore, of this empire made all force nugatory, and a contradiction in terms. It was not like "the kingdoms of this world;" if it had been, as Christ Himself said, "then would His servants have fought."

Now, this ambitious dream of universal dominion, especially when conjoined with renunciation of all violence as a means to the end, presents us with a prodigious anomaly, as contrasted with all previous history and experience.

I think I might insist upon either of these circumstances as in itself a paradox, but both together certainly constitute a very startling one. The audacity of the project itself takes away one's breath; it is about the last which, looking at the infinite and immemorial religious differences of mankind, hallowed and strengthened by time, custom, and tradition, human nature would be likely to entertain. It would be regarded—as indeed it still is by the bulk of mankind—as the most chimerical of enterprises. Nor do I know of any other well-attested instance of such a dream having ever entered the imagination of man, if we except the case of Mahomet, and Mahometanism may be summarily dismissed as no parallel at all : first, because it came after Christianity, and was in this, as in several other respects, a plagiarism from it; and secondly, because the means by which it proposed to attain its object, and which it so ruthlessly employed, was *force*, in its coarsest and most vulgar form.

Nor is it easy to conceive how, in the face of the universal religious condition of the nations at the time Christianity appeared, and the apathy with which the world acquiesced in it, a thought so presumptuous, however sublime, should be suggested. As one looked abroad upon the many-coloured panorama of the religions of the world, with their " gods many and lords many ; " saw the neighbourly terms on which these for the most part dwelt together ; how contentedly they " cantoned " out the world amongst them, and conceded to each other the limited dominion and the limited prerogatives they severally claimed—in all which their worshippers cordially acquiesced— he would assuredly say that the dream of the universality and supremacy of one religion was of all things the most visionary. Indeed it looked so hopeless, that the world seems to have quietly assumed its impossibility—the compression and extension of each area of belief seldom depending on any instinct or effort of religious propagandism, but on political revolutions or military violence. This last, indeed, did effect considerable changes ; sometimes destroyed a nation and its gods too ; sometimes drove both, equally forlorn and helpless, from their native seats. Colonisation, again, sometimes effected the same thing. The emigrants carried their gods to a new locality, by the same means and on the same terms that they took their other " goods and chattels." In these changes the gods and their worshippers behaved characteristically ; the last were *active* and the first *passive.* The gods did not " move ; " they " were moved "— as Isaiah says in his graphic picture of the huge images of Bel and Nebo " nodding " on the groaning wains that bore them into captivity—" a heavy burden to the weary beasts ! " But there was no display of active propagandism, or any serious attempts to overcome the *vis inertiæ* of traditional and local beliefs, far less any dream of the universal supremacy of any one religion.

Yet the paradox does not end here, for we must suppose this audacious speculation to have first entered the head, not of sages and philosophers, not of great legislators and conquerors, but of a *Jew;* who, if no more than a Jew, was one of a community who, as we have seen, doted on their exclusive privileges, and jealously guarded the mountain-passes which shut them out in religious isolation from the rest of the world ; who, if their ancient writings intimated that "from the midst of them" a religion would arise which should spread beyond Judea, and in which their own exclusive privileges should expire, had grossly misinterpreted these records, and would not hear of a religion that was to be *universal,* in any sense that would not still admit of the supremacy of that of Moses. Like the rest of the nations, they assuredly made no active efforts to realise any such dream.

An objector will probably say, "And is it not, in spite of the progress of Christianity, still a dream ? Would any one, looking on the infinite religious discords and controversies of the world, venture to say, without superhuman illumination, that these discords would one day be hushed, and one religion prevail ?" I answer, this is precisely what I am saying ; this *objection* is my present *argument.* I do not think any human being, left to his own intelligence, would have indulged any such dream.

But it is the *combination* of the two features I have mentioned —the predicted universality of the religion with the renunciation of all violence in attaining it — which constitutes the great peculiarity on which I am now insisting, and which makes it deservedly rank as one of the many paradoxes which require to be accounted for, if the New Testament was the work of un-aided men. Nor is it, as I have hinted, any answer to say that the religion of the New Testament has not always been propagated by merely moral forces, or rather it is an objection which much strengthens the argument,—as we shall presently see. It did restrict itself to such means in the days of its signal and most rapid triumphs, namely, for the first three centuries; and has done so since in all its most worthy and durable conquests. Nor, perhaps, can a single instance be pointed out in which it has not received more damage than benefit by the ill-judged and ignorant resort to other than its own weapons. Beyond question, if its nominal sphere has been sometimes enlarged by such methods of propagandism, the violence done to the genius of the religion has generated evils which, for ages, have obscured its lustre, and impeded its real progress and legitimate influence. But this is not the only, nor the chief reply to the objection. The objection, in fact, *answers itself.* My argument is based upon the paradoxical character of the original conception;—of a universal religion, in the establishment of which all coercion was to be abjured. Nothing depends on whether men have acted up to this conception or not. But that they notoriously have *not*, is of itself an argument for the *un*human character of the project itself. For it could only be because they despaired of the possibility of realising it in the prescribed methods, that they deviated from them, and violated the express letter of the Scripture rule. They have thereby simply borne witness to the genuine tendency of human nature; demonstrated how little likely men were to originate, how difficult for them even to entertain, such a conception. They have thus shown that it was foreign to all their ideas and repugnant to their passions and their impatience. They found it impossible to adhere to such a conception, though it had been clearly sketched out before their eyes. The veil of our common nature was upon their hearts, as the veil of old prejudices was upon the hearts of the Jews when the Scripture was read in their hearing: "seeing, they saw not," and "hearing, they heard not, neither did they understand."

9. It is another paradox, though only a corollary from the

preceding, that the New Testament, in thus peremptorily prohibiting all attempts to protect or propagate Christianity by coercion and penalties, recognises the rights of conscience in general as sacred, and consecrates the principle of toleration. It recognises at once what Christians themselves, with the book before them, too soon unlearnt, and were slow to learn again,—that religion, by its very nature, can be propagated by nothing but argument and persuasion.

Now, however various and multiform the religions of the ancient world, we look in vain for such a principle of toleration as this. Gibbon eulogises, and with some show of justice, the tolerance of the imperial government of Rome ; but it is easy to see that the praise, for anything more than political wisdom, does not belong to it. It never recognised, it never dreamt of recognising, the true nature and claims of conscience or religious liberty. Nor is it even true that the *kind* of toleration it at last practised was known to it when Rome was a homogeneous state and had a homogeneous religion. Then, like all the rest of the world, it could persecute with rigour ; it could banish from the state, under severest penalties, those who presumed to innovate in religion, and essayed to be " the setters forth of strange gods ; " who either introduced new rites into the old worship, or alien divinities for a new worship.[1] It was not till after the Roman power had absorbed into itself many nations of heterogeneous race and creed, that the problem was forced upon it as to how the various religions were to be treated. Without attempting to solve it on any religious or philosophical principles, without having any just notions of religious liberty at all, the political instincts of that great people, and the consummate administrative sagacity which so distinguished them and so fitted them for empire, suggested that the nations should be left to the undisturbed enjoyment of their various religious systems, and the Pantheon be open to all the divinities of the

---

[1] See passages proving this, from Cicero, Livy, and other writers, cited in Waddington's "Church History," vol. i. pp. 110–112.

earth; provided always the gods would live on terms of peace with one another, and engage that their votaries would be as quiet as their statues! So long as the gods were contented, each with his own belt of territory and his own *peculium* of incense and sacrifice, and their votaries refrained from troubling the imperial government, Rome was content to tolerate them all. Nor is there, in all the history of Rome, any greater proof of political genius than the instinctive wisdom with which, abandoning early predilections (in which she shared with all the rest of the world) for religious *uniformity*, she restricted her aims to what alone was possible; and exacting, with all the sternness of her iron rule, absolute obedience to the civil government, left the many-coloured religious panorama of the world just as she found it. Rome, doubtless, felt that not even Rome could rule the nations, if she attempted to reduce the religious opinions of men to one, and that a foreign, standard. Nothing but persuasion can change these; and indeed it is one of the proofs of the indestructible religious nature of man—the deep foundations in which religious sentiment is laid—that it is easier to rob him of his liberty than of his conscience, even though it be a superstitious one; easier to despoil him of his goods than of his gods, though he would so often gain by the loss; easier to enslave his body than coerce his mind. In the knowledge of this, the Romans were assuredly wiser than many a Christian ruler. For though their toleration was only a political compromise, and no true concession to the sacred claims of conscience, it was a discreet expedient in the absence of a toleration founded on better principles. They and their subjects had at least peace, though it was founded only on a truce between truth and error,—both of which the theory held equally sacred. But at all events they did not stultify themselves (as many Christian rulers, that ought to have known better, have done) in the attempt to propagate truth or suppress error by *force*. But that Rome had no true idea of religious liberty, or genuine toleration, such as is claimed for it by Gibbon, appears from these two simple facts: first, that all the gods and goddesses were regarded as equally eligible to a place in the Pantheon,— showing that *indifferentism* to all religions was Rome's conception of reverence for conscience, and a courteous bow to every idol—*ex quovis ligno fit Mercurius*—the true sign of an enlightened statesman; secondly (and it proves the point more conclusively), that no sooner did the haughty mistress of the world apprehend that Christianity aspired (even though without violence) to universal dominion, would make no compromise of equality, nor accept a place with the rabble of the heathen deities, nor sit cheek by jowl with Osiris and Jupiter in the Pantheon, than she instantly began to persecute it with a zeal and vigour which showed but too plainly what her notions of religious liberty really were, and within what narrow limits she practised it. She was prompted, in part, probably, by some misconception of the *nature* of that "universal dominion" which Christianity challenged, or jealous that if it was obtained, whatever its nature, it might endanger her own political supremacy.

The notion of toleration, as entertained by heathen statesmen, is excellently well implied in the epigrammatic sentence of Gibbon, "that in the estimate of the vulgar, every religion was equally true; in that of the philosopher, equally false; in that of the statesman, equally expedient;" and, therefore, *as* equally expedient, equally worthy of being cherished, and, as far as possible, protected from the proselytising zeal of every other!

When we reflect on the proneness of men to persecution, how almost universally it has been practised, how late, in point of fact, men have come to the discovery of its enormity, or anything approaching true liberty of conscience, the peculiarity of the New Testament on which I am now insisting would seem very remarkable. That it *does* prohibit all persecution, is beyond question. No one with the least particle of intelligence or candour will deny that, both by precept and example, by direct statement and oblique implication, everything in the form of force and violence is forbidden to every disciple of Christianity in terms perfectly decisive and perspicuous. This has never been disputed ; and if it be rejoined that Christianity has paid but little regard to the will of its Founder, and has persecuted as largely as any other religion in the world, I reply, as I have already done, that the more true the charge, the better for the present argument. It proves most conclusively that the peculiarity of the New Testament is not the *natural* expression of the tendencies of man. It proves that so strong are his impulses in the contrary direction, that in this, as in many other cases, they have led him, even when he has accepted Christianity, to violate the plainest laws and principles of its statute book, and to act in direct opposition, both to the precept and example of the acknowledged lawgiver. Nor is it without significance that when Christians in general, in blindly following that *nature* which the New Testament contradicts, had forgotten their Master's maxims on this subject, the true principles of religious liberty were recovered by renewed appeal to the neglected book. We stand indebted for the discovery of toleration, not to philosophers (who in general troubled themselves but little about religious liberty), but to the religious men who found it two centuries ago in the New Testament. It was hence they drew the obsolete maxims the world had forgotten.

That the New Testament should have contained these maxims, is the more wonderful when we reflect that it was *Jews* who consigned these principles to us. Their own religion was severe towards all wilful deviations from it ; and reasonably, if their government was (as they thought, and as the Old Testament professes it was) a *true* theocracy administered by God Himself; for every deviation from it was also, *ipso facto*, an act of high treason against their Divine King. And if it did not enjoin proselytism by violence (as it certainly did not), yet considering the rigorous laws against religious error among themselves, it was not very likely they would discover what they would naturally have no conception of,—the true principles of religious liberty as applied to the world outside them, and under conditions wholly different from those of their own institutions. Those principles are found in the books of the New Testament; and I venture to think constitute another anomaly in the structure and contents of that book, viewed in reference both to the tendencies and practices of human nature.

10. As regards the relations between Religion and Political Government, I cannot help thinking there is an observable contrast between the tone of the Bible (different as are the Old and New Testaments in this respect) and that which the founders of human systems of religion have almost universally advocated.

Though the position of the Old Testament in this matter would seem the very reverse of that of the New, the position of both is equally opposed to that which has approved itself to human judgment and practice.

In the Jewish dispensation, " Church and State " were not merely allied, but incorporated ; not united, but identified. I am not now arguing that it was a *Divine* institution ; rather, as usual, I am arguing on the supposition of its human origin, and considering how far it bears the traces of this, as compared with undoubted fabrications of man's religious handicraft.

The Jewish system of government was a genuine *theocracy*. God was presumed to have constituted Himself monarch of the State, and hence its contrast with every other form of government in the ancient world.   It was an anomaly.   Politics were identified with religion, the sacred and civil codes were essentially one, and the priestly functions assumed a paramount importance.   *God* was the invisible, but real Sovereign.   Moses himself was merely His "servant" and administrator ; he did not affect to be, like the Grand Lama, or even the Pope, the visible representative and vicegerent of God.   So emphatically, according to the original draft of the Jewish constitution, was Jehovah the Monarch, that when they demanded to have a "mortal" and visible king, "like the nations around them,"

His controversy with them was that they had "rejected *Him* from being king over them;" deposed Him, and placed an usurper on His throne.   "They have not," He is represented as saying to the great prophet, who then administered His kingdom, "rejected thee, but ME, from being their king."

On the other hand, the New Testament seems to assume an exactly opposite position.   Not a syllable is said on the subject; not a hint is given of any contemplated alliance or connection of Christianity with any form of political government. On the contrary, the line of demarcation between the "kingdoms of this world" and itself, as "*not* a kingdom of this world," is seemingly most sharp and trenchant.

In saying this, I do not mean to prejudge the question of the lawfulness or expediency of the union of Christianity with the State,—though I have strong opinions on the subject.   But to the present argument it is indifferent how the question shall be decided.   The very long and protracted controversy on the subject may perhaps be admitted to prove that the *silence* of the New Testament does not altogether preclude doubt upon it.   But the *silence*, and apparent *indifference*, are the features on which I lay stress, be they interpreted as they may; for we do *not* find them in the other drafts of religion which man's ingenuity has framed; and certainly not in the Jewish, out of the bosom of which Christianity immediately sprang.   This very fact, indeed, has had no small influence in inducing men to argue that it *must* have been the design of Christianity to maintain close relations with civil governments.   So intimate was the union in the Jewish economy; so customary the alliance in *other* cases; so often had the "kingly and the priestly functions" in ancient times been combined in the same person; and, even when those functions were severed, so general had been the conviction that the alliance between them ought to be of the strictest kind, that people were slow to believe that anything else was possible; or that the office of legislator and magistrate could be fitly exercised, unless consecrated by formal connection with religion. It was urged, therefore, that though the New Testament was *silent* on the subject, its silence must be supposed to "give consent" to an arrangement so apparently natural, and all but universal.

This (as is now evinced by the general current of modern speculation and policy) was a hasty inference. However reasonable it may be, if God by express revelation assumes the immediate government of a people (as was supposed in the Jewish theocracy), that " Church and State " should be incorporated, it would certainly be rash to conclude, without any such warrant, that it is lawful for every casual form of government and polity which man's caprice or ingenuity may set up, to enter into alliances equally variable with those religious systems which happen to have the suffrage of the government. This, the theory necessarily comes to ; for as each government is left to choose what religion it will establish, it as necessarily chooses that which it *deems* true ; and with what results we see. If there were no other argument against such a course, it would be a strong one, that it must be obviously inexpedient for the interests of Truth ; for as false religions are many, while the true can be but one, it throws the whole weight of political power and patronage into the scale of error, in the ratio in which false religions are a multiple of the true,—which has always been, is still, and must be the case.

It has, accordingly, come to be felt that the remarkable silence of the New Testament, in relation to this subject, is susceptible of a different interpretation ; that so momentous an inference as that just mentioned required a positive sanction, and that "silence" rather forbade than authorised it. It also came to be felt, that as the old dispensation was generally abrogated, it is but natural to infer that this feature of it, in the absence of all provision for its continuance, and of all sanction for any attempts to renew it, was abrogated too. Accordingly, after many ages of a contrary opinion, during which it was taken for granted that the practice of the ancient world generally, and the example of the Jewish polity in particular, were to be imitated by the nations which embraced Christianity, we see that a more cautious study of the New Testament, and more profound meditation on the genius of the Gospel, have gradually generated a conviction, which is becoming more and more widely diffused, that the older theory was erroneous; that Christianity was not designed to be formally taken under State patronage, or implicated with the fortunes of any earthly polity; that its sublime function was to make both kings and subjects Christians, and therefore the better kings and subjects, by moulding their opinions and characters. So far as it did this (and it must, so far as it is embraced and loved), it would be the inspiring genius of a nation, without being trammelled or shamed by the equivocal support of statesmen and politicians, often too ignorant of its nature or too often indifferent to its claims; who, applying their maxims to a purely spiritual institution, have been too apt to subordinate it to their ends, or to intrigue, bribe, and even persecute on its behalf. It asks no such equivocal patronage.

Like some subtile, but potent elements, which, though invisible and imponderable, freely enter into combination with all bodies without being identified with them, Christianity aspires to permeate every form of human polity without being enthralled to any. This leaves her free and unshackled to pursue her work of supreme beneficence, for the spiritual and immortal welfare of man, in her own way and at her own charges,—as becomes her; depending not on revenues extorted from reluctant hands, by tax or bribe or menace, but on the gifts of love freely cast into her treasury; in happy immunity from the bitter taunts to which man's folly has so sorely exposed her— that she preached love, but practised theft; laid unwilling oblations on her altars, and counted " robbery a burnt offering;" did not " take of the things of Christ and give them to man." but took of the things of man and gave them to Christ. As to those temporal benefits which she confers, which are but the

" by-work " of her beneficence, the fruits and flowers which " drop from her piled-up horn of plenty," as she passes along; —for these, priceless as they are, she counts herself sufficiently requited, if governments are wise enough thankfully to accept them, and leave her alone ; dreading nothing so much as that they should seek to make that fatal return of aiding her by incongruous methods, and blindly essaying to coax or cozen or force men into the affectation of yielding her that merely nominal homage, which to her is not only nothing worth, but an insult and a wrong.

Thus do men now reason.   And so extensively have these and such like views prevailed, partly as I have said from pondering the nature and genius of Christianity, and partly from a more thoughtful weighing of the significance of that *silence* which the New Testament maintains on this subject, that the tendency of *modern* thought cannot be mistaken.   Everywhere a reconstruction of the world's old theories about " Church and State " is going on.   New States will not accept " establishments ;" young States that had, in a certain degree, adopted them, are shaking them off; old States are beginning to feel that they had better have been without them, and that it will be wise to consider how they may be got rid of ; while there is hardly one thoughtful man out of a thousand who can be got to say more for them than this :—that, as they *exist*, it is not desirable to abolish them ; though he is often ready to add, that if a man were laying the foundations of a new State, he would be wise to have nothing to do with them.

Now, though my sympathies are, and ever have been, with modern views on this subject, it is not necessary for the present argument to express any decided opinion upon it.   The *singularity* of the New Testament "silence" on the point, let the question be settled how it will, remains.   The mere fact, visible to anybody who will read the book, is that there is not one syllable on the subject ; and it is in palpable contrast with all that one would have expected from previous experience.

The universal adoption of some "Church and State" theory in ancient times ; the example of the Jewish polity itself, from which the new religion sprang ; the quiet acquiescence in the time-honoured principle, when Christianity became a great power in the world, and kings were enrolled amongst her converts, clearly show what is the general tendency of human thought and opinion, and how little likely it was to leave no trace of itself in the new Testament, if human thought and opinion alone had to do with its fabrication.

But even if it be contended, as many still contend, that the New Testament by its *silence* only indicates that the position of Christianity is designedly neutral in this matter, and leaves the nations freely to adopt or reject the practices of their ancestors as may seem expedient ; yet, even so, its very abstinence from any utterance on the subject, considering what was the constitution of the Jewish polity, what the habit of the old world, as well as that of the nations who embraced Christianity, is remarkable, and is at variance with the general stream of human speculation and practice.

11. Another paradoxical feature of the Scriptures,—of the Old Testament and the New alike,—and not to be expected in any religion devised by man, whether we judge by the actual specimens he has left us of his religious manufacture, or from the abstract principles of human nature, has often been insisted upon.   I refer to their reticence in relation to the future and invisible world.   Here the Bible confines itself to the vaguest and most general statements that are consistent with its moral aims. It tells us little more than that there will be "joy and sorrow" in that invisible world; that such joy and sorrow will be the fruit and consequence of our conduct in this, as determined according to the rules of that moral government it discloses to us.   But there are no details ; nothing but what just suffices for our guidance and duty.   Now this abstinence is "not after the manner of men ;" for the human mind instinctively yearns for light on the darkness of the future world, and this yearning is

amply and constantly met in the religions which are of undoubted human origin.   Every man, indeed, on reflection, can
see how much more worthy of a true revelation is this reticence ;
—how much more befitting the majesty of Him "to whom
secret things belong," and whose "glory it is to conceal them,"
not to tell us what is merely calculated to gratify an idle curiosity, but those things only which "belong to us and to our
children," as necessary to our guidance and safety.   But it is
not a reserve to which human nature easily reconciles itself. To
show this, we have but to look into the fables of the Greek and
Roman mythologies, or those of oriental nations, or of our Gothic
ancestors.   Similarly, the pages of the Koran only too copiously
illustrate the same fact.   But a still stronger proof of this inordinate tendency of human nature, and consequently of the *contrariety* of that tendency to the tone of the Bible, is to be found
in the additions which, as human nature proceeded to corrupt
Christianity, it made to the disclosures of the New Testament.
So strong was the impulse of nature to break bounds in this
matter, that the book could not keep men within its own limits ;
and those who professed to take it as a guide, supplemented it
with all sorts of unauthorised revelations.   In the multitudinous
fables of monkish superstition ; in the dreams of the school-
men, who, with their strange faculty of reasoning without
premises, undertook to map out heaven and hell, and even to
describe a new province on the confines of both, of which the
New Testament says nothing ; who adventured to give us exact
descriptions of the felicities of the redeemed, of the torments
of the lost, and of those penal fires which were to purify the
souls that hovered in suspense between them ; nay, even in the
comments of more sober and temperate theologians, we see
how greedily the human mind revels in these speculations,
and what violence the writers of the New Testament (if they
were, indeed, simply human) must have done to its native tendencies, in abstaining from them.   Nor is it without instruction
to mark what is the character of these superstitious additions.

They consist for the most part of pretended discoveries as to the *physical* conditions of that future life; its modes and degrees of enjoyment or suffering; detailed descriptions of all that can appeal to the senses or the sensuous imagination. They do not tell us anything of *moral* significance. In this respect, indeed, they could add nothing to the disclosures of the New Testament; for these, scanty as they are on all else touching the future life, are full and express on the moral aspects of the subject. They tell us not only all that is needful, but perhaps also all that it is possible for us to know.

And this leads me to remark that, however just the stress so often laid on the reticence of the New Testament in relation to a future state, it sheds on one spot so intense an illumination, amidst the surrounding darkness, as to constitute another anomaly of Christianity as compared with religions of confessedly human origin. These are copious on the physical accessories of a future life; on such topics the New Testament is silent, but it points, as with a sunbeam, to that which constitutes *the* characteristic and essential felicity of that life; and in this is perfectly consistent with the reigning feature which from first to last distinguishes this book from every other—that it subordinates everything to the claims of God, of religion, and morality. It accordingly declares that the future state, to which it tells us to aspire, will consist of " new heavens and a new earth," the *characteristic* of which is, that " therein dwelleth righteousness." It leaves us to conjecture, indeed, what are the secondary sources of that felicity which belongs to such a world; though we may safely augur that they will be ample enough, both from the instincts of our moral nature, which associate virtue with well-being, and the tendency of virtue itself (confirmed, even by present experience) to draw after her, as part of her train and retinue, the best kinds of all inferior good. The metaphors, also, which the New Testament employs (though, doubtless, only metaphors), and which are derived from our sources of enjoyment here, seem to foreshadow the same thing. In the songs, sung to harp and lute, of the celestial choirs; in the ever-verdant trees of immortal fruit (the aliment of perpetual youth), which overhang " the river of life;" in the enamelled meadows of perennial green, through which the ever-brimming stream rolls its translucent waters ; in the pæans of victory and the ideas suggested by crowns of gold and wreaths of unfading amaranth, faint images are suggested of some of the adjuncts of the felicities of the celestial life—of the delights which salute and wait upon " the spirits of the just made perfect." But still the book makes no precise promise beyond the fact that man shall be immortally happy, because immutably holy, there. More it may have been as impossible to tell us, as to give us a conception of a sixth sense, or enable us to comprehend modes of existence and capacities of enjoy-ment absolutely transcendental to all our present experience. But as to the essential characteristic of all happiness—that which makes the " mind its own place," and enspheres heaven within it, the New Testament casts on this point an intense light. The felicity of that world will principally consist in perfect rectitude of soul towards God and all His creatures ; and in that favour of the Infinite Beneficence " which is life for evermore." Add that that world will contain only such as are made worthy of it ; that all sin, and error, and sorrow, are banished thence, and who would not call it heaven, even though, physically, no better than earth ?

Let any one compare the pictures of a future life given in the Koran, and he will see how prodigious is the difference. Though it is admitted there, too, that only virtue, such as the Koran defines it, shall be admitted to heaven, it has provided such a *species* of happiness, so voluptuous, so fondly tricked out with sensual delight, that it is hard to imagine that virtue can mean anything very different from vice. True virtue, to enjoy it, must be corrupted before it enters paradise, or is in some peril of being so afterwards. The pleasures, most gloatingly de-scribed, are merely Epicurean delights of this world intensified and multiplied. The unlimited command there of all the concomitants of an Oriental harem and banquet, make up almost the sum of the heaven promised to a devout follower of the Prophet. And in offering this sort of heaven, as Bishop Hampden justly observes, the Koran so contradicts that preliminary moral judgment by which we must determine whether or not a professed revelation is worthy of coming from God, that it alone refutes Mahomet's claims. In a draft of a future world drawn by man's pencil, the importance attached to conditions of physical enjoyment or suffering analogous to those which are found on earth, is natural; but it strongly contrasts with the supremacy given to moral elements in the New Testament.

The stress laid on moral pre-requisites, not only as the conditions but the chief essence of all true felicity, pervades the Scriptures, and is in harmony with its characteristic subordination of every thing to the claims of God and religion. It assumes that God is carrying on a Moral Government of the world, preparatory to a more perfect dispensation, wherein its principles will be fully vindicated and brought to their true issues. This world, therefore, is but the school in which man is educating for another and a better,—the quarry whence the "precious stones" which are to "adorn the spiritual temple" are hewn, the mines whence are dug the diamonds which are polishing for the coronets worn above. We need not wonder, therefore, at the emphasis which the New Testament lays on this aspect of a future state, or that it is almost silent on every other. Many portions of our very nature, many of our appetites and passions, would seem merely *provisional*, the transient means and appliances for the formation of habits which are to last for ever, which, when they have answered their purpose, perish, like the envelope which protects the chrysalis or the shell of the young bird; or if they survive at all, may probably reappear in forms and under conditions analogous, indeed, to the present, yet so different, that we can have no present conception of them.   If so, it is no wonder that Scripture says little or nothing of the physical accessories of a future state.   But if the *character* now formed is to be the chief instrument and condition of happiness ; "if heaven be now," to employ the fine image of Robert Hall, "attracting to itself whatever is congenial to its nature, and enriching itself with the spoils of earth ;" if, as Butler conjectures, it be not God's purpose to make His creatures happy, simply as *creatures,* but only in harmony with the laws of their moral being, and that it is a fond imagination of ours that Beneficent Omnipotence has the former for its sole object ; if (to use his words) it "be His design only to make the *virtuous* man happy"—and, indeed, it seems something like a contradiction in terms to suppose that even God Himself can make any other man so—then the supreme importance which the New Testament attaches to this subject, the intense light which it throws on this central point of its disclosures with regard to a future state, while it leaves the surrounding topics and the whole scenery of the heavenly world in darkness, is intelligible, and worthy of a true revelation.   But it is not "after the manner of men ;" and this peculiarity of the New Testament, as compared with drafts of the future state given by religious systems of human origin, needs and demands an explanation.

12. The last point I would urge is the difficulty of imagining how human nature should spontaneously have given such a picture of *itself* as we find in the dogmatic statements of the Bible.   There, every soul of man is charged with a total failure in the primary and cardinal obligations of a rational and moral nature,—those we owe to GOD ; as also, though not to the same extent nor in equal degree in all cases, with a failure in the duties we owe to one another.   The indictment in the former case is of the most absolute and comprehensive character. "God looked down from heaven upon the children of men, to see if any did understand and seek God.   They are altogether gone astray ; they are altogether become polluted ; there is none

that doeth good, no, not one." They are described as universally and by nature opposed to God, and alienated from Him, and therefore as also exposed " to His wrath." These are not the colours, I think, which human nature would spontaneously employ in painting itself; still less could we reasonably expect such a picture from many different authors in the same book.

It may be very true that interpreters have erred in supposing that the language of Scripture which asserts the "depravity of human nature" in relation to *God*, is equally applicable to man in his entire moral and social capacity,—as if *no* good of any kind remained in him, or was to be expected from him. This extreme view appears sufficiently refuted (if there were no other argument) by the words of Christ, in which, while declaring our nature to be "evil," He still implies that man knows very well how to do some things "that are good." "If ye then, *being evil*, know how to give good gifts unto your children, how much more shall your heavenly Father give good things to them that ask Him?" There are actions of human nature which we cannot, without absurdity, deny to be "good;"—actions prompted by benevolence and compassion; by generous and self-sacrificing patriotism; by the self-forgetting *abandon* of parental or filial love; by incorruptible honesty and truthfulness in the dealings between man and man. It is true, indeed, that these will want that quality which can alone crown them, if not radicated in religious principle, or if performed without a thought of God, and must assuredly be utterly without avail as a compensation for failure in the yet higher moral claims which the Creator rightfully makes upon us. Still they are beautiful, and claim our admiration accordingly ; nor is there any ground for the exaggerations of theologians on this subject. The Scripture representations of man in his ordinary moral relations with his fellow-men are, soberly interpreted, dark enough, and only too well justified by the history of the world. Its crimes, and consequent miseries; its wars and oppressions; its vices and selfishness, too surely show that there is something very wrong in human nature.   But, in truth, the better a man is affirmed to be in his social capacity, the better he knows what is morally right and fair, and the better he exhibits it in his relations to his fellow-men, the heavier is that indictment which the Bible brings against him of being disloyal to God.   For would it not aggravate that charge, if God could say with truth to any one of us, " You have known how to fulfil every relation in life,—except to Me.   You were a good son—you knew how to 'reverence and obey' your parents ; you were a good father—you knew 'how to give good gifts unto your children ;' you were a good neighbour, and shared your bread with the hungry ; you were a just master, and ' never robbed the hireling of his wages ;' you were just, 'and coveted no man's silver and gold ;' but ME, the Author of your being, who 'breathed into you the breath of life,' who bestowed upon you all the faculties you possess and all the blessings you enjoy, by whose bounty you have been fed, by whose mercy you have been spared,—ME you have not thought of ; or if a thought has obtruded itself, it has been unwelcome to you ; you have offered Me neither gratitude nor obedience ; you have not sought to please Me, or shrunk from offending Me ; never asked My counsel or sanction in any plan of yours, and have lived as though I were not."   Would it be any extenuation of man's guilt that he knew so exactly how to comply with the requisitions of the Second Table, while he so egregiously failed in those of the First ?   Now this great and universal apostacy the Bible charges, in the most direct and un-sparing manner, on the whole human race.

If the charge be true, if the " natural man " be thus universally oblivious of God, if he does "not like to retain" his Creator and Benefactor " in his thoughts," it is a charge against him of a far baser ingratitude than he could possibly be guilty of towards his neighbour, and a far more insolent disobedience than he could ever display towards any earthly superior.   Now, considering how unwilling human nature is to suspect, and much more proclaim, its own baseness ; how easily it deceives itself

into a good opinion of itself; above all, how quietly it takes
the thought of this very indictment, and how much more loudly
it resents any charge of baseness towards man than of any
amount of delinquency towards God, I doubt whether it would
spontaneously paint itself in the dark colours of the Bible. If
it could not "wash the Ethiop white," it would at least not
intensify the dye.

If it be said—as indeed the very repulsiveness of the Bible
declarations has made many say—that the picture seems grossly
overcharged; that the estimate of man's moral delinquency is
exaggerated; I must leave it to each man, looking at the history
of the world in relation to God, and the voice of his own consciousness, to judge of *that*. But if the Bible thus appears to
be a libel on human nature, it strengthens my present argument.
It certainly is a paradox that a draft of human nature, which
seems greatly to wrong itself, should be persistently given in a
book written by so many different men, in such distant ages,
and in the teeth of all natural prepossessions of egotism and
vanity.

Similar remarks apply to the doctrines by which the Bible
proposes to remedy the evils under which our nature labours.
The whole process by which man is to obtain forgiveness and
restoration is a process of humiliation. He is to cast himself,
without one attempt at justification or extenuation, upon "the
mercy of God in Christ Jesus;" assured that, if he does so, he
will be accepted; and from that lowest, but needful stage of
"self-abasement," be enabled to climb the whole arduous ascent
between sin and holiness, earth and heaven. I doubt much
whether a plan so unflattering to man's self-righteousness, and
so deeply offensive to his pride and vanity, would have been
devised by himself.

In truth, I believe there never was a religious system,—
especially when conjoined with the self-denial it exacts and the
austere heaven it promises,—which has been on the whole more
distasteful to the intellect and heart of man; and accordingly

it has met with a more general and bitter opposition among men than any other.

If it be affirmed, as sometimes it has been, that Christianity must have a subtile adaptation to the condition of human nature, to account even for that degree of welcome and that emphatic admiration it has met with,—so that its main peculiarities of doctrine have been mentioned as indicative of a deep knowledge of that nature, of its moral necessities and remedies, in those who proclaimed them,—all this is quite true too. It *is* adapted to human nature, as a bitter medicine may be to a patient ; and the question is, would human nature have prescribed it? Those who have taken it, tried its efficacy, and recovered spiritual health, gladly proclaim its value. But to those who have not, and who will not try it, it is an unpalatable potion still. Moreover, the myriads who have experimented upon it, and now see its adaptation to the moral wants, guilt, and weaknesses of human nature, have with one voice proclaimed that *before* they tried it, it was to them, as to the rest of the world, an "offence" alike to intellect and heart, as also the book itself expressly declares it *would* be. "The gospel," said Paul, "is to the Jews a stumbling-block, and to the Greeks foolishness."

The mere *character* of the doctrines of the Gospel—so remote on the whole from the ordinary track of human speculation (whatever faint analogies may be found with other systems), forms no slight argument that man would not have been likely to conceive them ; and the Jew, to whom they have ever been as gall and wormwood, as little as any. But the indictment against human nature, the unflattering portrait that is everywhere given of it, it is still more difficult to ascribe to human nature itself. Nay, more ; if the Bible be of purely human origin, we must not only imagine men spontaneously giving expression to a religious system in which themselves and all mankind are painted in the most odious colours, but telling the world at the same time that they know the portrait will be an

" offence " and a "scandal " to it, and encouraging all who receive it to expect " tribulation " for so doing !   Is this "after the manner of men " ?

Quite as extraordinary is the *tone* in which the "depravity " of man in his relation to God is asserted.   It is in no cynical, no satirical spirit ; there is nothing akin to misanthropy in it. This last is always bitter enough ; for it is itself the mere expression of a vindictive memory of the real or presumed injuries by which wounded vanity or self-esteem, or perhaps some better qualities, have been shocked ; and hence its morbid view of human nature in general.   Misanthropy thinks simply of man, and his relation to his fellows.   Of that great moral lesion of his nature with which the Bible deals—of *God's* controversy with him—it has not a word to say.   It is too human for *that.* In all philosophy and fiction, in the maxims of a Rochefoucauld, in the speeches of a Timon, there is not a word that indicates the faintest conception that it is man's relation to God that chiefly determines the question of his moral worthlessness or worth.

On the other hand, the writers of the Bible, in their tremendous impeachment of human nature, seem not to think as men at all.   They speak in accordance with what I have represented as the character of the Bible,—on behalf of God.   They are simply witnesses for Him.   There is not a shadow of petulance or malice or resentment in their utterances ; and yet if any men ever had cause for resentment, surely they had.   The most uncompromising charges of man's religious apostacy are made with judicial calmness and composure, mingled, indeed, with a deep compassion for those whom they thus arraign, and with urgent entreaties to " flee from the wrath to come ; " but there is nothing of human passion, or pique, or waywardness, or moroseness, discernible about it.   On the contrary, it is most evident that they thus arraign human nature, and point out the evils under which it groans, only with the conviction that the detection of the malady is essential to the cure, and with the hope of effecting it. The matter and the tone of the sacred writers on these subjects are unparalleled in all other literature.[1]

Lastly; a general presumption that the religion of the Bible sprang from some other source than that which gave birth to the religions which are incontrovertibly of human growth, may be further gathered from this,—that when man proceeded, as he has so often done, to modify or corrupt that religion, it has always been in the direction, and "after the similitude," of those religious systems which have his own signature upon them; till at last Judaism under the Jews, and Christianity under the Christians, were so far assimilated to the religions man had incontestably invented, that it has not always been easy to discern the difference. Thus human nature has borne significant testimony, both to the *alien* nature of that which it has so obstinately bent to its purpose, and to its own original and native propensions.

The process by which the Jews reduced the religion of the Old Testament to that condition in which Christ Himself declared that they had "made the law of God of none effect by their traditions," was much the same with the process by which Christians slowly, but surely, engrafted upon Christianity abuses which at last offended men like Erasmus almost as much as men like Luther; and in either case the deflection was in the same direction, for human nature was true to itself. Whately, in his admirable work on the "Errors of Romanism," justly objects to speak of them as if they were exclusively those of the Church of Rome. For similar reasons, I would not speak either of Jewish or Romanist errors, as if they were exclusively chargeable on some particular races or classes of men. It is not so; they are the errors of human nature, and might be reproduced, in various forms and degrees, in any age and by any men. From tendencies characteristic of that *nature* have all the evils in question come.

[1] Chalmers has well illustrated this peculiar tone of the sacred writers in his work on the "Evidences."—*Collected Works*, vol. ii. book iii. chap. ii. pp. 118-120.

That the corruptions and abuses, of which no candid Jew or Romanist will deny their fathers to have been guilty, were of a nature which tended to assimilate Judaism and Christianity more and more to the current religions which had extensively prevailed in the world, and whose origin was distinctly human, is evident on the slightest inspection. The Jews for ages, even down to the Captivity, were perpetually falling into the idolatries of the surrounding nations, though they were so severely scourged for it; and that great lapse was accompanied, as might be expected, with manifold corresponding corruptions in their entire institute. As for the New Testament,—it might at first sight seem, to a candid and intelligent reader, incredible that any similar degradation could take place in the religion it taught;—a religion marked by the purest morality, by the most simple ritual; a religion which seemed to give so little handle by which corruption could lay hold of it; which made so little appeal to the senses, had no esoteric mysteries, came out into the light, disclaimed all force, exulted in spiritual freedom. Any man might rationally have doubted whether it *could* have been converted into that system which immediately preceded the Reformation, and in which all these characteristics were reversed; in which hierarchical pomp, sacerdotal pretensions, a meretricious splendour of worship, were prominent characteristics; in which a huge wild growth of superstition had overshadowed and blighted alike simple doctrine and pure morality; in which the moral code was so relaxed that its proper claims were too often commuted for penance, or even pence; in which (as if to hide the transformation) the very statute-book of the religion was, in a great degree, suppressed, or kept in the hands of the priesthood; the service mumbled in an unknown tongue; ignorance hailed as the " mother of devotion ;" and all resistance to the spiritual tyranny thus erected, met throughout Europe with the most ruthless resort to fire and steel! Was it possible, one is ready to ask, that human nature could transform primitive Christianity into *that?* The thing was possible,

for it was done ; but it could have been done only because the
tendencies of human nature, so far from being likely to originate
the religion of the New Testament, vehemently reacted against
it. All that man did, when he took it in hand, was to spoil it.
Illustrations of this have been given in this and the preceding
lecture, when dealing with special instances of apparent contrariety between the Bible and human nature :—as, for example,
when speaking of its morality, which man has ever made more
accommodating ; and its scanty revelations of a future state,
which he has so voluminously supplemented. But in point of
fact the same spirit is seen through the whole series of changes.
All are in one direction. Man loved a gorgeous ritual, and the
simplicity of the Christian worship was soon enveloped in a
glittering cloud of ceremonies. He was addicted to idolatry,
and he was taught that there were a thousand tutelary saints
and angels to whom he might legitimately offer various species
of adoration. He was prone to " self-righteousness," and he was
told that austerities and penances, and even money, were effica-
cious supplements of a defective repentance and obedience.
His pride often aspired to superhuman merit rather than content itself with plain Christian obedience, and he learned to
attach an artificial sanctity to celibacy, to monastic seclusion,
and to the cell and roots of the anchorite. Christianity had no
priest except the one invisible High Priest, " passed into the
heavens ; " but man's weak heart had been accustomed to the
solace of many, and he soon inaugurated an order of priests
with more than the prerogatives of the heathen priesthood, and
more than its sacerdotal pretensions. Christianity had no
" sacrifices," except the " one offering " of the invisible High
Priest ; but as man had made " priests," so they must " needs
have somewhat to offer," and that somewhat was no less than a
sacrifice perpetually renewed by a stupendous miracle. And,
finally, to all this, human nature gave its consent, for it loves to
lay responsibility on other shoulders than its own ; and leaning
credulously on the priest, fully divided with him the infamy and

guilt of " priestcraft."   " *Populus vult decipi* " is but a prelude and invitation to the priest's " *decipietur*," and to a great extent an apology for it.[1]

In conclusion, if human nature gradually constructed the system of religion which overshadowed Europe just before the Reformation, out of the New Testament (as it undoubtedly did), it is to me a strong presumption that that same human nature, which showed its genuine proclivities in so long a course and on so great a scale, was not the sole or legitimate author of the New Testament itself.

[1] Whately, in his " Errors of Romanism," makes candid, but just admission of this.   Pp. 89–95.   London, 1845.

LECTURE III.

ARGUMENTS ANCILLARY TO THE SAME CONCLUSION.

LECTURE III.

THERE are certain peculiarities in the teaching and conduct of the writers of the New Testament (and it would be easy to select like topics from the Old) which are ancillary to the same conclusion. Considering the condition and antecedents of the founders of Christianity, and that, on the points to which I am about to refer, philosophers and religionists, in their attempt to reform human error, have very generally gone astray ; it is not easy to see how the suggestions of mere human sagacity kept ignorant men like the apostles in the right path, when it is so difficult even for the wise to find it.

The *first* point I would mention is the decision with which the principle is asserted, that conscientiously to reduce to practice what we already know, and so far as we know it, is the surest method of advancing in the knowledge of Divine truth. "To do the will of God," is in the New Testament the great source of further illumination. It rests indeed on a very general principle of our nature—which applies to all things that are *practical ;* and therefore to religion, which, if *not* practical, is nothing.

It did not escape the penetration of Aristotle any more than that of Butler,[1] that we are so constituted, that the only effectual way of learning things of a practical nature, is to work them into the soul by habit, and to give them expression in the life. The great exponent of this principle, as applied to religion, is our Lord Himself, who expressly proclaims it in the words, "He that doeth the will of God shall know of the doctrine whether it be of God." This is the true "Via Intelligentiæ," "The way of understanding," as Jeremy Taylor calls it in his celebrated sermon on the text. That text, indeed, does not mean, "Blindly accept whatever you are told, on human authority, is the will of God, and *act* upon it." Neither does it say, "If you are *doubtful* whether or not a doctrine is of God, nevertheless act upon it ; *that* is the way to know of the doctrine whether it be of God :" for that would imply a contradiction, telling us to do the will of God without any presumed knowledge of that will. But it plainly means what it *says*— that if we do what *is* the will of God, we shall in that way best learn the doctrine whether it be of God ; that is, come to a clear perception and plenary conviction of its Divine origin.[2]

[1] "It is well said, therefore, that the just man becomes so by doing what is just, and the temperate by doing what is temperate. But many there are who do not practise these things, but betaking themselves to talking about them (ἐπὶ δὲ τὸν λόγον καταφεύγοντες), imagine they are philosophizing, and that in that way they will be duly affected by them (καὶ οὕτως ἔσεσθαι σπουδαῖοι) ; doing something like what the sick do when they listen diligently to their physicians and follow none of their prescriptions. As therefore these do not get health of body by that sort of therapeutics, neither do those health of soul by such sort of philosophy."—Aristotle, Eth. II. iv.

Butler, with yet deeper philosophy, proceeds one step further. "Going over the theory of virtue," says he, "in one's thoughts, talking well, and drawing fine pictures of it ; this is so far from necessarily or certainly conducing to form a habit of it in him who thus employs himself, that it may *harden* the mind in a contrary course, and render it gradually more insensible ; that is, form a habit of insensibility to all moral considerations. For, from our very faculty of habits, *passive* impressions by being repeated grow weaker."—Analogy, Part I. chap. v.

[2] It is true that the rule to each *individual* man must be his own conscientious conviction, after diligent use of such means of illumination as are in his power, as to what *is* the will of God. But even so, it is the right

Religious knowledge, then, being *practical*, can be made effectual by no mere intellectual assent or conviction, but must be wrought into the very tissues of our moral and spiritual life; just as food can nourish us only as it is actually assimilated into our flesh and blood. *Practical* truth thus becomes our own in a sense in which no mere theoretical truth ever can be : and a soul, thus cognisant of it, is in a position to attain higher and higher degrees of it.

Nor is it difficult to see that the prescribed method naturally *tends* to produce this result. It does for the soul what the "rectification" of his instruments does for the astronomer. As that is necessary for the just observation of sun or star, so is this docile disposition necessary to place the soul in a right posture in reference to the great source of spiritual illumination. It lays the axe at the root of all prejudices and sinister aims, and necessarily implies that simplicity and candour, the lack of which it is that chiefly obstructs our mental vision.

I know that Christianity tells us (and I believe with perfect truth) that He who made this docility the condition of our progress, directly rewards it by express donation of increased light from Himself. But I do not, of course, urge this, because it would be to assume the truth of the claims of the New Testament. I simply remark that it was in a spirit of deep knowledge of the necessary conditions of spiritual and moral illumination, that it thus insists on the diligent "*doing* of the will of God," as the condition of all advance in the knowledge of Divine truth ; — just as he alone can truly discern the excellence and beauty of integrity and virtue who becomes acquainted with them by practice. Nor, even if it be supposed that the initial knowledge of the will of God, on the part of a

---

rule. For this faithful listening to conscience, after diligent examination, is at any rate the will of God ; and if conscience be sincere and diligent, will rarely lead men astray. At all events, it is the only possible rule, and for the reasons assigned in the context, the one best calculated to clarify the mind and prepare it for further truth.

genuinely sincere disciple, is still mixed with remaining error, is the rule less philosophically just. For the dispositions it enjoins and cherishes put us in the most likely way to defecate the mind from mistake and illusion ; just as in ordinary practical matters, candour and docility, when we come to test knowledge by *experience*, will usually soon show where a misleading fallacy lies.

2. A second point, in which the teaching of the New Testament alike transcends the antecedents of the writers, and the then prevailing impressions of the value of orthodoxy *per se* and the efficacy of rite and ceremony, is akin to the preceding : I mean the decision with which the writers insist that no religious knowledge is worth anything at all if it be not reduced to practice. If they insist on the vital importance of *faith*, it is impossible not to see that it is as a " motive power,"—as the informing spirit of action,—that they so commend it.

" Faith without works is dead," says St. James. It is, says St. Paul : for " though I had all faith so that I could remove mountains, without charity I am as sounding brass or a tinkling cymbal." " Can faith save ? " says St. James. Yes, says St. Paul, but it must be a " faith working by love,"—unfeigned love to God and man. And all this is but the echo of the same doctrine which is found in the Old Testament. " To man, God saith, The fear of the Lord, that is wisdom, and to depart from evil is understanding : " to which it were easy to add a score of like passages.

Now when we consider how very generally this great truth is forgotten by men of all religions, and too often by Christians themselves, who have been often taunted (and have not seldom given just grounds for the taunt) that they pay more attention to " faith " than to " works," to a creed than a life, and plume themselves on that dead orthodoxy which resembles true faith about as much as a mummy a living man ;—it is not a little remarkable that the New Testament should have been so perspicuous and decisive on a point on which Jew and Gentile generally went astray, and in which Christians themselves, yielding to those tendencies of human nature by which they at last assimilated their religion to that of the heathen, too often followed their example. The heathen priesthood (as elsewhere said [1]) were generally contented to abandon the field of practical morality altogether; and without much caring even about an orthodox faith, reduced religion to a thing of rite and ceremonial, in which the Christian Church, in a few centuries, too faithfully imitated them.

3. A third point, I think, worthy of attention, is the noble freedom from minute casuistry which characterizes the writings of the New Testament, and the astonishing wisdom and moderation with which such questions, when they *must* be confronted, are discussed. Of the *first*, there is not only abundant proof in the very general form in which the moral precepts of the New Testament are given,—frankly relying on the common sense and candour of the reader to interpret and apply them aright; but it is conceded even in the objections which adverse critics have made to that very generality. The New Testament, it has been affirmed, often lays down rules so vague as to be practically no rules at all. Few, I think, will acquiesce in this judgment. On the other hand, the objection is fairly met by a *reductio ad absurdum ;* for to specify all the specialities of circumstance which must modify and limit any moral precept would be to ask a moral teacher to perform an impossibility, and has never been exacted of any. Even the precepts, " Love your enemies,"—" Love all men,"—" Do to others as ye would that others should do to you," may be met by many *seeming* and some *real* limitations. But they are safe rules

---

[1] *Ante*, pp. 17, 18.

" But the religion of the heathen, as was before observed, little concerned itself in their morals. The priests that delivered the oracles of heaven, and pretended to speak from the gods, spoke little of virtue and a good life. And, on the other side, the philosophers, who spoke from reason, made not much mention of the Deity in their ethics."—Locke's " Reasonableness of Christianity." Works, vol. vi. p. 144. London, 1824.

enough for any honest man who sincerely wishes to act upon them; and so in other cases. The precepts of Christ and His apostles are all of this *general* nature—embodying principles of which common sense, if it be but conjoined with candour, can easily see the propriety, and leaving it to that same common sense and right feeling to determine the application. Sometimes, indeed, Christ does not hesitate, in order to give greater point and force to His maxims, to embody them in forms which look paradoxical; as where He enjoins us, when " smitten on the one cheek, to turn the other also;" or to "pluck out even the right eye," if it is the cause of "offence" to us. The former command, a captious critic would tell us, is a little too much for the world, or even for the Christian. But until he consistently interprets the latter, and many other such expressions, with the same extravagant *literality*, it would be but fair to apply the more rational interpretation to both; and to say that we have in the first a *rhetorical* expression of the spirit which Christ would inculcate on His disciples, and which ought to animate them, even when suffering most wrongfully.

But, at all events, the moral elements of the New Testament are notably free from those minute, no doubt often difficult, but as often frivolous discussions, which so many casuists have taxed all their ingenuity to multiply, and by which they have made their books as much the laughing-stock, as the oracles, of the world. Anxious to anticipate every conceivable assemblage of circumstances which may modify moral precepts, casuistry aims at a scientific completeness which is unattainable, for a thousand folios would not be sufficient for it. And, in general, it may be said that the more minute it is,—the more pretentiously exhaustive,—so much the more thorny, litigious, frivolous, and, in a moral sense, pernicious, it becomes. All this is but too notoriously exemplified in the voluminous collections of " cases" and "judgments" which make up the more ponderous systems of Christian casuistry; the questions, in the immense preponderance of instances, being either such as an upright heart and an honest conscience will intuitively decide from the general precepts; or such as, if they really justify doubt and involve difficulty, had far better be left to be argued and determined as the exigencies of practical life give rise to them, than formed into a *system;* for this, in order to make it complete, tempts men to raise ten thousand imaginary questions that would never require to be decided in practice, and which only tend to wiredraw the judgment, and not seldom ensnare, or even pollute, the conscience both of those who ask and of those who decide them.

But while there is in the New Testament a remarkable free dom from all those minute and supersubtile questions which make the staple of casuistry, yet when such questions (for, as just intimated, they *will* occur in actual life) incidentally present themselves, it is impossible not to be struck with the singular prudence and moderation with which they are treated. We have several examples in the Gospels, and others in the Epistles. The Jews, indeed, like all who have perverted a moral institute into a copious system of casuistry, had well-nigh evacuated the moral element of their law altogether; and Christ in the most trenchant manner explodes and ridicules that sophistry, equally captious and wicked, which had led to this result. Under pretence of giving to the " treasury of God," some of them would fain, in certain cases, evade the obligations of filial affection; by the frivolous distinction between the " temple and the altar," or " between the altar and the oblation laid upon it," they would absolve themselves from the obligations of an oath; and by straining the law of the Sabbath in a thousand absurd ways, they converted into an intolerable yoke what was intended to be a merciful rest and solace to the " weary and heavy laden." He might well say of the first, " Ye make the law of God of none effect by your traditions ; " of the second, "Ye fools and blind, for whether is greater, the altar or the temple? the altar or the oblation ? " and of the third, " The Sabbath was made for man, and not man for the Sabbath ; " " God will have mercy and not sacrifice ;" and, "Had ye known what this meaneth, ye would not have condemned the guiltless." Again, His answer to those who sought to inveigle Him into dangerous collision with the civil government, by asking, "Whether it was lawful to give tribute to Cæsar or not" (though blamed by some critics for reasons to me utterly incomprehensible), has been generally considered, as it seems to have been by those who put the invidious question, a masterpiece of that prudence which combines the "wisdom of the serpent with the innocence of the dove."

All these matters are decided on the broadest principles, in marked contrast with the mode of casuists in general, and especially of the Jewish casuists of that age.[1]

The same spirit rules in the Acts and Epistles. In these are discussed some questions of great difficulty, which would have provoked whole chapters of ingenious wiredrawing in the tomes of the Escobars and Baunys of a later age ;—questions which arose out of the novel circumstances in which Christian maxims and institutions had placed the world. In the treatment of these questions it is impossible, I think, to deny the justness of thinking and consummate prudence which the Christian teachers evince.

We see this conspicuously in the management of that vehement dispute which arose so early at Antioch between the Jewish converts who were still attached to Judaism, and could

---

[1] It is the same with the Old Testament. "What doth God require of thee," says the prophet, "but to do justly, to love mercy, and to walk humbly with thy God?" Throughout the book there is no countenance given to those refinements of casuistry which ever mark the *decadence* of a moral system. Nay, it is curious to see that while the Jews were continually degrading their own institute, and gradually piling up those traditions by which Christ expressly says "they had made void the law of God," the successive prophets not only show no sympathy with them (or rather the most marked antipathy), and not only perpetually recall them to that *spirit* of the law which they were sacrificing to the *letter*, but continually give their code a higher and higher spirituality, and make the claims of the moral over the ceremonial law more and more emphatic.

not reconcile themselves to its summary abolition, and the Gentile converts, who could not consent "to bind that heavy yoke" on their shoulders. The question was referred to a council of the Apostles, Elders, and Church generally, at Jerusalem. Though almost all the members—certainly all the principal— were *Jewish* Christians, yet in what a modest and gentle temper, in how conciliatory a spirit, on what reasonable terms, is the question discussed and decided! One cannot find a trace in *this* Council of that blind bigotry which has so often made subsequent ecclesiastical assemblies, and professedly Christian Governments, when dealing with ecclesiastical matters, so obstinate and intractable. If it be reckoned (though with some latitude) the *first* of the long series of " Ecclesiastical Councils," there is hardly one in all Labbe's huge folios of subsequent " Concilia " on which a Christian can look with such unmingled satisfaction. Whence came these rude men, in the starkness of their ignorance and inexperience, in the infancy of their institutions,—themselves only just escaped from life-long bondage to a system of most opposite characteristics,—to be thus superior to prejudice, and so prudent in their conduct as compared with all their successors, who yet had their light to walk by, and shut their eyes to it?

Similar observations apply to the several cases of casuistry which Paul had to decide. His judgments are singularly marked by robust good sense, moderation, and charity. Take the case of the convert, for example, whose lapse from Christian morality had brought scandal on the Church of Corinth. While the apostle uncompromisingly demands his expulsion, he none the less welcomes him back the moment he exhibits genuine repentance; and with exquisite pathos enjoins his fellow-Christians to assure the returning wanderer of their forgiveness, and to " comfort him, lest he be swallowed up of over-much sorrow."[1]

---

[1] Most exquisitely has Milton touched this trait of the evangelical discipline in the wonderful descriptions of the true office of excommunication, given in his " Tracts on Church Government " and " On Reformation : "—

What an entire absence is here of that austerity and spiritual prudery which soon after characterized Christian Fathers and Churches, and which proclaimed that *one* lapse into flagrant sin was an irrecoverable error, and must operate as an eternal bar to renewed communion!   How superior is Paul's decision both to that fanaticism and that laxity which on this subject and so many others alternately infested the Church, when man undertook to remodel the Gospel!   So little was that Gospel likely to come from him, that the moment he takes it in hand he bends its rules to one extreme or other; now to the side of extreme rigour, and now of scandalous laxity.

Another instance of a decision, equally marked by moderation and good sense, is the one respecting the propriety of "abstaining from meat offered to idols," as also that respecting the observance of "certain days;" on both which points divisions of opinion had arisen in the Church, aggravated, as usual, by the strong prejudices of those who still clung with the customary pertinacity of human nature to tradition and antiquity.   Paul decides that these things, in themselves, are neither good nor bad : "that an idol is nothing in the world;" that he who eats of meat offered to it, is "neither the better nor the worse" for it; that he "who observes" certain days, and "he who does not observe them," may offer an equally acceptable service to God,—*provided* "their conscience condemn them not in the things they allow;" and that there is nothing in such variety of opinion and usage that should break the

"It may be truly said, that as the mercies of wicked men are cruelties, so the cruelties of the Church are mercies. For if repentance sent from heaven meet this lost wanderer, and draw him out of that steep journey, wherein he was hasting towards destruction,—to come and reconcile himself to the Church ; if he bring with him his bill of health, and that he is now clear of infection, and of no danger to the other sheep ; then with incredible expressions of joy all his brethren receive him, and set before him those perfumed banquets of Christian consolation,—with precious ointments bathing and fomenting the old, and now to be forgotten stripes, which terror and shame had inflicted ; and thus with heavenly solaces they cheer up his humble remorse, till he regain his first health and felicity."

"perfect bond of charity." At the same time he affirms that though every man had a *right* to perfect liberty of judgment and practice in such matters, yet that a true Christian will in some cases impose a voluntary law upon himself, if his innocent liberty is likely to lead others into sin, " through their weak conscience." He will avoid that which may be "a stumbling-block in his brother's way;" and Paul nobly declares, "If meat make my brother to offend, I will eat no flesh while the world standeth."

And this " counsel of perfection " is based on the only true principle ;—not on the " weak brother's " *rights*, but on our own charity towards him, lest we be to him the accidental cause of sin. This we may be by inadvertence; for with true philosophic discrimination the apostle asserts that even an " erroneous conscience " still binds ; and that if, therefore, the "weak brother" imitates us, on our authority or by our example, in an action of the innocence of which *we* may be convinced, while he himself still doubts, he is not free from sin ; since he " who doubts," is self-condemned, if he performs any action while in that state of doubt about its lawfulness ; and that he only is "happy, who condemneth not himself in the thing that he alloweth." Well had it been for the world if principles so plain and comprehensive had guided the decisions of those who have treated of such matters in their books of casuistry. The famous doctrine of the "probable," and the rules for directing the " intention," with which Pascal makes himself and the world so merry, would never have been heard of.

But that the concession to a " weak brother " was merely a voluntary concession to his " weakness," and not to be construed to the prejudice of Christian liberty, is plain, both from Paul's founding it wholly on charity, and from his own conduct : for while he enjoins this magnanimity on proper occasions, he firmly rebukes Peter's equivocal compliance with Jewish prejudice at Antioch. *That*, too, was a compliance in things, *in themselves*, indifferent, and a hasty reasoner might have imagined that Peter was only doing what Paul avowedly did on some occasions,—"becoming all things to all men." But Paul was far too perspicacious to be imposed upon by any such false analogy, or to confound treachery to confessed truth and mean truckling to ignorance and bigotry with an indulgent charity! He felt that the question was, whether liberty should be,—not voluntarily foregone,—but unworthily sacrificed: he therefore says, "To whom we gave place, no, not for an hour."[1]

And on the same principle, had it been demanded of him, as a moral obligation, that he should surrender his *liberty* of "eating meat offered to idols," or abstaining, as he pleased; had he been told that he must look at the thing as morally wrong; we cannot have a doubt that he would have eaten the obnoxious viands, in the very face of his censors, on the first opportunity. To do or not to do a thing that we admit to be *indifferent*, is Christian prudence or imprudence according to circumstances; it may be Christian charity, it may be Christian folly. A magnanimous desire not to "give offence to weak consciences" is one thing; to be told that though a thing be indifferent, we *must* practise it; or that, though we think it indifferent, we are to regard it as morally right or wrong, is quite another.

Now where did this Jew, a "Hebrew of the Hebrews, and as touching the law a Pharisee," who had been brought up after "the straightest of that sect," and sat at the feet of Gamaliel, come by his discriminating and elevated casuistry? Not, we may be sure, from the Jews, who were so tenacious, not only of their ancient law, but of their most frivolous glosses upon it; —whose whole soul was immersed in ceremonial, and who had made void even the "weightier matters of the law" by their punctilious scrupulosity.

---

[1] The full import, and therefore rational vehemence, of Paul's protest on this occasion, is admirably drawn out in a remarkable Sermon (or rather Dissertation) by the Rev. Thos. Binney, entitled "The Law our Schoolmaster." *Sermons* preached in the King's Weigh-house Chapel. (1829-1869.) 8vo. London. Pp. 276-284.

Nay, how superior is the apostle's whole mode of looking at such questions to that in which the Christian Church afterwards, and for many ages, looked, and to a considerable extent *still* looks, at them.   How many "Churches" and "Councils" have contended to the death, not only for the exact observance of a given ceremonial, but even for the mode of that ceremonial, even for the shadow of that mode ; contended for it as for the most vital truth, and sacrificed not only charity, but liberty, to their crotchet.   Nay, how often for the sake of their senseless idol of "Uniformity" (which, in such matters at least, the apostle's whole reasoning shows to be of no consequence—of no more than those other "Mumbo Jumbos" which he reduces to the same category of "nothing in the world"), have men imprisoned and scourged and slain their fellow-Christians ;— not "weaker brethren," indeed, but men a great deal stronger in every respect,—except in the pernicious prerogative of persecution.   How came Paul and the other writers of the New Testament to be so much wiser than the millions of their successors, who had their precepts and example before them, and set them both at naught ?

Similar commendation, in my opinion, is due to the apostle's decisions in reference to another question on which the Corinthians consulted him ; I mean, marriage.   But on this I will not lay any special stress, inasmuch as many demur to the accuracy of the apostle's judgment ; and deem that, though confessing marriage not only "lawful," but "honourable in all," and to men in general, expedient, he has too much admiration for celibacy, and in some degree sanctions the extravagant views on that subject afterwards developed in the Church. I shall content myself, therefore, with simply expressing my conviction that those who thus argue do less than justice to his views, and with giving, in a few words, my reasons for so thinking.   The error of their interpretation seems to me to consist in supposing that the apostle, in the phrases they censure, is speaking of the expediency, or otherwise, of marriage

in general—marriage in all ages, and in reference to all men.
Now if this be inferred, it seems contradicted by what the
apostle expressly says in other places. He says, showing what
his opinion of marriage *generally* is:—" It is good for every
man to have his own wife, and every woman her own husband."
It seems more reasonable, therefore, to suppose that, in the
cases here referred to, he is speaking with special reference
to the circumstances of the Corinthians, who had consulted
him. Some may have asked him whether marriage, however
desirable, was expedient in times of persecution and "present
distress" like theirs; whether it was wise "to give" (as
Bacon phrases it) " such hostages to fortune, as wife and children." He decides that, in such circumstances, such as *could*
receive the doctrine would be wiser to abstain from such bonds
than to entangle themselves with them. In similar circumstances (whether in that age or *any other*) he would also seem,
by implication, to say, that such as could be celibates, and yet
chaste; pure, yet without a daily warfare with impulse and
passion, would in his judgment be better if they remained
celibates; but he acknowledges that, as a general principle,
" every man should have his own wife;" that only some men
can receive the above counsel of celibacy; and therefore con-
cludes that it is " better to marry than to burn;"—better to
face the inconveniences of marriage even in times of persecution, than to live in perpetual conflict with passion.

The apostle has also been charged, and that in somewhat
coarse terms, with treating this subject too exclusively in its
lower and more animal aspects. The answer is, first, that even
in these aspects, marriage has such momentous bearings on
human welfare,—on virtue and vice,—as to make it necessary
that the moralist should not overlook them; and secondly, that
the passages in question are not the only passages in which the
apostle lets us see what are his sentiments on this subject. It
is impossible to imagine a loftier ideal of purity, the tenderness,
the forbearance, the devotion which ought ever to characterise

connubial love, than he has given us in various parts of his epistles, and especially where he tells us that it ought to emulate the self-sacrificing love of Christ Himself. In truth, the sentiments of the New Testament in relation to women are so vividly contrasted with those of the ancient world in general, that they may be fairly adduced, not merely as an illustration of the argument of the present lecture;—namely, the superiority in many points of the teaching of the New Testament to what might be expected from the antecedents and condition of the teachers, but of its superiority to the teaching of the greatest sages of antiquity.

On another related matter there can be no doubt that Paul's decision is eminently that of common sense. I mean that in which he decides that, if a Christian husband has an unbelieving wife, or a Christian wife an unbelieving husband, the marriage shall not be dissolved on that account; and for this reason, if for no other, that it was possible continued intercourse might issue in the conversion and salvation of the unbelieving party. It had been well if all who have treated cases somewhat *akin* to this, had imitated his tact and good sense.

4. Another point, worthy of being noted here, is the place assigned to Charity in the New Testament. It is represented as the crown and glory of all religion. That eminence is not given to correct belief,—to that *faith* which is yet so highly exalted, and which so many in after ages would fain honour more than charity. Faith, though of paramount importance, is so only relatively,—as the necessary condition of charity and every other excellence. It is the *root*, as some other graces are the leaf and stem; but Charity is represented as the flower and fruit. It is the immortal product of them all, and still "abides," when "hope" vanishes in fruition, and "faith" is lost in "sight." It is the fulfilling of the law; it is that which faith *must* produce, or faith itself exists not. In the glowing eulogy of it in 1 Cor. xiii., we see that Paul extols it above every other Christian grace, above all intellectual orthodoxy,

above all "revelations," "visions," and "miracles;" above the "eloquence of men and of angels," above the self-devotion of martyrdom itself. Well might Lord Lyttelton ask whether this was like the language of ordinary fanaticism? How seldom has the Christian Church—how seldom has the individual Christian—risen to the elevation of this thought! How often has bigotry contemned it as a test of Christian character altogether, and indeed rather thought its opposite, if it but masked itself under zeal for orthodoxy, a surer proof of being sound in the faith!

And this glowing eulogy of Charity—of "love unfeigned"—is in harmony with another reigning peculiarity of the Christian religion, and which is characteristic of no other ; namely, that it makes benevolence and philanthropy,—practical philanthropy, the genuine fruit of this Charity,—the absolute proof and criterion of a sincere profession. However important its dogmas, even in relation to this very thing, the test by which it is determined whether or not they have been loved and embraced, is precisely *this*.'—The *characteristic* of Him who founded the religion, is that "He went about doing good ;" and He not only demands that all His disciples should imitate His example, but declares that the single trait by which He will determine whether they are such, is their conformity to Him in this point; that, like Him, they have ministered to the necessities and mitigated the sorrows of mankind. This is plain from the instances He gives in His own exposition of His rule of judgment. (Matthew xxv. 34–45.) However orthodox the faith, however apparently devout the life, it is adjudged that there *cannot* be either genuine faith or genuine devotion without this active

---

' The language of the Old Testament is almost equally strong in the inculcation of this duty of *practical benevolence*, as inseparable from all true religion. "Blessed is he that considereth the poor " (or the sick), "the Lord will deliver him in time of trouble." "He that giveth to the poor lendeth unto the Lord." See also Isaiah lviii. 6–11; Jer. xxii. 16; Job xxix. 11–16; and many other passages.

benevolence. The language of the apostles is to the same effect.[1]

And as no religion but Christianity has ever made benevolence so exclusively a *test* of the sincerity of profession, so none has ever practised it to the same extent. However short her disciples may have come of her requirements—and they have come very short indeed—we shall look in vain in any other than Christian lands for such efforts to succour sickness and poverty, ignorance and destitution, as she has made; such funds for the maimed, the halt, the blind, the orphan, and the widow, as the treasury of Christ has supplied. Hospitals and asylums were unknown in the ancient world. They were created by the Gospel.

Now I cannot but doubt whether men such as the apostles, or, indeed, *any* zealots such as religious history generally celebrates,—men intent on the proclamation of certain doctrines, and convinced of their momentous importance,—would have suspended the whole value of their darling orthodoxy on a practical issue, which (however vitally connected with it and necessarily flowing out of it), seemed, in the sole *test* given of it, to keep it out of sight altogether !

5. There is yet another point on which, as it appears to me, the writers of the New Testament exhibit a practical wisdom which from their antecedents and circumstances we could scarcely expect, and which, in like circumstances, has been rarely, if ever, manifested in the world's history. I allude to the singular tact with which the apostles managed to steer clear,—enthusiastic and zealous though they were in their new enterprise,—of those social and political rocks on which their bark might have been so easily wrecked. All history shows now easy it is for religious to pass into political zeal, or coalesce with it,—especially where men are suffering under oppression and persecution. The Jews in particular, from both sorts of zeal,—from fervid attachment to their laws, and hatred of that

[1] James i. 27 ; 1 Tim. vi. 17-19 ; Eph. iv. 28.

ignominious yoke against which they were always chafing, were inflammable as tinder. They were perpetually breaking out into insurrection, till, at last, resistance ended in their utter ruin. Hardly had Luther entered on his career than he was troubled with the fanaticism of Carlstadt, and soon after by far worse fanatics, who would have turned the Reformation into an instrument of political revolution, and thereby gravely imperilled his enterprise. In our own country, during the sixteenth and seventeenth centuries, how often did the movements which took their rise in religious zeal (sometimes an auxiliary, sometimes an incentive, to political discontent) flame out into resistance against the persecutions that would suppress it !

Now, when we consider that from the first the Christians were a sect not only "everywhere *spoken* against," but cruelly maltreated, it does appear marvellous that its leaders could escape all the mischiefs and scandals which might so easily have sprung from this source. It is attributable, no doubt, to their inflexible adherence to the course the New Testament ascribes to them. They were exclusively intent on a single object,—the propagation of the Gospel ; and though not insensible to the evils of their time, and quietly depositing *principles* in the world, which if received, and so far as received, would infallibly correct them, they seem to have instinctively felt that to enter upon a crusade for this object would be to imperil their religious mission, and retard that mitigation of political and social evils which its success would bring with it. None can accuse them of timeserving and subservience. They openly professed their resolution to prosecute their proper enterprise in spite of all the powers of the world,—and they kept their word. They accordingly denounced with unflinching decision whatever was inconsistent with it ; whatever stood between man and God's favour, between man's soul and its salvation ;—all idolatry, all impurity, all sensuality, all covetousness and dishonesty, all malice and uncharitableness, and these, of course, none the less, when they flowed from vicious social customs and political institutions.

But while inculcating *principles*, which if accepted and acted upon would have destroyed the essence of despotism and slavery, transformed every despot, in fact, into a just and beneficent sovereign, every slave-owner into a kind master, like Philemon, and every slave into a freeman in all but the name, like Onesimus,—nay, into a "brother beloved,"—they refrained from a crusade against despotism and slavery as political institutions. Both had so long and extensively prevailed, and the last was so universally sanctioned,—the roots of both were so entwined with the framework of society,—that they could not be extirpated by any summary process, nor denounced and resisted, except at the risk of transforming the religious into a political revolution. The apostles seem to have been contented, therefore, to wait; and while plainly proposing principles which *must*, if acted upon, secure liberty and extinguish slavery, left the seed to germinate in the soil. Such, at all events, appears to be the posture of the writers of the New Testament in reference to these evils; nor can we do them justice except by.recollecting that Christianity was a system suddenly inserted into the framework of ancient society, and that it was impossible, without certain ruin to its main enterprise, and infinite hazards even to its secondary objects, directly to encounter some of the political and social enormities of the time. It was the case of the "wheat and the tares" in the parable; they must for a while grow together. The evils of a corrupt social or political system, indeed, would certainly be corrected in each *individual* by the moral reformation which Christianity, if sincerely received, would effect; but the correction of the system itself, the assertion and vindication of men's social rights, and the limitation of exorbitant political power, could only be effected in two ways; by the gradual formation of enlightened opinion,—which was the work of time; or by violence and revolution, which certainly was *not* the work of apostles. They wisely chose the former; and, dropping the seed into the ground, waited for the harvest.

Thus we see a reason for what to some seems a paradox, namely, that the New Testament does not explicitly forbid slavery, nor command the converts to Christianity instantly to manumit their slaves. This fact, I think, every candid reader of the New Testament must concede. Nor is it wonderful; for slavery was a thing to which the world was so accustomed, that it would require time, and familiarity with the consequences of the social principles which Christianity inculcates, to educate men even to apprehend that it was an evil at all. Neither philosophers, nor the vulgar, seem to have had the slightest conception of there being anything wrong in it. Plato and Aristotle, the greatest ethical authorities of antiquity, appear to regard it quite as a natural and proper institution. Nor can we estimate the social confusion which might have resulted from the sudden adoption of a contrary principle, before either master or slave was in any degree prepared for it. But a general servile war would have been a natural, if not an inevitable consequence.

On the other hand, that the New Testament propounds principles which, if they be *acted* upon, must necessarily put an end to slavery, is not only obvious, but is abundantly proved by experience. As antiquity had no conception of the enormity of slavery till Christianity appeared, so no modern nations, ignorant of Christianity, have any such notion to this day. But wherever it *is* known, there the contest between itself and slavery is sure soon to begin; and the most signal triumphs over both the slave trade and slavery, which have ever been achieved, have been the distinct result of the influence it has exerted and the public opinion it has formed.

Similar remarks apply to the tone the founders of Christianity adop ed in reference to the despotic governments of the day. While initiating principles which, if they be accepted, must extinguish all tyranny, and eventually establish all political rights, the apostles did not attempt that premature realization of such objects which would but too well have justified the calumny so often falsely cast upon them, " of turning the world upside down." They enjoin, therefore, in the most general terms, submission to " rulers and governors" *de facto*, as the duty of the Christian, and forbid him to resist them by violence, on any pretence that in his judgment governments might be much better constituted ; least of all, to resist on account of the oppressions and wrongs inflicted on Christians *as such.* This last prohibition is, no doubt, *absolute ;* the wrongs of persecution are to be submitted to ; the martyr must not turn soldier, nor fight the battles of the faith with fire and sword. This would be incompatible with the very essence of the Gospel itself,—at once destroying its object, and transforming that " kingdom " which is *not* of this world into one directly resembling those that "arc of this world," in the most vital point. Beyond this the New Testament does not go ; it neither invites nor forbids discussion as to whether there may not be extreme cases which, on political grounds, will justify men in open insurrection against an unjust and cruel government.

Paul, in the thirteenth chapter of the Epistle to the Romans, is by many supposed to have determined the question in the *negative*, and to have enjoined unqualified " passive obedience " and "non-resistance ;" and there was a time in the history of our own country when these doctrines, in their most slavish form, were as slavishly preached from that chapter. But we all know that the fanatical champions of such a perverted loyalty were themselves effectually confuted by James II., and at last admitted there might be *limits* to the submission even of the most servile. Nor will a candid reader of the New Testament hesitate to say that this amended interpretation is very rational. The apostle, prescribing *general* rules, — rules applicable even to governments very far from theoretical perfection,—merely says what all sensible men, what every sound politician, every upright citizen, would say in every age, that it is the duty of a loyal subject to obey the edicts of government, without pre-judging the question whether there may not be cases in which insurrection may be justifiable, or even imperative; just as they would lay down the duty of obedience to parents as the general rule, without pretending that there could be no cases in which children would be released even from that obligation. As a general rule, all wise men assert these maxims as strenuously as the apostle did; and, considering the infinite suffering which usually results from any rash attempt at innovation by violence, and the terrible responsibility incurred by every self-constituted authority that proposes it, it is the only safe *general* rule.   But while all wise teachers, no less than the apostle, agree in this, no one would imagine them to be pronouncing upon, or even thinking of, the lawfulness of resistance in those extreme cases which alone, with any sane man, will justify revolution ; in those extreme cases, for example, where a king tramples on the charters to which he has sworn, and violates the articles and conditions which notoriously limit his prerogative; or again, where an absolute monarch, who has no well-defined limits to his power, abuses it to resist every limitation which the rising intelligence of his subjects demands, and will give no security against the most intolerable oppression.   The New Testament does not decide upon any such extreme cases, and it would be strange if any manual of *general* duty did : they are best decided when the terrible emergency occurs.   It would be of ill omen for the world if religious systems, or even manuals of morality and politics, instead of laying down the general rules of duty, entered into a nice discussion of all the cases in which they ceased to be obligatory, and canvassed all the possible justifications of resistance to authority.   That the writers of the New Testament were not thinking of any such cases, is sufficiently clear from their description of those governments to which their principle applies.   They must (whatever their defects) still be such as, on the whole, to be "a terror to *evil deers*, and a praise to them that *do well*."

Now suppose, if you will, that the New Testament is very defective as a manual of political rights (as I confess I think it is—for it has nothing directly to do with politics); say, if you will, that the apostles were timid and pusillanimous (though, I fancy, few who consider their history will say *that*); still, considering how easy it is for religious zeal to become factious, how often the attempt to innovate in religion has proceeded to political violence, especially under persecution; how pertinacious and exasperating the persecution directed against the founders of Christianity was, and how incessant the insurrections among their turbulent countrymen, the Jews,—I cannot help thinking it a very extraordinary thing that the apostles should have been such wary pilots, and steered their bark in safety amidst shoals and breakers where so many other mariners have suffered shipwreck.

May we not ask, as the Jews did, concerning their Master Himself, " Whence had these men this wisdom ? "   How is it that while they introduced a system which operated a greater revolution in the world than had ever before been effected, they yet avoided those excesses into which the passions of men in general, with far less enthusiasm than theirs, and under far less wrongs and oppressions, are so easily provoked ? How is it that while they made greater progress than Puritans or Huguenots, the apostles exercised a self-control, a sobriety, a moderation, which the most ardent admirers of those reformers and confessors of subsequent times will hardly claim for them ?

I will not say that the wisdom and prudence implied in the various particulars enumerated in this lecture could not have been manifested by other men.   I do not place these things precisely on a level as arguments, with some of those other traits of the Bible already mentioned, which seem to me absolutely against the grain of human nature. But I think that, taken altogether, the conduct of the apostles, as contrasted with that of the generality of those who have propounded systems of religion to the world, and as contrasted also with what might have been reasonably expected from such men, from their origin and their antecedents,—does exhibit a considerable paradox, to be added to the many others I have dwelt upon, and which justify the presumption that the New Testament is not simply a book of man's origination.

LECTURE IV.

SINGULAR COINCIDENCES BETWEEN SCRIPTURE AND HISTORY.

INDICATIONS OF UNITY IN THE BIBLE.

LECTURE IV.

THOUGH the argument from "prophecy" is beyond the
scope of these lectures, yet those strange "coincidences"
between certain ancient Biblical statements and historic fact
(on which the argument of prophecy is founded) are fairly
within it, and are among the many things this volume presents
us with that seem difficult to account for. These "coincidences" must, at all events, have been very striking, to lead so
many millions of intelligent men, and among them so many
possessed of the greatest acuteness and learning, to acquiesce
in them as nothing less than veritable instances of inspired
prediction.

Bishop Butler lays great stress on the general *harmony*
between the statements of Scripture and historic facts, not only
in the "prophetical" portions, but in the "ordinary" narrative;
and contends that its general correspondence with the world's
civil and religious history, as gathered from extraneous sources,
is a strong argument for its veracity.   He says that if a person
previously quite ignorant of the Bible, and uncertain, after
perusing it, whether it purported to be fact or fiction, were told
of the entire series of harmonies between it and history, he
could not but be much impressed with their variety and extent.

It is but a very limited portion of this large field that I have
space to touch ; and even of the so-called *prophetic* conform-

ities between Scripture and history, but which I simply call "coincidences," I shall content myself with selecting a few of the more prominent by way of specimen. Nor as regards the greater part of them, will there be the slightest room for that favourite subterfuge, that the "sayings" of the book, instead of being long anterior to the events to which they seemingly point, were in fact written long after them, and are, therefore, not only not prophecies, but not even *coincidences*. The events to which I shall principally refer confessedly transpired long since the books were written. If not, some of these documents must have been written very recently; at a date, indeed, to which no sceptical imagination, however daring, has yet ventured to assign them.

Instead of taking a man ignorant of the Bible, I will modify Butler's supposition, and suppose him alike ignorant of history and the Bible. I will further suppose him indoctrinated in the former by a candid instructor who did not believe in the latter, and sedulously kept it out of sight ; and that he is afterwards informed of the coincidences between what he has learnt even from such a Mentor, and the undoubted utterances of the Bible.

Let us suppose him then taken through a brief course of Ancient History, and that the outline of the Jewish annals is given (traditionally) thus. He is told by his guide that in the times immediately preceding authentic history, the nations of the earth, so far as could be ascertained, savage and civilised, were alike sunk in the profoundest religious degradation, having " gods many and lords many," gods of all sorts and sizes, of all form and feature, of wood and stone, brass and iron, gold and silver, malign and benevolent ; but that from the earliest times of which we have any genuine records, there was one people, the Jews, who professed the most decided *monotheism*, and alone (as far as reliable history made known to us) preserved that doctrine in the world ; that, nevertheless, they shared so fully in the general proclivities of mankind to idolatry, that they did their very utmost from time to time to extinguish their better light, and again and again fell into all the grossness of the worship of the nations that surrounded them : though they still clung obstinately to the *theory* of monotheism, always returned to it, and confessed its truth, even while they failed to practise it. Our neophyte will be told that in the course of their history they were often reduced to great straits, and more than once led into cruel captivity by other nations,—events which they foolishly and superstitiously attributed to their forgetfulness and neglect of the doctrines and duties of their religion ; that though they were doubtless mistaken in that, yet it was a *curious* fact that, though they were frequently conquered, and, as was the case with so many other ancient nations, torn away from their native soil, and subjected in foreign lands to the influences which had so often broken up and at last absorbed other communities, this singular people did not share in the same fate of disintegration : that though mixed up with other nations, they were not incorporated with them ; remained a foreign element interfused through the communities in which they existed ; and that *that* has been in effect their condition, through every variety of their fortunes, since their final conquest and dispersion, about 1800 years ago ;—still wandering everywhere, but having a country nowhere. He will be told that their entire system of laws, though its moral elements were perhaps superior to those of any other ancient codes, was on the whole so peculiar and so burdensome, that they continually broke away from it ; that some of them acknowledged that it " imposed a yoke which neither they nor their fathers were able to bear ; " and yet that they have obstinately clung to it notwithstanding. He will be told that small and insignificant as they always were, and weakened and dispersed as they have been through a great part of their history, they had cherished from remote ages a foolish delusion that from among them should arise an eminent Personage, who should not only reign over *them,* but over all nations : that *His* kingdom should never be destroyed :

that some among them had ventured to speculate as to His characteristics and fortunes ; that some said He was to be from the first a *triumphant* king ; others, that He was to reign only after dire defeats and sore troubles ; others, that He was to combine the character of priest with that of king ; while it was also insinuated by some sour and unpatriotic spirits that, considering how obstinate the nation had ever been, how slow to learn and how apt to forget the lessons of heaven, it would proceed to reject the claims even of this illustrious Personage ; but that if it did, it would be " provoked to jealousy " by seeing Him accepted by other nations.   All these things, the pupil will be told, may be supposed the illusions of diseased fancy ; though (curiously enough, and by a very odd coincidence) about the *time* and at the *place* which certain dreamers among them had fixed upon as the date and spot at which this personage should appear, a most remarkable Man did really claim to be the king in question ; that He *was* rejected by the Jews in general, and what is still more odd, after being crucified by the Gentiles (though at Jewish instigation) as a malefactor, was eagerly accepted by immense numbers of widely diverse nations among these Gentiles ; invested by them with attributes of royalty greater than ever belonged to royalty before, and voluntarily honoured with a homage such as king had never received.   He will be told, further, that though the Jews were upbraided (no doubt, very unreasonably) with the rejection of their fabulous king, and nothing but superstition suggested that they would be punished for it, yet curiously enough, and by another odd coincidence, their capital very shortly after was burnt, their polity destroyed, and their nation finally dispersed.

If our professor of history maintains his candour, he will inform his pupil, that though the strange empire erected by this pretended Monarch, and founded on Religion, gathered strength from day to day, till the temples and shrines of the Roman empire fell before it, and has since successively received the allegiance of many nations of the most diverse character and condition; yet the foundations of this new Power in the world were laid without any resort to force on its own part, and in spite of the most violent resistance on the part of the world at large; that it was scorned by philosophers, hated by priests, and opposed by tyrants. It will be added that to account for its success would be to account for the infinite caprices of mankind; but that the mystery may, perhaps, in part be solved, by candidly admitting that its first votaries and emissaries were singularly upright and virtuous men, and that their impulse was for a long time felt in the religious empire they set up. Our pupil will be told further that the ancient empire which had most vigorously opposed this religious empire was at length destroyed, while this last gradually usurped its seat, and succeeded to the power it wielded, in the same spot, though in another form; that after many vicissitudes of fortune, this power, too, had waxed very corrupt, seemed to be growing decrepid in consequence, and would doubtless soon " vanish away." But if our professor be cautious, he will perhaps add, that after so eventful a history, it is not possible to speculate very confidently on the future; that the " superstition "on which this empire was founded had a curious property of *revivescence :* that, as Tacitus said of it in its early days, it was an " obstinate " superstition, tenacious of life, and apt "to break out again ;" that it had hitherto been proof both against murder and suicide; that accordingly its emissaries, apparently without any ordinary human motive, might be seen still doing what no other religionists, Jewish or Gentile, had ever been foolish enough to do,—busying themselves in every corner and region of the earth, savage and civilised, in proselyting the world to their belief;—to which end they had actually given some ancient voluminous documents in Hebrew and Greek, on which they profess to found it, a voice in two hundred languages ; more, by many scores, than any other of the professedly sacred books in the world had ever spoken in !

If now our historic student begged to have a sight of those

same documents, and on inquiry about their date, were told that though there was some doubt about some of them, it was absolutely certain that they were all in existence nearly 2000 years ago, and the most ancient certainly more than 2500 years ago, would he not be surprised to find so many "coincidences" between them and "history" legibly inscribed there ? that all the facts, so cautiously narrated to him, were there described, as what *was* to be ; that even those parts of the books which are most ancient (or if the rationalists will, the least modern, for they are still ancient enough for my purpose), palpably contain such "coincidences ;" that, for example, the Pentateuch speaks of the captivity and dispersion of the Jews as their *characteristic doom*, while it expressly stipulates for their continued national "life" notwithstanding ; and that their final dispersion did not occur till they had rejected the proffered Messiah, many centuries after the *last* of the Hebrew documents had been written ? Would he not be struck on finding, that if they frequently apostatised from their religion, it was said they *would* do so, and be punished by repeated captivity and dispersion for it ; as also that if they repented they would be restored, and that this change in their fortunes was repeatedly exemplified in their history before their last dispersion ? Would he not be more struck still, to find that, if in spite of their dispersion, they have been still preserved, it was expressly said that they should be so ; and no less, that the characteristics of their promised king which our neophyte had been taught to regard as the fond illusions of national vanity were copiously described, conjoined with others which no national vanity would ever have suggested, and which national vanity, therefore, not unnaturally misinterpreted ? Would he not be surprised to find that if, at the very time and place, when and where the Jews expected this great personage, one appeared claiming to be such, and who seemed to unite the contradictory attributes of greatness and lowliness, these documents, many hundred years before, had made statements which tallied with the expectation; that, if the Jews rejected Him, it was hinted they *would;* that if the nation was conquered, their temple and polity destroyed, and their old doom of dispersion, but without extinction, finally inflicted, it was in conformity with declarations that all this *would* be so; that if the Messiah proffered to them, but rejected by them, was accepted by the Gentiles as the founder of a new religion, it was implied that He *would* be? Would he not be astonished to find that if that new religion succeeded against the combined power, philosophy, and superstition of the ancient world, and destroyed the ancient paganism, it was "coincident" with declarations to that effect? that if it became corrupt as it became prosperous, and arrogated in a new form, the power, as well as the pomp, of the great empire on whose ruins it had risen, it is "coincident" with statements that it would? that if, notwithstanding, this religion not only exhibits signal recuperative power, but (unlike other religions) is irrepressibly aggressive, and bent on preaching its "gospel" to "the ends of the earth," it is expressly declared that it would be so? What would our tyro say on discovering these things? I fancy he would say what I am now saying, that whether these things be *prophecies* or not, this book is full of the strangest, most mysterious, most unaccountable "coincidences."

Nor, as already said, is it possible to get quit of these "coincidences" by the method which has been applied to certain parts of Daniel's prophecies and some other portions of the Old Testament—by saying that the documents were written after the facts, and are therefore history and not prophecy. For the greater part of the "coincidences" to which I have referred are between documents and facts, as to which it is uncontested that the former were prior to the latter by many centuries. What shall we say then? A man may affirm, as Butler says, that the "conformity" between the documents and the events "is by accident; but there are many instances in which the conformity itself cannot be denied."

We can scarcely imagine the conformities in question to be the result of *accident*,—as little as in the case of Daniel's prophecies. But then we cannot, as in *that* case, dispute about the date of the documents. Nor can it be pretended, any more than in *that* case, that they are due to political sagacity. Indeed, it is more easy to imagine that the seer of Babylon might conjecture the (comparatively) imminent, and far less complex events of the reign of Antiochus Epiphanes (though most people will agree with Porphyry that it was *impossible* he should do so), than that any man should have sagacity enough to anticipate events in the world's history, so distant in time, so peculiar in character, so complicated in their relations, and involving the fortunes of so many different nations, as those just referred to;—a notion which reaches the *ne plus ultra* of incredibility when it is remembered that the documents proceeded from different hands and were written at widely remote eras. Several of the authors, on this hypothesis, must have been gifted with a sagacity which it is utterly incredible should have belonged even to any one. What, then, is a man to do in this case? Is he determined to adopt the argument of Porphyry in relation to Daniel? If so, I see but one course for him. He must take the same line as Porphyry, and say that the documents were posterior to the facts. He must affirm that the writings of the Old and the New Testaments were compiled not only as late as many renowned critics of the present day maintain, but much later; not only that the books of the Pentateuch, and the greater part of the prophets, were written after the Babylonish captivity, and the Gospels somewhere about the end of the second century; but that none, whether of the Old or New Testament, were composed till a few hundred years ago; if even they can be supposed to be composed yet! If, with the very books in his hands, he finds it hard, however sceptical he may be, to come to this last conclusion, he must at least emulate the courage of Père Hardouin, who professed to believe that the whole series of Greek and Roman classics was the work of the monks of the middle ages! If Porphyry's argument be sound, if veritable prophecy be an impossibility or incredibility, and if it is equally impossible to ascribe the "coincidences" in question, between the various statements of the Bible and the course of the world's history, to either accident or sagacity, there remains nothing for it but to believe that the documents were compiled long after the Christian era commenced, and perhaps within the last few hundred years. The sceptic must find their cradle where the eccentric Jesuit found the cradle of all the classics, in the monk's cell; and with about as much reason. Nor is it impossible that if the course of the world goes on so perversely to multiply "coincidences" with the Bible, as it has done in the past, and as it is still doing, a sceptic 2500 years hence may believe that our modern Hardouin, in assigning its documents to the middle ages, has made them too ancient after all, and prove that they are not even composed in our day; just as Porphyry proved the prophecies of Daniel to be subsequent to the days of Antiochus Epiphanes. He may prove 2500 years hence that the books, in spite of our having them under our very eyes, could not have been compiled before A.D. 2000.

If, on the other hand, there be no doubt that the books are of the date generally attributed to them,—all the Old Testament composed many centuries before the Christian era, and the New within a century after it,—it is impossible to say why the critic should find any great difficulty, in the face of the "coincidences" on which I have insisted, in admitting that the writings of Daniel may have contained equally curious "coincidences," without supposing them copied from history.

In accounting for the conformity between certain complex movements in the moral history of the world, and the anticipations of the Bible, it is impossible to take refuge in an argument often resorted to in relation to some special "coincidences" between its language and the subversion of *this* or *that* nation or empire; namely, that such an issue, some time or other, is so probable, from the general analogies of human history, that it may be expected, and therefore predicted. The events to which the present lecture refers are too peculiar in their *tout ensemble*, too unique and strange, and in many points too contradictory to the natural and ordinary speculations of men, to allow of such an hypothesis being applied to them.

The argument just adverted to, and which was a favourite argument with Bolingbroke and many who followed him, is of no real force even against that special order of " coincidences " it is employed to annul. It does not account for the conformity between the documents and the facts. As Davison has well shown in his Lectures, the *specific* characteristics of national catastrophes threatened in Scripture have nothing in common with the vague anticipation that at *some time* or other, in *some way* or other, the most flourishing nations will decay and fall. This is presumed to be their lot, by a universal natural law, which a considerable induction of facts makes plausible enough ; though many distinguished historic critics, and Lord Macaulay among them, doubt whether it be founded on anything better than fallacious analogies in the natural world,—forming a precarious basis for any such sinister vaticination. But whether there be any such *law* or not, the Scripture " coincidences " in this kind have nothing to do with it. They are not founded on any historic " parallelisms " which, according to the remark of the philosophic Thucydides, may, " while human nature remains the same," be assuredly anticipated. Davison shows that in many of these cases the language, so far from being equally applicable, as Bolingbroke affirms, to any nation of the world, is strictly limited to one ; so that it is impossible, in interpreting it (though it *ought* to be possible, if this theory be correct), to " shuffle the cards," transpose the subjects of prediction, and apply the descriptions of the doom menaced against different nations indiscriminately. Repeated captivity and dispersion, with all their attendant miseries, were to be the lot of Israel, but their national life was to be a "charmed life" notwith-

standing.   Nineveh and Babylon were to be absolutely destroyed, and to become a by-word for "desolation," and a
"habitation" of doleful creatures, in perpetuity ; and they have
been.   Egypt was not to be destroyed, but to be what she has
been, "a base nation."   The sons of Ishmael were to be rest-
less wanderers in their *own* land, as the Israelites were to be in
every land *but* their own ; and so it has come to pass.[1]   The
only way of neutralizing the "coincidences" in these cases is
to contend, as Porphyry does with regard to Daniel, that the
documents were antedated.

But this, I submit, is impossible in the case of the chief
"coincidences" adduced in the present lecture, not only from
their nature, but because the priority of the several documents
to the principal facts is uncontested.

I now pass to the *second* subject of the present lecture.

If there be any *unity* in the Bible, if the appearance of coherence, and of reciprocal adaptation, in its several parts, be
not a dream of fancy, or some unimaginable result of chance,
then one part of my thesis, that the Bible is not such a book as
man "could have constructed, if he would," is beyond all contradiction ; for that *condition*, on which alone the conclusion
could be denied, namely, that its unity might possibly be the
effect of collusion amongst its authors, is absolutely precluded.
The volume is the product of about forty different authors,
writing under every conceivable diversity of circumstances, at
far distant dates ; and who were therefore unconscious of each
other's purpose, and incapable of acting in concert.   The
earliest of these writers is separated from the latest by an
interval of at least a thousand years,—to content myself with a
very modest limit, which even the most courageous rationalist
will hardly dispute.[2]

[1] See Appendix No. IV.

[2] In spite of the infinite discordance of rationalist criticism, as to the dates
of the Hebrew sacred writings, the earliest of which it refers to all periods
between Samuel and the return from Babylon, comparatively few would

Before proceeding further, however, it may be as well to say
that this phenomenon of a quasi-sacred book so composed,—
of such miscellaneous contents and various authorship, and that
took a thousand years in its completion,—is itself anomalous,
and must be ranked with the many other anomalies which discriminate the Bible from all other so-called sacred books. None
of them can be ascribed to a series of writers extending in long
procession to a thousand years ; and whose writings, moreover,
traverse large portions of secular history,—are imbedded in it,
and run parallel with it.   This sharply discriminates the Scriptures from the books of Confucius, and many others. The
Koran was the work of Mahomet alone.   The striking difference
in this respect between Mahomedanism on the one hand, and
Judaism and Christianity on the other, is well put by an able
writer, who certainly cannot be accused of understating the
claims of Mahomet, and who, if he has erred at all in appraising
them, has erred on the side of candour and charity.[1]

deny that some of the more important were in existence long before the
former epoch.   Nor does it much matter to my present argument if it be
denied ; for as the more sceptical of these critics postdate the books of the
New Testament in the same manner, to the middle or close of the second
century, there will still be an interval of nine or ten centuries between the
earliest portions of the Bible and the latest.

[1] " Each again of these three great monotheistic religions has its written
revelation.   Herein comes one of the most marked distinctions between the
three, and a specially marked distinction between Christianity and Islam.
The book which contains the revelation of Islam is the work of the founder
of Islam.   It proclaims itself as the word of God, not indeed written by the
hand of the prophet, but taken down from His mouth, and spoken in His
person.   It is a revelation which began and ended in the person of its first
teacher, which none of his successors dare add to or take away from.   But,
as that revelation does not take the form of an autobiography, it follows that
there is no narrative of the acts of the prophet which can claim Divine authority.   But the sacred books of the Christian revelation are biographical ;
they are not the writings of the founder of Christianity, but records of His
life, in which His discourses are recorded among His other actions.   Certain
other of the writings of His earliest followers are also held to be of equal
authority with the records of His own life.   The Jewish law comes to us in
a third shape ; it is a code incorporated in a history, a history which ortho-

This then is itself a *unique* feature of the Bible, which must be added to the many other paradoxes of this strange book. It is not easy to account for it, and it is plainly out of *analogy* with religious history in general.

But to resume the more important subject of this lecture, which is to point out certain indications of unity in the Bible.

As a matter of fact, and about which there is no doubt, immense multitudes of the human race, of the most diverse nations,—nations differing by every conceivable variety of custom, history and culture, but including amongst them all the most pre-eminent in modern science and civilization, — have somehow come to regard the Bible as intelligibly one ; as possessing unique and pervading characteristics of sentiment and doctrine, structure and style ; a coherence of purpose and design, which both discriminate it from all other books and proclaim its own identity: all this in spite of that wonderful composite authorship, and very gradual formation, just referred to.   In this delusion, if it be one, many of the greatest names in all these communities,—names illustrious in every sense, for genius, for learning, for intellectual power, for moral worth,— have deliberately, and after prolonged study, shared.   It is true that the bulk of those who have believed this have also regarded the book as containing, in some sense, a " Divine Revelation," and therefore as being divinely inspired, either in whole or in part.   But it is not necessary here to canvass the justice of this conclusion.   Whether such a view be true or false, is here irrelevant ; I am simply considering whether there are solid

dox belief looks on as an autobiography.   But in this case the revelation is not confined to the first lawgiver himself, or to his immediate followers : an equal authority, a like Divine origin, is held to belong to a mass of later writings of various ages, which are joined with those of the original lawgiver, to form the sacred books of the first dispensation.   In short, the Mahommedan accepts nothing as of Divine authority, except the personal utterances of his prophet, taken down in his lifetime.   With the Jew and the Christian the actual discourses of Moses and of Christ form only a portion of the writings which he accepts as the sacred books of his faith."—" British Quarterly Review," Jan. 1, 1872.   Pp. 111, 112.

grounds for this so general impression of the unity of the book. *A priori*, indeed, we may be almost sure there *must* be some plausible reasons for it, otherwise it would be difficult to imagine either how the idea of a " Divine Revelation" should have clung to this fabric of fragments, or if such a crude notion had been adopted in ages of ignorance and superstition, why it should not long since have vanished away in that searching scrutiny to which it has been subjected. One would expect that the folly of any such view would have been proved a thousand times over out of the book itself, which, if it be a fortuitous aggregate of heterogeneous writings, must, from its very mode of formation, give such infinite advantages to its assailants.

Whether the Hebrew literature, for example, as some have supposed, was much more voluminous than its extant fragments, or really consisted of very little that is not incorporated in the books of the Old Testament itself,[1] there would seem no reason, if it was the product of simple natural causes (like those which developed the Greek, Roman, and other literatures), why the idea of *unity* should have so obstinately attached to a certain number of its fragments, of widely different contents and of far distant dates.

The Greek or Roman literature probably contains a hundred times the mass of all that is extant in the ancient Hebrew. Yet it is not within the compass of the human imagination to conceive, that if only a portion of either literature, equal to the Bible, had survived, but containing fragments by as many different authors as have composed *that*, such a volume could have been supposed to be one. By no process, let us shuffle the more copious existing materials as we may, or exercise the most discriminating arts of selection, could we compile a *mélange* equal in bulk to the Bible, that could for a moment cheat any

---

[1] A few works of Hebrew authorship, as for example, certain historic, poetic, and didactic compositions (more especially those ascribed to Solomon), are no longer extant : but there is no reason to suppose they were very numerous.

ordinary mind into the belief that it formed an organic whole; much less impose on many millions of mankind of different races and epochs, including among them thousands of the most illustrious for genius and learning. By no manipulation, by choosing a poem here and an oration there, a piece of history as one element in the fabric, and a play as another,—so as to give, on the whole, something like the same variety of form, matter, and authorship which we find in the Bible, and as far as possible a similar diversity of dates,—could we effect even the faintest approach to that semblance of unity which such vast multitudes have found in the Scriptures.

Nor is the wonder at all diminished if we suppose that the Hebrew literature contained little but what has been incorporated in this one book. If that was all their literature, and the effect of purely human causes, it would show, indeed, that the Hebrew pen was not very fertile ; but there would be no more reason than before why the Jewish people, and still less so many *other* people, should fancy that nearly all the scanty literature (though on widely different subjects, and by authors living centuries apart) was linked together by a common object and pervaded by an essential unity.

Should it be supposed that the Hebrews regarded nearly all their literature as sacred, and so conceived it to have *unity;* this is contradicted by fact, for they certainly did not incorporate in the book all else they wrote,—whether much or little. Moreover, the books that have been selected for this honour (as I have had occasion to notice more fully in a preceding lecture) are full of matter which national vanity must vehemently resent, and, if it could, would willingly forget. This is notoriously the case with the largest and most important of them, with the Pentateuch, books of Judges, Samuel, Kings, and Chronicles, the prophecies of Isaiah, Jeremiah, and Ezekiel. If the facts they record be not true, they are the most cruel collection of libels with which any people was ever branded; and if not history, but romance,—if merely the natural, and yet most *unnatural* product of certain perverse minds among them,—one can hardly imagine the patriotism of their countrymen excessively solicitous to find either "sacredness" or "unity" about these books, much less jealously to watch over their inviolate preservation, and least of all to revere them as originating in nothing less than Divine inspiration!

However, even if the Jewish ascription of unity to these writings could be solved by any such theory, it would not account for the equally obstinate belief which has led so many other nations, utterly without sympathy with them, nay, by original traditions and associations, in intense antipathy to them, to imitate their fatuity, and cherish the same delusion.

Somewhat similar observations will apply to the multifarious contents of the New Testament, and still more to the Old and New Testaments together.

It is then, I think, a natural *presumption* that there must be some very plausible reasons which, under the most diverse circumstances, have led such multitudes (including among them so many of the greatest minds, exercising the most deliberate judgment) to see a prevailing unity in this series of fragments. Unless this had been the case, that obstinacy of belief which attaches to the supposed unity of these writings could hardly have been proof against the rigorous criticism which has subjected them to an infinitely more severe ordeal than any other writings in the world. The works alone that have been written *against* them would make a library far greater than all the literature of Greece and Rome, taken many times over.

No such unity as is justly attributed to the writings of such men as Confucius or Mahomet, furnishes any parallel. The cases differ *toto cœlo*. The Mahometans, for example, very rightly regard the Koran as one, for it is so : let the discrepancies, or contradictions, or extravagances be what they may, it was the work, though composed and given to the world in fragments, of one mind. The world did not make the unity, it simply acknowledged it. But if the Bible be *not* one, those who believe it to be so have made it so; and if they made it so without reason, we ought to be able to assign some sufficient cause for this singular consentaneousness of hallucination. If the Bible is a mere collection of "shreds and patches;" if its books really originated in purely natural causes, and have no internal cohesion, other than belongs to human writings produced in the course of many centuries by the same nation; there would seem no more reason why the book of Deuteronomy, the prophecies of Isaiah, the Gospel of Mark, and the Epistle to the Romans should have been imagined to form parts of one book, than why a collection of a score or two of fragments from any other literature should be so considered. The Bible, in fact, is a "Miscellany"—a very various one. The question is, why, with so wide a *consensus*, it should ever have been supposed to be anything else?

Among the indications, then, of this unity, must be reckoned, though it is only a *presumption*, the general and obstinate persuasion that it exists.

But whatever presumption of unity may be inferred from this singular concurrence, it can be of little avail unless confirmed by indications in the contents of the book itself. A few, and only a few of these, I will now enumerate. Some of them I have had occasion to advert to under another aspect and for another purpose, namely, when endeavouring to show that the Bible is distinguished by certain uniform characteristics, which could not be expected, *a priori*, in any book of man's making. Now, some of these, not simply as *unique*, viewed relatively to human nature, but as *pervading* the book, also suggest its unity. I shall simply remind the reader of some of them without dwelling on them. For example: 1. The fact that the Bible is, as Butler says emphatically, "the book of God," in the sense of being exclusively dedicated to Him and His claims. 2. The subordination of its contents to this conception. 3. The indissoluble connection everywhere maintained between religion and morals. 4. The uniform reticence of Scripture on topics which merely tend to gratify curiosity, and on which other books of professed revelation have been singularly copious. Some other particulars in the first two lectures, considered as uniform traits of the book, in the same manner suggest its unity.

A trait closely related to the first three of these peculiarities, and in like manner *pervading* the book, argues the same thing. It is this: that God is there represented as establishing a great spiritual kingdom, an "imperium in imperio," separate from His universal providential empire, but also existing in the midst of it, in which are enrolled, without any restriction of political or social or intellectual differences among men, or rather in contempt of these, as well as of all conventional distinctions, all who from the heart unfeignedly recognise, in proportion to their light, the principles of that spiritual government, and act upon them. Those who, wherever they are found,[1] unfeignedly love and obey God, and give Him, in thought and act, the supremacy He claims, are represented as the true aristocracy of this world,—the *élite* of humanity. He is represented as gathering all such into one community; "enriching heaven from the spoils of earth," and constituting a "kingdom" which, as "it *cannot* be moved," so is it worthy of being "immovable." For it is to be composed exclusively of those who, trained for self-government by inflexible rectitude of will and habitual subjection to an enlightened intellect and conscience, can dispense with the mechanical bonds and ligaments of this world's government and those irksome restraints and discipline which imply a

[1] "Of a truth I perceive God is no respecter of persons; but in *every* nation he that feareth Him and worketh righteousness, is accepted with Him."—Acts x. 34, 35. This and other texts, conclusively and delightfully prove to me that there are those who will be saved by the Gospel who yet never heard of it—by means of that sincere, conscientious use of the *modicum* of light afforded to them, which is the germ of all "faith" and goodness. The helianthus is said to turn towards the sun, though clouds may partially veil him; and the sincere soul, like the plant shut up in darkness, will struggle towards the light, even though it stream only through hole or cranny; and that determines it to be "a child of light," though it can only attain its maturity under other conditions.

remaining reluctance to duty; in fact, an imperfect virtue which needs to be still artificially guarded. This kingdom, being *spiritual,* is therefore a true and genuine dominion, where loyalty is the loyalty of the heart, and obedience the obedience of the will.

Now I am not arguing that this is a conception that will be actually realised, though I believe it will. But that it is a very sublime one,—looking on all other kingdoms as but the shadow of the true, the field of the world as but the nursery of a paradise better than Eden,—few will deny. I might have adverted to it in the earlier lectures as a trait which, considering man's religious history in general, he was not *likely* to exhibit in any system of religion conceived by him. But not wishing to press any topic too much, I refrained from looking at it in that light, nor will I now insist that the conception is beyond what the human mind might have originated. Nay, for aught I am at present concerned, it is quite open for people to say, though I think few but Plato's Thrasymachus would say it, that there is nothing sublime about it; that physical power is as good as moral ; that they would as soon reign over a kingdom of slaves as of freemen, or of men who obeyed reluctantly as of those who obeyed from love. All I am now arguing for is that such a peculiar conception *pervading* the Bible, though it be made up of fragments by different writers, with chasms of centuries between them, may be urged as an argument for its unity. And it is further strengthened if we consider, not only that the conception pervades the successive fragments of the book, but that it is developed very gradually, and grows with the book itself. Such a conception, had it been equally prominent from the beginning, might not have been less *unique,* contrasting the Bible with other books ; but it would hardly have been so strong an argument for its unity, for the several writers might be thought to have derived their conception from one another. But the very mode in which the idea is developed precludes this. It is by many gradual steps. The light "shining more and more to the perfect day," and passing from twilight to dawn and from dawn to noon, is the fitting image of its growth.

The general results which the multitudes who have studied the book with the most diligent and persevering efforts to comprehend its meaning, pretty generally coincide in, are these :— that man, reduced to a condition of guilt and misery which estranged him from God, received a promise coeval with the calamity itself that some Deliverer bearing the nature of man, and of "woman born," should be sent into the world, charged with the functions of rescuing him from the consequences of his apostacy. Nothing more is said; the oracle is silent for a long time. The promise, indeed, is not vague; it is clear as far as it goes : the subsequent announcements are like it; clear, but imperfect, marked by very gradual augmentations of light. A particular race, we are told, is selected to be the depositary of the great fact, and of the elements of all true religion, while the world in general is sunk in the darkest and most hideous idolatries. That such a temporary ark for the great truths of religion was absolutely necessary, would appear, not only from the fact that the rest of the world was involved in religious delusions, but that man universally was so prone to them, that even the "chosen nation" itself, in spite of all its peculiar safeguards, again and again obstinately relapsed into idolatry.

Centuries after the first promise was given, a voice was heard declaring that the promised Deliverer was to be of the lineage of Abraham, but with no restriction of benefit to *his* race : on the contrary, it is said that in "him shall all the families of the earth be blessed." Long after, another oracle declared that He was to be in the line of Jacob. At this patriarch's death, it seems obscurely intimated that amongst his many sons Judah is the one in whose line the promised Messiah is to appear. The oracle is again silent for long; but in due time further intimations are given which successively limit the meaning of the promise, and the light converges to a focus. We are told that the Deliverer is to come in the line of David;

the place of His birth is also intimated, and writers, one after another, gradually disclose many other circumstances concerning His character and history; that He is to be a lawgiver, as was Moses; that He is to be a pr'est, not of the lineage of Aaron, but of the tribe of Judah, and with some undisclosed attributes which are to assimilate his priesthood to that of Melchizedek. They also gradually give hints as to the nature of His kingdom; that, though springing out of the Jewish dispensation, and grafted upon it, it was to be by no means conterminous with it or limited by it; that, on the contrary, it was to be cosmopolitan, throw down the invidious "partition" walls between Jew and Gentile, and open the privileges of God's people to all nations. They also intimate with increasing clearness the spiritual and moral characteristics of this kingdom : that, founded on truth, it would aspire to exercise dominion over the hearts and consciences of men ; that literal compliance or reluctant obedience had no moral significance, much less mere outward rite and ceremony ; that these last could be of no value except as really expressive of devotion to the moral truths they symbolized ; and that this spiritual economy would have the reality and substance of what had before existed only in " type "and " shadow."

After the last of the writers of the Old Testament had spoken, there was a silence again for no less than four centuries, and when the New Testament opens, it is to tell us that the great Deliverer was come ; that in Him the various tokens, which had been predicted of Him in the course of so many ages, met. In confirmation of this it proceeds to give the history of His life, death, character, and many details of His teaching and doctrine. He assumes the character assigned Him, and declares He is come to set up that spiritual kingdom of which so many seeming prognostications had been given,—the "kingdom not of this world." Unlike other monarchs, He claims nothing less than the obedience of love ; and, in fact, His true dominion begins where all others end—in that interior realm of thought and feeling which earthly potentates cannot reach.

The New Testament goes on to give us the history of the commencement of this kingdom in the world; attracting to itself, and incorporating with itself, all such as spontaneously accepted this new allegiance, and were willing to live in accordance with the laws its great Spiritual Potentate prescribed. It tells us that these, continually increasing in number, are to form a kingdom which shall silently subsist among all other kingdoms, and be unshaken by the causes which ruin them; that it shall survive them; and that, at last, all its subjects, gathered from the heterogeneous kingdoms of this world, and invested with immortality, shall be translated into a world that shall be meet for such occupants,—"a new heaven and a new earth, wherein dwelleth righteousness."

That the idea of such a kingdom, however chimerical it may be deemed, is a very sublime conception, few, I think, will dispute: that even now, as a matter of fact, Christ exercises a more various dominion, and attracts more love than any monarch of history; has more subjects that are willing to signalize their loyalty, if need be, by dying for Him; is, I think, as little liable to dispute.[1]   But it is not on the truth of any such conception that I am now insisting: let it, if the reader will, be a dream. I am merely pointing it out, as one of the singularities of the book, that this conception is found there; and that being gradually developed by a number of authors, writing at far distant times and places, and without any possibility of concert, it confirms the argument for its *unity*.

That this representation of the contents of the book, so far as I have gone, coincides with what the great bulk of those who have most sedulously studied it *imagine* to be its significance, will be admitted; that in most men's judgment it clearly declares more than all this, and tells us much as to the means

---

[1] The reported sentiments of Napoleon I. in reference to the grandeur and solidity of Christ's empire—and he had well learnt by experience its contrasts with his own—are admirably commented on by Liddon in his Bampton Lectures, pp. 222-225. 8vo. Ed. 1867.

by which the Founder of this spiritual kingdom proposes to work out His design, and give efficacy to His doctrines, will also be generally granted. But I have confined myself to the conclusion which the vast majority, who profess to interpret the book as a *whole*, concur in finding there.

Shall we say that it is all a dream,—that the book contains nothing of the kind,—or that all who have thought so have gone mad together? If this be thought incredible, then how shall we account for the delusion ?—By chance ?   Who can compute the chances against it ? By concert of the writers ? The mode in which the book has been constructed, its gradual composition, makes this impossible.

I do not here enter on the question whether the facts of history have at all corresponded with the representations of the book. I have briefly touched on the subject in the previous part of this lecture, and content myself with saying that the degree in which that conformity may be truly affirmed is one of the singularities with which the book is encompassed, and of which the philosopher may be asked to give some account. At present, for anything my argument requires, Christianity may be a failure in the world; the "spiritual kingdom," of which the book is supposed to speak, hardly commenced, or regarded as an absolute delusion.

But *in proportion* as it may be deemed chimerical, let us recollect in *that* proportion is the incredibility of such a chimera entering any head, much less the heads of a succession of men, whose writings must be supposed to have only an arbitrary connection, and who lived centuries apart from one another.

I turn to another topic. On the supposition that the Bible is an accretion of casual writings, arbitrarily linked together, and without any pervading unity, it would not appear easy to account for the many latent "correspondencies" (as they may be called) between statements which occur in very different portions, and often at wide intervals, in the sacred books,—any more than for the "undesigned coincidences in the historic portions, which also tend to prove the same thing. These "correspondencies" seem too remote in place or time, or too oblique in their reciprocal reference, to be the result of human art, and yet are connected by such refined links that we cannot regard them as accidental or arbitrary insertions. I will content myself with taking two or three instances, just as specimens, though I might give as many scores.

The expression, "And the veil of the temple was rent," is dropped in the most casual manner. And where? It occurs in the midst of the most intensely interesting narrative,—that of the crucifixion and death of Christ, which it suddenly arrests. Apart from the reality of such an occurrence, and a conviction of its significance (this last only to be cleared up to the reader, however, by subsequent disclosures of the bearing of Christianity on Judaism), it seems inconceivable how a writer, whether of fiction or of history, should have paused at such a moment, and without any comment, to insert this parenthetical irrelevance ; or if he invented the incident as a deep stroke of art, that he should not have paused to *connect* it with the narrative which it so abruptly interrupts. Yet when we consider the symbolic significance of that " veil,"—how it was designed to seclude the " Shechinah " from the gaze of all but the high priest, and from him in every hour of the year but one ; that it indicated that restricted access to God which the new dispensation was designed to abolish for ever; that its characteristic function ceased at the death of Christ, and contemporaneously with the cry, " It is finished ; " that the rending of it proclaimed that henceforth the way to the " Holy of Holies " was laid open, and every one, " worshipping God in spirit and in truth," was welcome to the " throne of grace ; " we see that the incident becomes profoundly significant. It quadrates with the intimations given in the Old Testament of the symbolism of the " Holy of Holies," and with the reasoning of the author of the Epistle to the Hebrews, who without mentioning on his part the incident of the Gospels, shows us what the veil was designed to typify. But it is the *isolation* of the incident, in itself considered, the perfectly unnatural manner (supposing it either not true, or the writer not aware of its sig. nificance) in which it is intruded in a narration of such transcendent interest, without preparation and without comment, that suggests the idea of "undesigned correspondence" with those other statements of Scripture with which it is so consentaneous.

Another correspondence, or rather series of correspondencies, is found in the mode in which Melchizedek is connected with Christ. I may remark in passing that the original abruptness with which that "priest of the most High God" is introduced to us, the equally sudden manner in which he is dismissed,— all that we know of him being confined to that one incident in Genesis,—is (as may be said of so many other incidental passages of the Biblical narrative) an argument for historic reality; it being, apart from that reality, a thing perfectly unimaginable that a writer would have thought of thrusting into the narrative an *invention* so utterly irrelevant; and, moreover (as regarded by a Jew), not very flattering, since, as the writer of the Epistle to the Hebrews shows, Melchizedek is represented as receiving the homage of the great progenitor of the race. However, the name of Melchizedek emerges but a moment from deep obscurity, and night falls upon it again. It is as a shadow passing for a moment along an illuminated portion of a wall on a dark night : the outline of some figure silently steals out of the gloom into the line of illumination, and vanishes into the darkness again. The eclipse here is long indeed; for we hear no more of Melchizedek for many hundred years, and then once, and once only, till after the close of the Old Testament canon. In the second verse of Psalm cx.,—generally regarded —and even by many critics slow to trace Messianic vestiges— as a prophecy of the Messiah, a solitary voice proclaims, "I have made thee a priest for ever after the order of Melchizedek." The oracle is again silent for about another five hundred years;

and then Christ once more recals it, by asking the Pharisees the meaning of the first part of the Psalm which records it, and not obscurely indicating that the reference is to the Messiah, though without saying who that Messiah is.   Some thirty or forty more years pass after Christ's death, and then for the first time an ingenious interpretation of this obscure phrase, and of the allusions to Melchizedek generally, a *raison d'être* of their place in the Jewish history, is given to the reader.   Whether it is the *true* interpretation or not, I am not now discussing ; but I think it is impossible even for a sceptic not to admit that it very ingeniously draws the parallel between Melchizedek and Christ.   The points of resemblance are various, and suggest an account of the obscure and detached allusions found so far apart, which, if not true, does credit to the writer's powers of invention.   The history makes Melchizedek superior to Abraham (who was the head of the Jewish race, and from whom the Aaronic priesthood was to descend), in representing him as receiving " tithes" of the " father of the faithful."   From the abrupt manner in which he is ushered into the history and vanishes from it, from no mention being made of his lineage or posterity, he serves to adumbrate the mysterious origin of Christ, and His mysterious future when He left the world.   No mention being made " of father or mother," his priesthood did not depend on lineage, whereas it was essential to the validity of the order of the Jewish priest that he should be able to trace his pedigree to Aaron.   Further, as Melchizedek (so far as appears) derived his priesthood from no predecessor and bequeathed it to no successor, he, unlike the Jewish priests, exercised it for an indeterminate period.   In all this he is a shadow of Christ, who was not in the line of Aaron, and fulfils His functions without restriction of time.

I am not attempting to prove that the reasoning of the author of the Epistle to the Hebrews is correct, though I fully believe it is.   I am simply solicitous to point out the singular " correspondencies " which are here found between hints so obscure and so various, given at such distant intervals and by such widely different writers, and which it is hardly imaginable that any fortuity (contrivance is out of the question) should have brought together. Who will compute the chances against all these notices, fragmentary and unconnected as they are, in the different documents, being thus ingeniously combined ? [1]

To take one other instance. Let us consider the account in Matthew and Luke of the Temptation of Christ. It is an isolated narrative. Nothing seems founded upon it in other parts of Scripture, nor is any distinct reference made to it. His whole life, indeed, considering how it was spent, might be called one long temptation ;—to anger, scorn, impatience, repining ; temptation such as none can conceive, if He could indeed penetrate all the depths of evil in the hearts of men, and shudderingly recoiled from all contact with it. There does not, therefore, seem anything that would naturally suggest this peculiar scene. But when it is recollected, on the other hand, that it is elsewhere declared to be absolutely necessary, and part of Christ's function, that He should endure, in all their variety and extremity, the temptations to which *we* are subject ; that, having been thus tried, He might sympathise with us,—be " able to succour them that are tempted," to " have compassion on the ignorant and them that are out of the way," be capable of being " touched with the feeling of our infirmities, having been in all points tempted like as we are, though without sin ; " and when we recollect, on the other hand, that if *we*, like Him, would be victorious over temptation, we are told we must take into our hands the "sword of the Spirit, which is the word of God,"—re-calling and applying in the hour of conflict all the motives which it presents ; it is impossible not to feel how *congruous*, at least, all this is with that brief scene in which all the keenest bolts from the quiver of the Evil One,—those aimed at the chiefly vulnerable parts of our nature—at appetite, cupidity, vain-glory, ambition and presumption,—are said to be launched against

---

[1] Appendix No. V.

Christ; and where in every case the victory is represented as won by the same weapon, the appeal to the word of God: " It is written—it is written—it is written."

I am not now arguing for the reality of the narrative, nor pretending to solve any of the difficulties which, at first sight, would seem to preclude the possibility of Christ's being the subject of temptation. Suffice it to say that He is represented as being truly *man;* and therefore whosoever receives that fact, whatever else he may believe Him to be, must acknowledge that He was liable to temptation. Nor is it difficult to show that, however impeccable, He might at least receive from the *presentation* of temptation—under the pressure of those sufferings and privations which so generally give it its power over us—that vivid sense of *our* temptations, and of the conflict they necessitate, which only experience can impart.[1]

But I am here merely pointing out how this singular episode, standing out as it does in bold relief, with no key to its bearing on any other transactions of Christ's life, harmonises with the representations of subsequent pages of the New Testament and its development of the entire doctrines of Christianity. It seems not difficult to perceive a *keeping* in the whole, for which neither fiction nor fortuity will account.

Of course, the argument for the unity of Scripture, which I am now pressing, is not founded on the singularity of any one instance of "correspondence," but on the aggregate of them.

---

[1] We see this illustrated in some degree, and in one point or other, even in our ordinary humanity. There is many a poor but virtuous man who would sooner face starvation than rob; but if he has been, on some dire occasion, compelled to make the election, he will ever after have a very different measure of *that* temptation—though he was incapable of being conquered by it—from that of him who, also honest, has never known anything but ease and plenty. And there is many an honourable merchant, who would sooner be a martyr than a forger; but if solicited, in an hour of impending ruin, to save himself or family by some act of dishonour—though he might be in no danger of succumbing to the temptation—he would know how to appraise it as he never did before.

They abound in almost every part of the book, and would easily fill a volume.

To the same effect I might, perhaps, adduce the great number of instances in which what are called "types and shadows" in the Old Testament are interpreted, and apparently without violence, to point to certain facts and doctrines of the New as their "reality" and "substance." Large parts of the complex machinery of Jewish institutions have, at all events, seemed to immense numbers of the wise and learned to be too curiously and artificially "analogous" with the chief facts of Christianity—to have too much of a "mortise and tenon" relation about them—to be accounted for by accident or by a besotted exegesis. "This," says Davidson,[1] "is the virtue and striking property of the Mosaic types, especially that principal one of sacrifice, that they do reflect so clear and unequivocal an image of the Gospel system, when once they are confronted with it. Their cryptic characters are illuminated, and their latent import is called forth."[2] Still, as it is probable, on the one hand, that few would attach the due value to this argument for the unity of Scripture, until they had already admitted arguments more direct and obvious; and as, on the other, it is a topic which the extravagance of allegorical interpreters in all ages has only been too prone to abuse, I will not dwell on it further.

I might also mention, in this place, as confirmatory of my present argument, the general effect of those undesigned "coincidences" of statement which have been traced between different portions of Scripture; inferring not only the *credibility* of these separate portions, but, if that be admitted, a consequent reciprocal connection between the books in which they are found. These coincidences have been elaborately traced in

---

[1] Lectures on Prophecy, p. 100.

[2] This subject is beautifully illustrated in the sermon of the Rev. Thomas Binney, to which I have already made a reference, "The Law our Schoolmaster." (See particularly pp. 295-300.)

the Evangelists as compared with one another, in the Acts as compared with Paul's epistles, and in the several books of the Pentateuch. There is no reason to suppose that they are yet exhausted. and they may hereafter disclose relations of similar significance between other parts of the Bible. This mine, which has yielded so many contributions to the evidence, was only opened by Paley, in his " Horæ Paulinæ," about eighty years ago ; and the copious and important additions which have been made by Blunt and others, give us ground to think that the vein is by no means worked out.

I might further argue the "unity" of the Bible from a certain *tone* and *manner* which generally pervade these writers, and which are not found in the same degree in any other; as also from a certain resemblance of *style*, which, however undeniable the differences that discriminate the various authors and attest their individuality, is perceptible in the compositions of Scripture in general ; a diapason which runs through all its complex strain of harmony. It is heard, as the surge of ocean is heard above the many-voiced winds which sweep over its surface. It is not without reason that critics have spoken of the " Bible style."

But as this lecture is already sufficiently long, and as the two last topics, however they may suggest some arguments for the " unity of the Bible," are more naturally connected with its peculiarities of structure and of style, I reserve what I have to say upon them to subsequent lectures.

Mean time, if there be unity in the Bible, then, from the mode of its composition, it is not a book that man could have made, if he would.[1]

[1] Appendix No. VI.

LECTURE V.

REPLY TO SOME OBJECTIONS FOUNDED ON THE FORM AND STRUCTURE OF THE BIBLE.

LECTURE V.

THOUGH my principal object in the present lecture is to obviate certain *objections*, I hope it will not be entirely without matter which may contribute to the main purpose of my present line of argument.

It is impossible to open the Bible without being struck with the variety of its form and contents. It was composed by manifold authors, writing at far distant dates, in different languages, in the most diverse circumstances, and with the usual peculiarities of individual genius. Though there is, as I have said in the last lecture, a general resemblance of style which pervades the Scriptures, there is also the distinct idiosyncratic impress of many minds. If there be harmony, it is the harmony of a large orchestra where the instruments, however in unison, are yet plainly distinguishable from one another. Further, these authors write on an immense variety of subjects, and the form of their compositions is as various as their matter. Narrative and poetry of various kinds, history and biography, odes and hymns, writings devoted to simply didactic purposes, familiar letters—all are there; in short, nearly all the compositions which, as addressed to the several faculties of the human mind, and evoked by them, naturally distinguish every national literature; but marked in this case, as we shall presently see, by peculiarities which do not belong to ordinary compositions of (loosely speaking) the same *genus* in other literatures. In truth,

the Bible is so multifarious that, as has been well said, it is
rather a " library " than a " book."

If there be that unity about so multiform a thing, for which I
have argued, the inference from such unity is strengthened in
proportion to this variety,—for it is in that proportion incredible
that man produced it.   If there be unity at all, it exists in
spite of this variety.   It is a unity, like that of some natural
system—that of the human body, for example—where elements
the most dissimilar in form, property, and function, are found
in juxta-position, and order reigns amidst seeming confusion.
If any such unity be denied, and the book be supposed a mere
conglomerate of heterogeneous things, this makes it all the
more unaccountable that so many millions of intelligent men
should have been deluded into the belief of its unity.

But this very variety of authorship, form, and matter, has
often been urged as an objection to its supposed Divine origin.
" Can we imagine it worthy of Deity," it is said, " to give a revelation in scraps and fragments, ' here a little and there a little,'
through successive ages and in the most dissimilar forms ? "

Though I think with Butler, that we are not very competent,
except in a few points (as regards morality, for example), to
judge *a priori* of what a revelation is likely to consist, still less
of the forms which it may possibly assume, I conceive it is not
difficult to repel, or at least neutralize such an objection, by the
following considerations.

If it be supposed incredible that God should reveal Himself
by so complex an instrument, then the best way is to test the
objection by an appeal to "analogy."   The prodigious variety
and consequent seeming confusion of Scripture are certainly in
conformity with the corresponding variety and consequent
seeming confusion in which the phenomena of nature are submitted to man's study and contemplation.   Nor are the conditions on which he has to perform his office of " minister and
interpreter" in either case very dissimilar.[1]

[1] In a future lecture, this, as appears to me, instructive "analogy," will
be more fully illustrated.

But I am not sure that the objection, if it be really the most *natural* conclusion human reason could arrive at, might not be pressed into the service of the line of argument adopted in these lectures. For it at least bears witness that man would not have chosen so elaborate and complicated an instrument of a professed revelation.[1]

[1] A similar objection has been founded on what is for the most part a necessary consequence of the complexity and variety of the Bible,—the unsystematic distribution of its contents.   On the other hand, this very quality has seemed to others a mark of superhuman wisdom.   Boyle has thought it worth while to reply at some length to the objection ; Whately and many others have largely vindicated the peculiarity itself.   Perhaps, as the quality is the *natural* consequence of the structure of the Bible, and its gradual growth, and as, on the other hand, it is often found in other professed revelations,—more stress has been laid on this topic than, *per se*, it deserves. The trait in question is not in itself a perfection ; it may consist, like the phenomena of the universe, " with order," but " ill understood ; " or it may imply real confusion ; it may be the effect of comprehensiveness and variety of purpose, or of ignorance and an inconsequent logic.

But if it be made an objection that it is *incredible* that God could have chosen such a method, then I conceive that the reasoning of Boyle, in his reply to the fourth and seventh Objections to the style of Scripture, and that of Whately, founded on the ends that may be palpably answered by such an arrangement, is amply sufficient.   The principal answer, indeed, as before, is derived from " analogy."   We see in what way God *does* school us in the world He has made ; how seemingly unsystematic the distribution of the phenomena man is called to study ; and how seemingly slow and desultory the lessons he is taught to learn.

But the ends to be answered by such a method are various and important enough to make the objection sufficiently precarious apart from this.   It is quite true that the doctrines and precepts of Scripture are scattered up and down as different occasions call for them, or suggest them ; that sometimes they are conjoined, sometimes detached, —doctrine without the practical inferences to which it leads, precepts without the doctrinal truths from which they flow ; sometimes they lie latent in the bare facts of the narrative, and are to be deduced by our own sagacity, or by comparison with other passages ; sometimes they are taught or confirmed by oblique allusion, and seem all the more impressive for so incidental a reference to them ; sometimes, as they represent progressive truth, they are necessarily developed in fragments, and thus the more important dogmas of the Gospel pass through all stages of illumination, between twilight obscurity and the bright noonday. But then, on the other hand, this method impresses truth more deeply on

But, in truth, I doubt whether deliberate judgment would attach any force to such an objection at all. If a man of large and cautious mind permitted himself to speculate on what form a Revelation might not unnaturally assume, I am by no means sure that he would not anticipate, on a survey of all its require-

the mind by the varied forms and constant iteration with which it is presented; it gives "line upon line and precept upon precept;" it imposes on the reader the duty of diligently exploring and collating the different portions of Scripture, if he would rightly comprehend its contents; it involves a perpetual discipline of the intellect, and the exercise of caution, patience, and humility. It prevents the mind from stagnating, through too constant familiarity with, or parrot-like repetition of, one unvaried, however accurate and logical, compend or syllabus of religious truth. "God's wisdom," says Whately ("Errors of Romanism," *Essay* iv. *Sect.* 6), "doubtless designed to guard us against a danger which I think no human wisdom would have foreseen—the danger of indolently assenting to and committing to memory 'a form of sound words,' which would in a short time have become no more than a form of words—received with passive reverence, and scrupulously retained in the mind—leaving no room for doubt, furnishing no call for vigilant investigation, affording no stimulus to the attention, and making no vivid impression on the heart. It is only when the understanding is kept on the stretch by the diligent search—the watchful observation—the careful deduction—which the Christian Scriptures call forth by their oblique, incidental, and irregular mode of conveying the knowledge of Christian doctrines —it is then only that the feelings, and the moral portion of our nature, are kept so awake as to receive the requisite impression." He elsewhere illustrates the same subject by a very striking image. On the supposition that theology had been taught in Scripture in the form of a logically arranged compendium, he observes that, "The compendium itself, being not like the existing Scriptures, that *from which* the faith is to be learned, but *the very thing to be learned*, would have come to be regarded by most with an indolent, unthinking veneration, which would have exercised little or no influence on the character. Their orthodoxy would have been, as it were, petrified, like the bodies of those animals we read of incrusted in the ice of the polar regions; firm-fixed, indeed, and preserved unchanged, but cold, motionless, lifeless. It is only when our energies are roused, and our faculties exercised, and our attention kept awake by an ardent pursuit of truth, and anxious watchfulness against error—when, in short, we feel ourselves to be doing something towards acquiring, or retaining, or improving our knowledge,—it is then only that that knowledge makes the requisite practical impression on the heart and on the conduct."—*Peculiarities in the Christian Religion.* Essay vi. p. 361.

ments, a very great complexity of structure and variety of form. He might conjecture that, to answer so many diverse and complicated ends, it must be not simply a perspicuous, logical abstract of the great truths which constitute its essential value as a Revelation, but an exhibition of those truths in the most versatile and flexible forms, adapted to minister to the spiritual wants and aspirations of universal humanity; that being the book of all time and of " every land," it would be suited to all the faculties of human nature, and all the intellectual and moral varieties in individual men ; capable of arresting not the intellect alone, but the memory, the imagination, the affections, and the heart ; that it would contain spiritual aliment for the wisest and the weakest among us,—wisdom here, so profound, that the deepest intellects cannot exhaust it ; there, so easy, that the child cannot miss it; aphorisms which may well employ the meditative powers of a Bacon or a Pascal, poetry worthy of kindling the congenial fancy of a Milton, and parables which even Bunyan's allegories cannot equal ; that its narratives would form such a picture of human life, that the learned and the ignorant, the rude and polished, age and childhood, the happy and the sorrowful, would hang over them with equal delight, as they saw reflected in that mirror the image of their own various nature, and the methods of Divine providence in dealing with it.   He might conjecture that it would be a book which should exhibit the most various truths in the most various forms—" line upon line and precept upon precept "—so as both to be its own best commentary, and bid defiance to any successful tampering with its text ; a book which, in addition to all this, should contain within itself—in its very structure—in its undesigned harmonies of part with part, and in remote coincidences with the history of that world with which its own is implicated, some of the very chief proofs of its own superhuman origin ; and, lastly, that it would be composed in such a style (everywhere generically the same, while yet bearing the specific imprint of the different minds that were employed upon it) as to adapt itself, with flexible ease, for transfusion into every dialect of man.

If really fitted to answer all this variety of ends, it must, like the outward universe, be exceedingly complex in its structure and various in its contents; nor need it surprise us that these last, like those of the material world, should exist in seeming glorious confusion; but in confusion like that of Eden, where was every tree that was good for food, or that could minister to beauty and delight—not planted with the stiff formality of a little Dutch garden, but as described in the vivid words of him who sang it as if he had seen it :—

> " Flowers worthy of Paradise,—which not nice art
> In beds and curious knots, but Nature boon
> Poured forth profuse on hill and dale and plain,
> Both where the morning sun first warmly smote
> The open fields, and where the unpierced shade
> Imbrowned the noontide hours."

Now assuming, for argument's sake, the Bible to be a Revelation, I apprehend that our supposed critic, on inspection of the principal elements of which it consists, their proportions, and the different purposes they seem adapted to answer, would say that it met in a high degree the conditions of his speculation. I have no space to enter into such extended investigation here; but I am tempted to take a single illustration from the manifold adaptations to the surmised ends of such a Revelation, presented in that element of the Bible which is by far the largest and the most important,—I mean, *narrative.*

The staple of the book is history and biography,—which in fact make up about four-fifths of the whole. This alone sharply discriminates it from all other so-called sacred books,—from which the historic element is almost wholly absent. The Bible, on the other hand, is professedly embedded in human history, runs parallel with it, and if true, forms the most important part of it; for all the principal dogmas themselves purport to be *facts,* and make the most significant part of the history it records.

Now, in the first place, this form of composition is one of the most easy and impressive vehicles of conveying moral instruction ; it illustrates precept by example, and appeals to the imagination as well as the reason.   It makes good the maxim, old as Aristotle and no doubt much older, that the things most effectually and quickly learnt are those which are " learned with delight."   It is capable of being at once understood and relished by the young and old, the learned and the ignorant, and in some measure equalises the condition and capacity of those who read it.   We all know that history has been called " philosophy teaching by example :" in the case of the Bible it may be truly called "theology teaching by example ;" for everything is regarded in the light of those great principles which characterise the entire book, and which subordinate everything to the claims of God, as the Creator and Sovereign of the universe.   It constitutes, therefore, a perpetual commentary on God's providential government, and shows us, by innumerable examples, how to interpret those lessons which the varying events of life, its joys and sorrows, its temptations and trials, are calculated to teach us.   There is hardly an event, hardly a character, that has not its parallel in that immense picture gallery of historic and biographic sketches which the Scripture opens to us.   The whole of life seems mirrored there ; nor can the attentive and candid reader fail to be struck with the fact that such a panorama, in which all the conditions of human life seem exhibited, should be painted in so small a compass.   The examples range through all the ranks of social life, embrace all varieties of character, and illustrate, by analogous cases, almost every conceivable combination of circumstances in which man can be placed.   It is hardly possible to imagine ourselves in any situation, in which that immense repertory and storehouse of monitory or touching examples will not furnish a precedent either for our warning, consolation, or guidance.

I shall presently have to notice a prevailing feature of this history, which greatly augments its usefulness, as an exercise and study : I mean its essentially *dramatic* character, by which bare historic facts, usually without a word of comment or reflection, are given, leaving us to draw the inference from the general principles elsewhere developed, or by reference to similar cases.   It is easy to see that this character of the history increases its value as a source of instruction ; and the mode of teaching is in this, as in many other respects, in analogy with that of nature.   It solicits the mind to exert its own intelligence, instead of making everything quite plain, and leaving us to be the mere passive recipients of knowledge.   It is hard to say whether the common mind is better pleased with inferring a general conclusion from a particular example, or referring a particular example to a general principle : in both ways the book ministers to a concurrent activity of mind in the student of it.   This feature of the Bible also affords an inexhaustible fund of apt illustration to those whose function it is to interpret the book to the ignorant.   Probably it would not be difficult to illustrate the whole gnomic wisdom of the Book of Proverbs by quoting parallel examples from the historic books of the Bible.   In this way the Bible is not only adapted to be a text-book of morals and theology, but is its own best interpreter; nor is there perhaps any commentary more useful than one made out of the Bible itself, by a careful collation of all parallel passages.

Other reasons for the prevalence of the historic form will readily suggest themselves.   It plays a most important part in relation to the "evidences" of the truth of the Bible.   It yields the far greater part of those "undesigned coincidences" which constitute so important a portion of apologetics.   Of this species of evidence, lying enfolded in the leaves of the Scripture history—and lying unnoticed for near eighteen centuries, —the most brilliant example is still the "Horæ Paulinæ." But though the collation of Paul's "Epistles" with the "Acts" gives the most striking specimen of this argument, it is one that may be gathered from many other books of Scripture, —as many works, similarly constructed with that of Paley, show. The wonder is that no one lighted on the entrance to this subterranean gallery before. Pascal, indeed, makes a casual remark that some such evidence might be extracted from a comparison of the incidents of the Gospels; and Doddridge has an acute observation, which contains, in fact, an anticipation of Paley's argument. But the idea was certainly not wrought out till Paley's admirable work appeared.[1]

[1] Professor Leathes, in his able " Lectures on St. Paul " (p. 64), has justly remarked that it is a curious instance of the fluctuations of controversy, that an attempt is now often made to " turn the tables " on Paley, by alleging minute historic discrepancies between the " Epistles " and the " Acts " as a set-off against the " undesigned coincidences." It is true; but surely it is not difficult to see the futile character of the " set-off." To suppose it can be such, is to show an incompetence to discern the nature of the argument from " undesigned coincidences." Of the alleged historic discrepancies, some may be due to corruptions of the text; many have been satisfactorily solved; others are in course of solution, and we cannot tell how far the solutions will ultimately go. Of many others, we have reason to believe that they exist only in the objector's imagination, and are due to the omission of some facts which, if known, would clear them up; and, supposing, in some few insignificant cases, that they are the result of mistake, ignorance, error on the part of the writers, even this will not affect the substantial truth of the history. But an argument from the " undesigned coincidences," when these are once established, admits of no such abatements: they are not a variable quantity; they are too numerous and exquisite to be referred to accident, and lie too deep for fraud,— unless fraud intended to defeat itself, for they were never discovered for eighteen centuries. The argument, indeed, from historic discrepancies is in one respect like that from the " undesigned coincidences;" for they both suggest that the writers could not be in collusion; but even this is proved far more effectually by the latter. In a word, they are of a totally different argumentative nature and value from the mere discrepancies, and tell far more powerfully for the historic validity of a document than mere discrepancies can tell against it.

It is as if a man thought to prove that a child's puzzle map was no such thing, though the " cloven tallies " fell so exactly into their places, because one of the pieces was chipped, another missing, a third had a misprint of a place on it, and so on. These " discrepancies " may be accounted for; but nothing can account for the " coincidences " except that they belong to the

In a similar way, many of the *driest* portions of the historic books,— the genealogies for example,—minister to the same end. The mere frequency and copiousness of such matter, untinctured with the smallest trace of mythological influences, and attended, as it often is, with a break in the continuity and interest of the narrative, is, *pro tanto*, a voucher that the writings in which they occur are neither fiction nor myth. A writer of fiction would never dream of introducing so large an amount of this unattractive matter, without one picturesque or poetical detail to relieve it ; far less obstruct the narrative for the purpose. We can understand the moderate use which Homer or De Foe may have made of such matter : that is, just so far as to impart a general air of verisimilitude. But whole pages together of nothing but names are so preposterously beyond all imaginable necessities of illusion, and so destructive of all interest in the reader, that we may safely infer that the introduction of such matter, to the extent we find it in the Bible, will admit of no such solution. As little will it admit of a mythical origin ; for though myths may be a gradual and insensible growth of the popular imagination, they are yet true to the principles on which they have been constructed and embellished—to amuse or instruct ; and neither the one purpose nor the other can be answered by whole chapters containing nothing but long cata logues of names.[1]

On the other hand, many of these portions of Scripture, regarded as history, have another important bearing on the evidences. The genealogies, however dry they may be, often

map, " undesigned " indeed by the child who puts it together,—just as the oblique " coincidences " in Paul and Luke are evidently undesigned by them ; but not by the maker of the map.

[1] " It is to be added, also, that mere genealogies, bare narratives of the number of years which persons, called by such and such names, lived, do not carry the air of fiction ; perhaps do carry some presumption of veracity ; and all unadorned narratives, which have nothing to surprise, may be thought to carry somewhat of the like presumption too."—*Butler's Analogy.* Part ii. ch. 7.

throw light on some obscure passage in a remote part of Scripture; or clear up some difficulty in a totally different book by a totally different writer, and of a far distant age.[1]

Another point in which the historic form conduces to the "evidences," consists in the challenge which it offers to criticism, by so often intersecting secular history. It is assuredly most extraordinary that the sacred history, supposing it other than it purports to be,—that is, fiction, or myth, or both,—should so boldly have defied the scrutiny of the world by deliberately traversing profane history, and yet have emerged from the most "fiery ordeal" of criticism ever applied to ancient documents, with scarcely the "smell of fire" upon it. It comes into constant contact with profane history, both in the Old Testament and the New, but especially in the last. It everywhere inserts its alleged facts into the plane of contemporaneous or nearly contemporaneous events, without the smallest hesitation, or preparation, or apology, or timidity,—as though it was quite certain that none would or could challenge the accuracy of its representations. Yet one would imagine that the immense difficulty of preserving consistency, or any approach to it, in such attempts —to say nothing of the greater difficulty of inducing those who must have known the true history, to acquiesce without protest in the feigned incidents mixed with it, as history too—would deter the most audacious impostor. In fact, far more limited attempts of this nature have been unmasked by less than a hundredth part of the unrelenting rigour of criticism to which the history of the Scriptures generally, but especially that of the New Testament, has been subjected. In this last case, though every advantage is given to the sceptic from the large remains of profane history with which the sacred history may be compared, and though the most acute minds, animated by the keenest desire to find flaws, have exhausted their skill in endeavouring to find them, the effect is absolutely inappreciable. On the other hand, unexpected confirmations of its accuracy are frequently

---

[1] See Boyle. *Style of the Holy Scriptures: Answer to Objection IV.*

found in the discovery from time to time of documents, medals, and other relics of antiquity, in which fresh light is cast on the harmony, even in minute points, between the Scriptural representations of profane history and those of secular writers. Now if Scripture history be either fiction or legend, or aught else but history, this " reckless scattering of names and dates," this profuse introduction of historic persons and actions ("where nothing," as Paley says, "but truth can produce consistency "), ought to be fatal to it.   It ought to be as easy to tear this artificial web to tatters as so many other flimsy fabrics which have been subjected to the ordeal of criticism.

The immense importance of the historical form of the Scriptures to the *evidence* is obvious, if we allow (what few deny) that the facts of *profane* history, implicated with the New Testament, are true.   Is it possible to conceive that those who then lived or those of the next generation, with every disposition and motive to reject the impostures or legends with which those facts, on this supposition, are so impudently connected, would have acquiesced in them if not true?   Is it possible, for example, if the history of Paul in the " Acts " be not true, that it could have been affirmed that he had been brought before Agrippa, had appealed to the facts of the evangelical history, and to Agrippa's own knowledge of them as " not done in a corner,"—without provoking vehement reclamations ?   Would it not have been said that these things had *not* been done, either " in a corner" or anywhere else ?   Would those who could so easily have shown the effrontery of this cheat, and who had every reason to do so, have been silent ?   And so of numberless other things, which it is certain that the contemporaries of the apostles, or the men of the next generation, would have instantly contradicted, instead of accepting them as history.   It is inconceivable that events, professedly of a public character, can be thus closely implicated with persons and transactions occupying a large space on the theatre of the world, without being either instantly contradicted, or beyond contradiction.

The prevailing historic form is attended with yet another advantage as regards the evidence. If it gives every facility to its adversaries for proving it false, the artlessness of the narrative, its vivid air of reality, its simplicity and apparent honesty, impress ninety-nine readers out of every hundred with a conviction that the writer is speaking truth. The natural air of unsophisticated testimony is often irresistible, and it certainly belongs as conspicuously to the Bible narratives as to any.

There is, if I mistake not, another prevailing peculiarity about the *history* of Scripture, which it is worth while to note, as it is a symptom of reality, and is in analogy, at any rate, with the actual history of men, whether they be conceived as communities or individuals. I refer to the general disregard of what art exacts in fiction, and instinct so often suggests in myth, as essential to its appropriate interest; namely, a well-rounded narrative, in which, even if there be some want of skill in the management of the intermediate incidents, or ill-judged digressions, or too long a suspension of the catastrophe, there is, as there should be, a well-defined beginning, and, above all, a well-defined end,—a *dénouement* such as shall satisfy the imagination. Now, Scripture history is generally little solicitous about this, and is thereby in accordance with human life.

The history of individuals and communities, as given in the Bible, and as transacted in the world, is something like the last voyage of Paul, in the Acts. The ship moves, indeed, but is driven hither and thither by baffling winds, and meets with strange variety of fortunes and disasters;—an image of that devious course which, under the providential government of God, marks the general history of human life. As there is nothing "so unlike a battle as a review," so there is nothing so unlike real history as the plot of a skilfully constructed novel, or a well-adjusted drama, where the *unities* are fairly preserved, and the catastrophe unexceptionable. In each man's life, and in that of each nation, we find "passages" which seemingly "lead to nothing;" though we are sure it is not so, inasmuch as they are part of the discipline and schooling of men—part of the "*plan de Dieu*"—however we may fail to see the connection between the means and the end. We often see incidents of apparently the most trivial character leading to the most momentous issues, and events which thrilled the contemporary world with awe or admiration, as often collapsing to nothing; profound sagacity stumbling over some simple obstacle, and projects long cherished in vain, and at last given up in despair, made, by a sudden turn of events, unexpectedly feasible. Civil and political history, which records these things, is of a corresponding complexion. In reading it, we encounter numberless digressions and episodes, which seemingly interrupt the course of it, and which are inserted, not because they have any vital, or, indeed, any visible connection at all with the main purpose of the story, but because the historian is bound to record what did happen, whether it always conduces to its interest or not. In fact, in human life and human history, we see but fragments of the "acts" and "scenes" of that vast drama which every rational atheist believes to be transacting on the theatre of the world.

Now it is of just such fragments that the historic portions of Scripture, for the most part, consist; connected, indeed, but just as the incidents of human life and of political and civil history are connected, by relations of cause and effect, of proximity of time or place, or contemporaneousness; but not by the laws of unity which imagination prescribes in her works.

There are comparatively few narratives in the history of the Bible to which these remarks do not apply. In reading them, therefore, we are continually struck with abrupt terminations of the story, with seemingly isolated facts or passages, which end in a *cul de sac*. We find ourselves continually putting questions which our unsatisfied curiosity asks in vain. We wonder what was the history of Jacob and his sons, and what their relations, during the twenty years of Joseph's exile? what the degree and effect of those suspicions which, from that explosion of feeling which took place when Simeon was missed and Benjamin seemed in peril, had, it would seem, been smouldering so long in the patriarch's bosom? what became of Isaiah, Jeremiah, Ezekiel, and so many other prime actors in the history of the Jews? how the Acts came to break off with such provoking abruptness in the very crisis of Paul's fate, leaving him a captive at Rome between life and death, without a word to indicate the catastrophe? These are specimens of a thousand questions which we ask in Biblical and ordinary history alike.

If there are any notable exceptions, the histories of Joseph and David may be deemed such. Yet even in these, though they are marked, perhaps (especially the former), by a greater completeness and more copious details than any of the rest, how many digressions and irrelevancies are there, which would never have been admitted by writers solely intent on the interest of their story; and how many vicissitudes and complications which seem to obstruct it. These things, however, are reflected in real life and real history. These circuitous methods, these long delays and slow preparations, this flux and reflux of fortune, are constantly seen in the biographies of those whom God has conducted from obscurity to greatness.[1]

[1] Davison, in his "Lectures on Prophecy," remarks that the history of David is particularly worthy of study, as an example of fulfilment of a prophecy,—the predicted elevation of David from a shepherd's hut to the throne,—by the interposition of a long, intricate, and most diversified series of incidents, without a miracle; by a series of events in themselves perfectly natural, and not out of the ordinary path of Providence. As I am not now arguing on the supposition of either prophecy or miracle, I here refer to this portion of Scripture history, simply as an image of the complex play of human passions and interests—the slow processes, the abrupt transitions, the sudden metatheses,—which true history has so often exemplified; as, for example, in the fortunes of Masaniello or Cromwell. The results are wrought out, as it were, dramatically, but with an intricacy of incident, a going backward and forward, a variety of vicissitudes and oscillations, on which the dramatist does not venture, for fear of too long suspending the action or marring its unity.

One remark seems necessary to qualify Davison's observation. When he says that the history of David is developed without the intervention of a

But though these are very beautiful episodes in Scripture history, and exhibit more of dramatic completeness than almost anything else in its pages, they are sufficiently assimilated to the ordinary history of Scripture, and to that of life, to bring them under the criterion in question. If they be *not* history, one is lost in wonder at the contrast between the prodigal invention which has feigned such an infinitude of incidents, and so naturally interwoven and expressed them in so small a compass, and yet has introduced so much digressive, and, so far as the main story is concerned, irrelevant matter. As history, indeed, we can understand it; but if the authors were composing fiction or embellishing myth, one does not comprehend how writers should have been both so exquisitely skilled, and such utter bunglers in the same art. What, for example, can be more incongruous than the intrusion, into the history of Joseph, of the fragment of Judah's story in chap. xxxviii. of Genesis; or than many of the interludes,—and especially the insertion of genealogies,—which break the continuity of that of David? All natural enough if these things belong to the domain of fact, but not very intelligible on the other hypothesis.

Assuming then, for a moment, and for argument's sake, as I have here done, the truth of the Bible, and seeing how many ends, principal and subordinate, may possibly be contemplated and attained by the very same instrumentality, objections from the artificiality of its structure, or the multifarious character of its contents, need not trouble us. But though I have reasoned only hypothetically, I think it is scarcely possible for a candid mind to consider the apparent convergence to many related ends which is found in so complex a structure—how naturally the

miracle, he probably means what we *commonly* call such, not the entire absence of the supernatural; for *that* is not absolutely excluded. Prophecy, prophetic vision, and appeals to the oracles of professed Divine appointment among the Jews, form an appreciable, though a small part of the history of David. Understanding him in this sense, he might, with equal justice, have adduced the history of Joseph, as carried on from first to last without miracle, and as an equally striking illustration of the slow and intricate, yet certain, methods of Providence.

various parts seem to argue mutual dependence and support, as seen in the many volumes which have been written on its self-derived evidences—without having some suspicion at least excited that all this is not a result of accident; and, if so, that some wisdom greater than that of the several authors and compilers must have presided over the whole, determined the relation of the parts, and directed them to their end.

If Scripture be a revelation of God's will, the *substance* of its contents, no doubt, will have quite another and far higher object than to give incidental proofs of its truth. Its design will be "to make men wise unto salvation." Yet in conformity with so many analogies in the works of God, where we see manifold purposes often attained by one and the same set of organs and instruments, it may engraft on its primary purpose many subordinate purposes, and attain the latter in attaining the former. Accordingly we see, in point of fact, how large a portion of the arguments in defence of the Bible are derived from itself. Nor to the cumulative power of that argument is it easy to set any limit, as the contexture, peculiarities, and relations of the several books come to be more searchingly investigated. If these views be correct, the book may be compared to some ancient temple, the elaborate ornaments of which, though the temple itself be designed for a higher purpose than to evince the skill of the architect, yet do bear witness to it. The shield of Achilles, though chiefly intended to protect the hero's life in battle, and to turn every weapon by its adamantine temper, yet proclaimed, in the pictured wonders which encircled its margin and covered its ample field, the skill of the divine artificer who had forged it.

But whether these considerations have any force besides answering an *objection* or not, there are two or three prevailing peculiarities about the writers of Scripture history, and especially the Evangelists, which have always appeared to me perfectly unintelligible, except on the supposition that they are not to be placed in the category of merely human authors. Of these peculiarities I shall treat in the next lecture

LECTURE VI.

ON CERTAIN PECULIARITIES OF SCRIPTURE STYLE.

LECTURE VI.

THE first of the peculiarities to which reference was made at the close of the last lecture is one which characterises the Bible *generally*, not only far more than any other book, but to such an extent as can hardly be imagined by any one who has not made the subject his express study. The quality I refer to is that of exhibiting character in a purely dramatic form; by simply relating naked facts and incidents without comment, without criticism, without description of manners, without enumeration of qualities; in a word, to the utter exclusion of that analysis which is so favourite an exercise of the human mind, and without which, not once in ten times, can it prevail on itself to let facts speak nakedly for themselves, or give the reader credit for sagacity enough to draw his own conclusions. As it is a very unusual way of writing, so it is incomparably the most difficult. Genius of high dramatic order is of very rare occurrence; and it is certainly not among Jews, whether in ancient or modern times, that we should expect the most profuse exhibition of it. To portray character by simply exhibiting it in action, by its own sayings and doings, is very rare even in the most famous novelists. Even by the greatest masters of the art—Walter Scott, for instance—characters are often introduced by a long and sometimes wearisome preparation of analytic description; ticketed and labelled with such and such properties, as if the author wished to engrave more deeply on his own mind the lines of the character he had conceived, or to frame a sort of model to work by, before dramatically exhibiting it ; or as conscious that his actual exhibition would inadequately convey to the reader the ideal he would paint. Even Shakespeare himself—that Prince of Dramatists, of whom one is accustomed to think (as a friend once expressed it) not so much as a "sublimation of what other men may feel in a weaker degree in themselves, but as something of another order"—even Shakespeare, not seldom, puts into the mouth of an interlocutor a vivid picture of the character he is about to exhibit, or gives it in the course of the drama, as though for the purpose of aiding the reader's conception. As to history,—we know that elaborate portraits of the principal characters have exercised the utmost skill of great masters in this department of literature, from Thucydides and Tacitus to Clarendon and Macaulay. They would have thought themselves strangely wanting to their subject, and to themselves as philosophers, if they had not given us such " characters, " and also essayed to analyse the motives by which their actions were determined. All this is natural, and we expect it ; and, in truth, the element is found rather in excess than in defect in all the principal histories. It is only too copious,—misleading the reader and prejudicing him for or against the characters, beyond what the facts, impartially judged, would justify ; and he is thus led astray by false lights into erring estimates. With the biographer this fault is proverbial. In many "Lives" the reader can hardly get an opportunity of fairly observing the professed subject of the biography for two pages together. The author stands between them with perpetual comment and reflection, stricture and admiration, so that, as people say, "we cannot see the ground for the flowers" or "the wood for the trees." To novelists, the extreme difficulty of representing character dramatically is some excuse for dropping so often into dissertation and reflection. The historian and biographer are not, indeed, under precisely the same temptation, for the facts are made for them. Yet practically it comes to the same thing ; partly from the intrinsic difficulty of presenting mere facts without becoming dry and dull, partly from the strong temptation to play the philosopher to excess. The historian is anxious to show that he can penetrate into the causes of events, as well as narrate the events themselves.

But whatever be the temptation to depart from a severely dramatic exhibition of characters—and in some degree it is necessary,—the writers of the Bible seldom do. The greater part of the book is history; and yet, in the vast majority of instances, the characters are brought out by simple speech and act, and not at all by description. They are not, like many portraits, half idealised by the artists; they are photographs, and photographed in the moment of action. A few instances of this quality must suffice here; but they might be given *ad libitum*, and would amply justify my assertion of the enormous *extent* to which this element is a characteristic of the Bible.

Take, for example, the character of Peter. When he is "called to be an apostle," nothing is said of him, either good or bad; nothing either of his intellectual or moral qualities. Neither is any comment of this kind made in narrating the actions by which his whole natural character comes out. It comes out nevertheless in the clearest possible light, and as distinctly as if there had been a whole dissertation upon it. He was evidently of that order of men whose strong, impulsive nature does not wait to consider the prudence, and is apt to forget even the rectitude, of an action, in the presence of any sudden appeal to feeling of whatever kind, and who may be heroes or cowards, impelled to generous and magnanimous conduct, or hurried into foolish blunders, or even crimes, as external circumstances prompt them; and both the one and the other, because they want self-possession to pause for the decisions of deliberate judgment. The instant view which such a mind takes of the circumstances which invite and provoke precipitate action determines it, and leads now to rash confidence, now to panic terror. This lack of *retenue* and self-possession, this emotional susceptibility, which dwells on the border-land of virtue and vice, and may easily pass from one to the other, was the natural characteristic of the apostle ; and all his actions, though the Evangelists say not one word about the trait, are dramatically true to it.   While his fellow-disciples, perplexed with the incomprehensible character of Christ, doubted whether He was the Messiah or not, and, wavering in their opinions like their fellow-countrymen, were dumb to the question, " But whom say *ye* that I am ? " Peter gave expression to the conclusion which his impulsive nature had prompted him to form, and exclaimed, " Thou art the Christ, the Son of the living God." His bold confession is rewarded by an emphatic commendation of his faith.   But the instant after he blunders into an error, which calls down upon him rebuke as strong as the eulogy that had just preceded it.   Sharing in all the convictions of his countrymen, that the expected Messiah would come as a mighty king and conqueror, and that therefore He whom he had recognised as Christ, however disguised for the moment, would soon break forth from the cloud and shine in the full blaze of His glory, he could not brook the idea of the humiliation and ignominy which his Master deliberately said awaited Him, and exclaimed, " That be far from Thee, Lord : this shall not be unto Thee." He is rebuked with, " Get thee behind Me, Satan ; " and is told, in spite of the boldness and decision of his recent confession, that he had no apprehension of the Divine purposes, and that he judged of them by a merely human standard.   When Christ was seen at midnight walking on the stormy waters, Peter, hearing His reassuring voice, passed at once from the state of superstitious dread in which " they had all cried out, thinking that they had seen a spirit," into a transport of love and faith, and exclaimed, " If indeed it be Thou, bid me to come unto Thee on the water ; " strong in his conviction that He who had performed, and was now exhibiting such miracles, could sustain him there.   But with that same facility of receiving impressions from every new occurrent, no sooner does he find himself exposed to the boisterous winds around him and the unstable element beneath him, than he feels all his courage and faith ooze away, and cries, "Save, Lord, I perish!" It is a scene which is really the very counterpart—one might almost call it symbolic prefiguration—of the similar, but more signal exhibition of mingled presumption and weakness on that memorable night on which he declared, "Though all should forsake Thee, yet will not I;" and before daybreak had "denied Him with oaths and curses." "Though I die with Thee, yet will I not deny Thee," said he, with full honesty of purpose, but in profound self-ignorance. "Before the cock crow thou shalt deny Me thrice," were the monitory words with which his Master received the declaration. When Christ was apprehended, Peter it was who hurries into rash resistance and "draws the sword." But in spite of this show of resolution, in spite of all his protests, and with that warning voice as it were still ringing in his ears, such was the power of sudden terror and danger to cow his spirit, that he forgot alike all that he had said to his Master, and all that his Master had said to him. Though he yields to his abject panic, no sooner does he hear "the cock crow" than another revulsion of feeling takes place, and horrified with the thought of what he had done, he passes at once into the most violent paroxysm of remorse, and "going out, wept bitterly." When, after the supper, Christ gave His disciples the touching symbolic lesson conveyed "by washing their feet," all of them seem to have passively submitted to His condescending ministration, till He came to Peter. Stung with jealousy for his Master's honour, he could not refrain from expostulating, "Lord, dost thou wash my feet?" Jesus answers, "What I do, thou knowest not now, but thou shalt know hereafter." Even this does not silence the impetuous disciple, who exclaims, "Thou shalt *never* wash my feet!" But no sooner does Christ remind him of the necessity of complying with His will, if he would be really a disciple of His, and says (with an allusion probably to the need of a deeper purification), "If I wash thee not, thou hast no part with Me," than his mood changes at once, and he exclaims, " Lord, not my feet only, but also my hands and my head."   When Mary Magdalene announces to Peter and John that she had found the sepulchre empty, they both instantly ran thither.   John, more fleet of foot, gets there first, but stands outside irresolute, apparently arrested by awe and wonder: the ardent Peter rushes at once into the sepulchre.

At the Sea of Tiberias, after the miraculous draught of fish, no sooner does John whisper to Peter that the seeming stranger who had spoken to them from the shore must be " the Lord," than the impetuous disciple girt his fisher's coat about him, and without waiting till the bark had drawn its freight to land, casts himself headlong into the sea.   When at the ensuing meal, his Master so tenderly, yet so deeply probed (and probed that He might heal), that wound which Peter's lapse had inflicted and which still bled inwardly, by the thrice repeated question, " Simon, son of Jonas, lovest thou me ? " Peter, though grieved at the repetition of the question, is no less impulsive than of old : strong in the consciousness of the sincerity of his love in spite of all his failures, and proof against that self-distrust which, after such a fall and such an exposure, would have kept many a man dumb, he confidently appealed to the omniscience of his Lord—"Thou knowest all things, Thou *knowest* that I love Thee."   And here, by the way, in this very scene of surpassing pathos, besides the characteristic trait of Peter, we see other indications of that quality of the Scriptures of which I am now speaking.   The exquisite delicacy of the reproof to Peter,— without one word of upbraiding or unkindness,—is in dramatic keeping with the whole character of Christ ; and so also is the reticence of the historian as to the *significance* of the incidents themselves.   There is not a syllable about the occasion which led our Lord thus to question Peter, no direct allusion to the circumstances which would seem to have led to such question- ing ; yet doubtless in the mind of Peter and of the disciples then (as of every intelligent reader now), one thought was present that has no mention in the narrative. It is impossible not to interpret the whole scene by the light of the preceding history, though not a word is dropped by which the connection might be indicated. Are there any other historians in the world who would have exercised this abstinence? Would it be possible for one who was fond of tracing "causes to their effects," and making all plain to the reader, or who was intent on eulogising the subject of his biography, to miss so fair an opportunity? As Tholuck in his commentary on John very justly observes: "The reproving look which Christ had cast on Peter after his denial (Luke xxii. 61) was still burning in his soul; he was deposed, as it were, from his earlier official dignity, and must be restored to it again. The *mode* in which this is done is one so full of spirit, so far beyond the reach of invention, that any presumption of a mere fiction in the case is put to the blush."[1]

But to resume the traits which are characteristic of Peter. No sooner is he reinstated in the Master's good opinion, and has heard that affecting prediction of the "death by which he was to glorify God," than with the same impulsive eagerness which had so often brought him under reproof, he asks, looking to John,—"And what shall this man do?" His curiosity receives for reply, "What is that to thee? follow thou Me."

After the resurrection, the apostles are represented as suddenly recovering from the profound dejection into which the shipwreck of all their hopes had cast them, and assuming an air of indomitable confidence and dauntless courage,—a change, the unaccountable abruptness of which has compelled even sceptics like Strauss to acknowledge that "*something remarkable*" must have occurred thus to transform them. Peter, as might be expected from his character, comes to the front among them, boldly avows before the Sanhedrim his Master's resurrection, denounces the guilt of the Jews who had crucified Him, pro-

[1] Clark's edition, pp. 423, 424.

claims his purpose of fulfilling his Master's commission, and to all menaces of punishment for so doing, makes the noble declaration, "Whether it be right to hearken unto you more than unto God, judge ye."

That the Gospel was intended not for the Jews alone, but for all nations, and that the exclusive privileges of the "house of Israel" were to cease, was first communicated in vision to Peter, and he proceeded to proclaim it to Cornelius. Astonished as he was, he did not parley with his prejudices, nor recoil from the summons to abandon them. Yet in connection with this very subject, he later on gives one little last indication that the old infirmity of his nature was not quite cured, the "old man" not yet "crucified." Though he had declared at the "council" at Jerusalem,—as absolutely as Paul himself,—that the Gentiles were not to be trammelled with Judaical restrictions, yet that same disposition, which was the source of so much that was laudable and so much that was blamable in him, once more, and for the last time, made him stumble. He was betrayed, it seems, at Antioch, into a cowardly surrender of his convictions and judgment, through fear of certain Judaising brethren who had come down from Jerusalem, and who perhaps were watching him with jealous eyes. The apostle (as Paul tells us) had freely "eaten and drunk, and kept company with Gentiles," till these precise brethren, who could not go that length of latitudinarianism, came; and then Peter, with that same faintheartedness which had so often made him flinch in sudden temptation, "withdrew himself," and slunk out of his Gentile company, afraid of shame and reproach at the hands of the Jewish zealots. How natural is the picture, when we consider his antecedents, and especially his "denial!" On this occasion he received the open rebuke of Paul, who on his part consistently displays that adamantine firmness of temper which his whole life illustrates. *His* character, too, is dramatically presented to us, and if there were space for it, it might be instructive to trace it as minutely as that of Peter. He never " conferred with flesh and blood " in face of a present temptation.

Peter's vacillation on this occasion was just the remains of that same weakness which made him bluster, and stammer, and grow pale, and lie, when suddenly and publicly charged by the " maid " in the hall of the high priest's palace. True religion will gradually subdue the original tendencies, but it rarely quite extinguishes all traces of them.

> " Naturam expellas furcâ, tamen usque recurret."

But consistent with nature as Peter's character is throughout, it is still only by his actions, nakedly set forth without criticism or comment, that we know it.

Here be it recollected that I am not arguing that the *naturalness* of the narrative gives us reason to think that we are reading history, and not fiction or myth. All the Bible history does that. Far less am I assuming that the *facts* were as they are related, and the Gospel therefore true. I am simply pointing out a very constant trait in the manner of the Biblical writers—the all-prevailing dramatic form, and the almost entire absence of reflection or comment, by which they are marked. They state bare facts, and let these speak for themselves.

Another slight, yet striking instance may be pointed out from the Old Testament. I refer to the history of Laban. He is most incidentally introduced, and, as usual, not a word is uttered by way of advertising us what we are to expect of him. He turns out to be a mere muckworm, sordid and rapacious in the extreme. The very first trait we have of him is in his interview with Abraham's steward, after the brief interview with Rebecca, his young sister. Whatever might be Eliezer's business, a single glance is sufficient to win Laban's favourable attention. We are told that " when he saw the earring, and the bracelets on his sister's hands, and when he heard the words of Rebecca, saying, Thus spake the man unto me ; that he ran unto the man, and said, Come in, thou blessed of the

Lord, wherefore standest thou without?"   Though Laban, no
doubt, like the rest of the patriarchs, was "given to hospitality,"
it is impossible not to surmise that the vision of the earring and
the bracelets reinforced and gave *empressement* to it.   But if
the historian meant to intimate it by this little trait, nothing, as
usual, is said.   At all events, no injustice is done to Laban in
surmising it, for almost every incident—every act and speech—
in which he is concerned through the after history (though the
historian himself bestows not a single epithet upon him), is of
a piece with the beginning: he is dramatically represented
throughout.

Another trivial instance, trivial in itself, but worth noticing
from the very obliquity of the incident, is found in the letter
with which Lysias, the captain of the Roman forces in Jerusalem,
despatches Paul to the governor Felix.   Lysias seems, on the
whole, to have been a very fair specimen of the Roman official,
and anxious to do his duty.   He very promptly rescued Paul
from the tumult which the exasperated Jews had raised against
him, and took every precaution for his safety.   Of course it was
hardly in the nature of a Roman subaltern, or indeed of any
official in any age, not to give as favourable a report as possible
to his superiors of the manner in which he had discharged his
trust.   Nor is the statement of Lysias absolutely untrue in any
particular; but there is a most natural and politic turn given to
one part of the transaction, on which his conduct, if exactly
reported, might have brought him into trouble.   We know how
jealous was the Roman government for the maintenance, in all
its vast dependencies, of the privileges of the Roman citizen,
the violation of which was regarded as an atrocious crime,—a
crime which Lysias, it seems, was very near committing.   "This
man," says he, "was taken of the Jews, and would have been
killed of them; then came *I* with an army and rescued him,
having *understood that he was a Roman*."[1]   But Lysias does *not*
say that when he first rescued Paul he did not know that he

<hr>

[1] Acts xxiii. 28.

was a Roman, and that he acted merely from the ordinary and proper motive of maintaining the peace of the city. Far less does he say that he did not know that Paul was a Roman citizen until,—having decided, without any inquiry at all into the matter, to scourge him,—he accidentally hears from the centurion the quality of the man he was about to subject to such ignominy, and "that he must take heed" to what he was about. Then, being evidently frightened, he sees Paul in a new light, and treats him with much consideration. But in the letter to Felix, not a word of this interlude in the transaction appears. His whole conduct seems to turn on his patriotic zeal, and solicitous regard to those inviolable privileges of a Roman citizen, which he had so nearly violated himself. He may also have thought that any possible reference on the part of Paul to the peril he had been in, might as well be anticipated by his own politic version of the affair.

Instances of this kind, from the Old as well as the New Testament, might be multiplied by the score. How shall we account for this method of composition in the Scripture history, —that of exhibiting character and conduct so almost exclusively by dramatic traits? I have said (what all literature shows) that it is a talent very rarely possessed in its highest form, and that in the case even of the highest dramatic genius it is seldom that there is such absolute abstinence from the by-play of comment, reflection, and description, as we find in the great bulk of the Bible narratives.

I fancy I hear some one say : " There is no great mystery in the matter ; the authors were describing bare *facts;* they were neither fictitious writers, possessed of wonderful fertility of invention (which, if they *were* fictitious writers, they must have been, since they have compressed in the moderate compass of the Bible such an infinity of matter so strongly marked by the characteristics in question); nor were they philosophical historians, intent not only on setting forth facts, but anxious also to set forth their own sagacity in penetrating causes, and

their skill in portraying human character. They were simply
annalists, who set down such facts as came under their observation; and this mere copying of nature, this simple photo-
graphing of facts, does not imply that they were great artists—
for the sun can do as much—but simply people who kept their
eyes open.   Any *real* account, however simple, of the actions
of a man, will give the same *dramatic* effect, because it is the
man in action, and he will be sure to be true to himself." Very
well; I should be quite content with that answer.   I have no
doubt it is, in the main, a correct one; but it concedes at once
the *truth* of the sacred history in by far the greater part of it.
Not only so, but it rids us in some measure of another difficulty
by which these histories are embarrassed; namely, how it is
that obscure men of such mediocrity of mind and deficiency of
culture as those to whom the conditions of the problem restrict
us, were able to write these wonderful histories.   If they were
merely copying what was under their eyes, making a transcript
of facts which had fallen under their personal scrutiny, a great
part of the difficulty would be removed.   But while perfectly
content to accept this solution, and to let the argument rest
there, I must say, in the interests of *truth*, that it does not fully
account for the phenomenon now before us, whether we look
at the narratives of the Old or the New Testament.   Mere
chroniclers have not had the same good fortune to seize upon
the admiration of the world in the way the sacred writers have
done.   They are not equally expert at *photography*.   Somehow,
neither in the selection, nor the grouping, nor the description
of their facts, nor in exquisite simplicity of style, can they come
into comparison.   Nor have they in general been able to infuse
into their composition the charm or grace attained by many
writers of ordinary poetic or prose fiction.[1]

[1] It is curious to see how little the exquisite simplicity of Scripture
narrative has been appreciated by many critics of past ages, whose literary
vanity has employed strange arts to transform and elevate it ! Few have
outdone in this respect the Jewish historian Josephus, whose affected imita-

But the fact remains, that the dramatic exhibition of character —character walking out of the historic picture-frames, and

tion of his classical models has often led him completely to spoil the Scripture story. If any one wishes to see a specimen, he may consult his preposterous version of the pathetic speech of Judah to Joseph. Campbell justly says : " It is impossible for any one whose taste can relish genuine, simple nature, not to be deeply affected with the speech of Judah as it is given in the Pentateuch. On reading it we are perfectly prepared for the effect which it produced on his unknown brother. We see, we feel, that it was impossible for humanity, for natural affection, to hold out longer. In Josephus it is a very different kind of performance ; something so cold, so far-fetched, both in sentiment and in language, that it savours more of one who had been educated in the schools of the Greek sophists, than of the plain and artless patriarchal shepherds." Many like attempts to make the Scripture look *fine* have been made since. One of the most imposing is that of Père Berruyer, who essayed to recompose the " Histoire du Peuple de Dieu " in a more florid style than that of the Bible ; in the style, in short, of Clelia or the Great Cyrus ! A single sentence given in the "Curiosities of Literature " will be enough for the reader : "Joseph combined with a regularity of features, and a brilliant complexion, an air of the noblest dignity ; all which contributed to render him one of the most amiable men in Egypt." Moses is too "common-place" and "barren," thought the good father : and it is in this style he supplies his deficiencies.

But of all the methods of spoiling Scripture which Christian ingenuity has invented, that of " Paraphrase " has been the most common, and one of the worst. All books suffer indeed from this device of dilution ; and as every "abridgment " of a book has been called a " foolish abridgment," so may every paraphrase be called a foolish paraphrase. Most books need comment, explanation, illustration ; but if that be the object, paraphrase is the worst way of effecting it, since it treats what is difficult and what is perspicuous in the same way, and reduces the whole to the same marsh level. But while it would be difficult to name any book which is the better for a paraphrase, the Bible suffers most of all in virtue of its general brevity, simplicity, and weight of expression. Plenty of scope for legitimate comment and exegesis there undoubtedly is, in its more difficult portions; as in Job or Hosea, where the language is elliptical and sententious, and the transitions of thought obscure ; or in the Epistles of Paul, where the reasoning is close and compressed ; but it is not easy to imagine them improved by mere paraphrase. When they are clear, they are simply marred by dilution ; when they are obscure, they are better treated by ordinary exegesis. Yet, strange to say, this weak device has been rather a favourite with many excellent expositors ; and, worst of all, they have been especially fond of practising it on the pellucid *narrative* of Scripture, which, of all composi-

speaking and living before our eyes,—is a strongly prevalent characteristic of the Biblical history ; to an extent, indeed, constituting an unique feature of it.   That the quality should be found, not only in one writing, but in the historic writings of Scripture generally (of widely different dates, and composed by minds so variously constituted and educated), augments the singularity.

There is another characteristic of the Biblical writers in general, so completely alien from " the manner of men," that it might almost as well have been discussed in the lectures on the "anomalies" which the book presents in relation to human nature, as here.   But perhaps it is as well to take it in connection with the present subject.   I allude to their freedom from vanity, egotism, and ambition,—foibles to which that class of mortals called authors are supposed to be addicted as much as most men, and by many a little more.   But in the Scripture writers generally there is not only an exemption from such foibles, but for the most part an absolute suppression of feelings that would have been most *natural* to them.   Though we see intellectual and other differences among them, which prove

tions, least needed it, and is most injured by it.   That men of so much good sense as Patrick and Doddridge should have given in to it is surprising. The prolixity of the former is amusingly commented on by Macaulay in his History, when speaking of the project for "shortening the collects." " If," says the historian, "the object had been to *lengthen* them, no man could have been better fitted than Patrick."   He then gives a brief specimen or two of the good bishop's aptitudes for paraphrastic dilation.   " He maketh me," says David, "to lie down in green pastures : He leadeth me beside the still waters."   Patrick's version is as follows : "For as a good shepherd leads his sheep, in the violent heat, to shady places, where they may lie down and feed (not in parched but) in fresh and green pastures, and in the evening leads them (not to muddy and troubled waters, but) to pure and quiet streams ; so hath He already made a fair and plentiful provision for me, which I enjoy in peace, without any disturbance."
Campbell, in his lectures on "Systematic Theology," says : "I own, that of all the kinds of expositors I like least the paraphrast. . . . In the very best compositions of this kind that can be expected, the Gospel may be compared to a rich wine of high flavour diluted in such a quantity of water as renders it extremely vapid."

that they were not mere automata (according to one—not very rational—theory of inspiration), they might very well have been such, looked at only in this one aspect.

Though these traits are particularly observable in the " Evangelists," they are also discernible in the writers of the Old Testament generally, and especially in the case of Moses. If the books ascribed to him were *not* his, the wonder is increased a hundredfold, and constitutes in itself a strong plea for their general veracity. It is *possible*, indeed, that supposing Moses the writer, we may impute to a very exalted virtue the perfect frankness with which he recounts all his failings, his reluctance to enter upon his great work, the various instances of his impatience and the penalty which chastised it,—as well as his self-suppression ; though, considering his wonderful achievements (which writers like Ewald eulogise as much as any of the orthodox), it is perhaps not easy to imagine such self-obliteration in a merely mortal virtue. But what are we to think if *other* men composed the writings? That the great founder of the Jewish nation and polity should *not* have been the theme of unbounded panegyric by those who wrote of his achievements is inconceivable, unless the writers were either different from all other writers, or utterly destitute of every sentiment of admiration, gratitude, and patriotism. Never has Jewish patriotism, *out* of the Bible, so treated this great leader. The Jewish writers beyond that circle, as is customary with those in all nations who record the achievements of illustrious ancestors, know how to use the loftiest hyperboles of panegyric and to embellish their narrative with all sorts of traditional glories. It is well said in the Speaker's Commentary (Introduction to Exodus. Vol. I. part i. p. 240): "Such a representation of Moses is perfectly intelligible as proceeding from Moses himself ; but what in him was humility would have been obtuseness in an annalist, such as is not found in the accounts of other great men, nor in the notices of Moses in other books." It is also well remarked by Isaac Taylor, in his "Lectures on

Hebrew Poetry," that the Hebrew poets never seem to dream of winning admiration by the opulence of their imagination, nor of charming by their sublimity : they have no descriptive Poetry like that of modern poets, where description is the very object ; no heroes celebrated, no national ideas set forth, in epic or dramatic fiction."[1]

But the traits in question are most conspicuous in the Evangelists.   Never did men write on such exciting topics,—on topics of such transcendent interest too (as subsequent *facts* prove them to be, for the world has never been at rest since), —with such wonderful suppression of all personal *animus*, or apparent carelessness as to whether they were believed or not. The bird that deposits its egg in the sand, and leaves the hot soil to cherish it or the foot of the wayfarer to crush it, as may happen, might be their emblem.   The ostrich is not " more hardened against her young ones," to use the expression in Job, than these writers seem towards their intellectual offspring. A few incontrovertible traits will illustrate this peculiar character, or rather *want* of character,—the " neutral tint,"— that belongs to them.

They simply retail facts, or what, at all events, they declare to be facts ; facts, too, which were certain to produce, as they ever have done, and do still, the most vehement ferment in the world, whether they be believed or denied.   Yet the authors say nothing by way of preparation or apology ; stoop to none of the rhetorical arts usually employed to conciliate attention, to soften hostility, to obviate prejudice.   The writers have to deliver certain facts, and whether men will receive them or not, is not their business, but theirs whom they address. This more than judicial imperturbability, this want of *susceptibility* (as we should naturally call it), would surprise us in any writers ; but in men who had devoted themselves to the maintenance of a great cause,—a cause, if we may believe them, of transcendent importance,—and under circumstances which, in

<hr>

[1] Pp. 57–60.

all other cases, inevitably kindle enthusiasm and make men fanatics even in spite of themselves, it is incomprehensible. Yet these men seemingly maintain an air perfectly stolid; and we should even call it *stupid*, if we did not know the character of their compositions, and the effect which these have had on the world. They content themselves with the most colourless and passionless statement of what purport to be *facts*. They might be mere machines, for anything that appears in their manner to the contrary.

Not only does this unnatural calm singularly contrast with the wonderful facts they relate, and their own estimate of them, but not even opposition and persecution can provoke them out of it; no, nor even the cruel wrongs done to Him whom they called their " Master " in a far higher sense than any party or sect ever called its Founder such. Not even His suf-ferings—not even His death--could inoculate them with the spirit which is universal in the world; and which, where in-nocence has to be vindicated, and great iniquities denounced, is invariably regarded not simply as excusable, but meritorious. As Pascal says, they have scarcely a word of passion or resent-ment even for Christ's worst enemies.[1] The facts, indeed, which they profess to relate (dramatically exhibited, after the usual manner of Scripture) determine the moral character of those they describe as agents; but there is no word of indig-nation or invective, such as is the infallible resort of parties in conflict. They call no names, make no clamorous reproaches;

[1] " Le style de l'Evangile est admirable en tant de manières, et entre autres, en ne mettant jamais aucune invective contre les bourreaux et en-nemis de Jesus Christ.   Car il n'y en a aucune des historiens contre Judas, Pilate, ni aucun des Juifs.

" Si cette modestie des historiens évangéliques avait été affectée, aussi bien que tant d'autres traits d'un si beau caractère, et qu'ils ne l'eussent affecté, que pour le faire remarquer; s'ils n'avaient osé le remarquer eux-mêmes, ils n'auraient pas manqué de se procurer des amis qui eussent fait ces remarques à leur avantage.   Mais comme ils ont agi de la sorte sans affectation, et par un mouvement tout désintérressé, ils ne l'ont fait re-marquer à personne."—*Pensées de Pascal.* Ed. *Faugère.* Vol. ii. p. 370.

indulge neither in curses nor querulous objurgation. Pilate, for example, is represented as afraid of the people; and it is about the worst they have to say of him.

When, in the "Acts," the apostles of Christ are represented as beaten and scourged, the historian might well have been excused if he had broken out into vehement invective against the cruelty of their persecutors. "He has nothing to say, but that they went to another city."[1] Though the Evangelists represent Christ Himself,—seemingly wearied out at last with the wickedness of those Scribes and Pharisees who dogged His steps and scanned His words with unsleeping malignity; who accused Him of working His miracles by "Beelzebub," and tried to extract even from His deeds of compassion matter for cavil, and to turn them into instruments of His destruction; —though they represent Christ Himself, I say (wearied out at last), launching at these hypocrites bolts of blasting, scathing invective, such as never before fell from human lips; denouncing them as those who took away the "key of knowledge," and would neither enter in themselves nor "suffer others to enter;" "who devoured widows' houses," and "for a pretence made long prayers;" who "compassed sea and land to make one proselyte, and after they had got him, made him two-fold more the child of hell than themselves;"—though they describe Christ once thus transported as never before, yet they themselves, who must have deeply felt His wrongs and sympathised with His resentment, have nothing to say even against the Scribes and Pharisees ! If they are *not* relating facts, but inventing them, or selecting or adorning legends; if Christ never used the words above referred to, but these writers have put them into His lips,—it is clear that it was no want of the power of vehement invective that kept them mute—no lack of eloquence which imposed this restraint. This manner, *un*human,— not to say *in*human,—if they "spoke as men," by which they confine themselves to bare facts, and do not tinge

<hr>

[1] See Paley.

them, as human nature usually does and cannot help doing, with personal feeling, is certainly a paradox of peculiar significance. Even the calmest historian, much more he who has suffered in civil or religious strife, cannot thus school his tongue; and would not, if he could.

As these writers seem above resentment for their own wrongs or the wrongs of their fellow-disciples, or even of Him whom "they called Lord and Master,"—whose sufferings they have yet described with such inimitable touches of pathos,—so they seem to be equally free from all else that we should include in "party spirit." They show, indeed, plainly enough, in the course of their narrative, whom they think in the right and whom in the wrong; with whom they sympathise and with whom they do not: but for anything that appears in the way of comment,—from the absence of the usual modes of expressing personal bias, of softening or concealing the faults or consulting the interests of their own party,—they might have no more feeling for their friends than for their enemies. They record with the same wonderful phlegm the errors and failings of their colleagues and partisans as the cruelty and malignity of their adversaries, and make no more apologies for the former than for the latter;—a thing which to him who has the slightest tincture of "party spirit" is utterly incomprehensible.

When two of the disciples, provoked at the inhospitality of some Samaritan village to their Master, not only broke into strong language, but wanted to back it by stronger deeds, we are told that they received a severe rebuke for it, and the record abides to their shame;—he who records it being generally regarded as one of the guilty parties.

If Peter falls shamefully, they do not even suggest what his compassionate Master said for them all,—"The spirit indeed is willing, but the flesh is weak." With like frankness of spirit, they acknowledge the pusillanimity they all displayed when they "forsook their Master and fled;" the denial of one, the treachery of another, and the cowardice of all: they confess the stupidity which so long made them "slow of heart" to believe in His claims or to understand His doctrines, and commemorate with impartiality His chidings at their unbelief.

Now many of these traits may be said to be without parallel in the history of faction. The excesses of the tongue, in all religious or political parties, are notorious. The bitterness of ecclesiastical and theological strife has even passed into a proverb, and has been branded by the name of the "Odium Theologicum;" and it makes it the more wonderful that the authors of the Gospels are free from it. It cannot be pretended that human nature was more exempt from it then than now; for no sooner do we get away from these writers than we have it in abundance in the early Church. When Paul, after his signal success at Corinth, left that Church awhile to itself, he soon found human nature asserting itself, as it has always done, and as it does still. The Church was broken up into violent factions. Some were "for Paul," and some "for Cephas," and some "for Apollos," and some "for Christ;" and in the usual unamiable fashion of party spirit, they proceeded to considerable lengths in abuse of one another. The apostle, just like the writers of the Gospels, is above everything of the kind. With that absolute loyalty of surrender to Christ which characterises his whole history, he contents himself with saying, "And who is Apollos, and who is Cephas, or who is Paul, but ministers by whom ye believed?" and recommends, as the cure of all faction, that self-oblivion in Christ which he himself so remarkably exemplified. Like the Evangelists, he is willing to be "nothing," that Christ may be "all in all."

Again, the Evangelists make no attempt to remove what writers of a hundredth part of their power of delineation might have seen would be likely to occasion difficulty to their readers. They do not attempt to explain or get rid of any apparent discrepancy, either in their own statements or (if they knew them) in the statements of one another. They tell the most wonderful things with the same composed air as the most trivial incidents; nor, as has been well remarked, does one kind of miracle surprise them as more stupendous than another.   They bespeak no indulgence, as is the usual way of narrators of the marvellous, for the degree in which they tax the credulity of the world ; nor deign to give any reason why the things which they narrate, however improbable, should be received.   In a word, remembering the thrilling things they relate, the whole manner of these writers is full of paradox.

But this is not all, nor perhaps even the most wonderful feature in the Evangelists.   I have spoken of the dramatic way in which narratives of the Bible are conveyed, as a very general characteristic of the book; it is attended, as usual, by a proportionate self-oblivion, or, at all events, self-repression of the writers.   But what shall we say of that more than dramatic skill by which the Evangelists have not only lost themselves in their subject, but have managed to make mankind equally lose sight of them?[1]   They are, one may say, never thought of. One does not realise their *greatness* as masters of description. They have so hidden themselves in their theme, that they leave us neither the power nor the inclination to trouble ourselves about them.   Yet as mere portrait-painters,—far more if they were, as some say, really the *creators* of Christ, whether by sheer invention, or by the skill with which they selected and laid on the colours which vague and fleeting myth supplied,— one would think that they must have arrested more of the attention of the world.   On the supposition just mentioned, indeed, they ought to be regarded as little less than demigods.

[1] " There is another species of simplicity, besides the simplicity of structure and the simplicity of sentiment above mentioned, for which, beyond all the compositions I know in any language, Scripture history is remarkable. This may be called simplicity of design.   The subject of the narrative so engrosses the attention of the writer, that he is himself as nobody, and is quite forgotten by the reader, who is never led by the tenour of the narration so much as to think of him.   He introduces nothing as from himself. We have no opinions of his ; no remarks, conjectures, doubts, inferences ; no reasonings about the causes or the effects of what is related."— *Campbell on the Gospels.*   Vol. i. p. 67.   London, 1825.

If Christ be but a *phantom*, to which they have given greater substance than belongs to any character in history; whose imaginary career (more romantic than romance itself) they have made so many myriads accept as historic verity; for whom they have created an empire over the minds of men mightier and more durable than king or conqueror ever established before; to whom homage is given by far more various races than were ever combined under one sceptre; and who exacts more from the willing love of His subjects than all the tortures of tyranny ever exacted from their fear;—if that " phantom " Christ was really the handiwork of the Evangelists, the men who achieved that unparalleled feat ought certainly to be the wonder of mankind. If it be said: " No, *these* did not create Christ. He is indeed a phantom, or little more; but it proceeded out of the mist of myth, and is the product of some utterly nameless and forgotten obscurities, after whom the Evangelists wrought ; they merely copied from their designs : " —if *this* be said, it may be answered, first, that the wonder is rather increased than diminished. For we have at least the *names*—though little else—of those who composed the Gospels ; a few, though very few, particulars of their history. But according to this theory, those who really founded the solid empire of a visionary Christ have hidden themselves more effectually than even the authors of the Gospels have done ! Secondly, it must still be said on this theory, that if the authors of the Gospels be no more than portrait-painters, it is the portrait they have left us of Christ that has chiefly secured Him the homage of the world. The hints and whispers of myth on which the Evangelists worked (if they really wrought from such things) would soon have been buried in oblivion had they not so preserved them. Of the many attempts which have been made, even by His own most devoted followers, to paint Him, none but the " four " have been able to win a thousandth part of the same admiration for Him.

Now, I repeat that, on any such theory, the world ought to

be struck dumb with admiration at the perfection of dramatic representation which must have been possessed by these writers —of whom yet we never think at all as the wonderful geniuses they must have been—if they either created or merely painted such a character as Christ. They have so completely buried themselves in their subject, that even by a reflex act we find it difficult to speculate on the endowments which, on any such theory, they *must* have possessed. It is not so in any other case. Of all human writers, Shakespeare is the one who (next to the Evangelists) exhibits in greatest perfection this power of forgetting himself in his characters; or rather, of so transfiguring himself, as to lose in them, for a time, his own individuality. And while his spell is on his readers, he is equally lost to *them* also. Still, it is only for a short time that he is under such eclipse. Genius exacts its own. He does not wrong himself. His superlative dramatic skill is not defrauded of the admiration and homage due to it. Once remitted to ourselves, we see that Shakespeare is on every page : and, transferring to him the interest we felt in his works, ask ten thousand questions about him which we would fain have answered. We stand for awhile absorbed in the characters of Macbeth and Othello : forget Shakespeare and ourselves in the sorrows of Ophelia and Desdemona ; yield to every varying emotion which the great enchanter conjures up ; and then, when his phantoms have stalked across the stage, cease to think of *them*, and concentre our thoughts on the enchanter himself. In closing his plays we say what, probably, no man ever said of Matthew, Mark, Luke, or John : "What a prodigy of intellectual power is this man! What knowledge of human nature ! What affluence of genius ! What imperial command of language ! Surely he is the leviathan among mortal intellects—on earth there is not his like." If it be said his work is greater than that of the Evangelists, we must deny it ; and on the supposition that the Gospels are not *history*, point to the *effects* of the writings of their authors for proof. Though all they wrote, put together, would not make more than a couple of Shakespeare's plays, yet how much greater the effect! Shakespeare's delineations terminate in the *ideal;* the Evangelists, on this theory, have transformed the ideal into the real, and made the world mistake it for history! If they created the character of Christ, or even painted it from floating mythical materials, as Shakespeare did that of Macbeth, they far outdid him. Why does no man break out into raptures of admiration about *them?* I apprehend the reason must be, that *if* they are but painters, they have given such a life-like representation, that the generality of people cannot help thinking the illusion real. The mirror is so perfect, that the image is no longer discerned to be such ; the medium so translucent, that it eludes the sense.

But on the ordinary hypothesis—even that of their being simple historians,--the trait I am now particularly insisting on still comes out with transparent vividness. They are not only self-oblivious, but we forget them too. Even on this generally received, and, as I believe, *true* hypothesis,—that they are transcribing from the life, and not inventing or adorning an ideal at all,—this feature is very wonderful.[1]

Somewhat similar observations might be made on the Apostle

[1] It is said of Robinson, of Cambridge (Robert Hall's predecessor, and himself a man of remarkable genius), that being asked to take part in the ordination of some young minister, he thought he saw (as will be the case sometimes, even in young ministers) certain tendencies to foppery ; and among other indications of it he observed a disposition to exhibit a rather brilliant ring on the little finger of the candidate's right hand. In the course of his charge he took an opportunity, as he well knew how, to give him a hint which he would not forget, but which no person in the audience but himself would understand. " My young friend," he said, " as a Christian minister, you must consider yourself as a mere servant, occupied in holding up to the gaze of visitors some master-piece of portrait-painting. All that you should desire to do is to exhibit it in the best light, and with as little intrusion of yourself as possible. You will be anxious to be entirely hidden behind the picture-frame. As you hold it up, you will not, if it be possible, allow even a *little finger* to be seen." The Evangelists have certainly acted on this principle to the uttermost, and have not even allowed "a little finger " to be seen.

Paul;—not, indeed, that there is *self-repression* in his writings (for that was impossible in compositions of such a nature), but in his mode of *self-exhibition.* In his epistles we naturally find his personal peculiarities—his modes of thought and feeling laid bare before us. Yet, in one respect, he is just like the other writers of the New Testament. He loses himself, as the Evangelists do, in that great Personage,—that reality or that shadow,—by which the world has been saved or—beguiled ! Nor is there anything more wonderful, considering Paul's antecedents—his early history, his education at the feet of Gamaliel, his burning zeal for the law, his ambitious hopes, his brilliant prospects—than his sudden, absolute surrender to Him whom, but the day before, he had esteemed as a justly-crucified malefactor, the very thought of whom naturally stirred all the gorge of this Pharisee of the Pharisees. Yet so entire is the apostle's absorption in Christ, that his whole life is henceforth without a thought but for Him. It is bound up in Him. For Christ he cheerfully endures " the loss of all things; " for Him he casts all the hopes of his life away, and counts them " but dross that he may win Him ; " exposes himself to every kind of suffering, to bonds, scourges, imprisonment, to a vagabond life of toils and privation, and to a death of agony and shame, for the love of Him. According to his own strong saying, " To him to live was Christ." If he ever becomes assertive, urgent, indignant, vehement, it is for Christ, not for himself. There is not a particle of egotism about him. He is willing to be forgotten by the world, or to be remembered only as the butt of its scorn and anger ; to have his labours depreciated, his achievements questioned or appropriated by others ; and his dearest recompense,—the affection of those for whom he yearned and laboured,—snatched away ; all is alike to him if Christ may be but honoured, whether it be " by his death or his life," and if His Gospel may be " by any means " preached, even though by his enemies, and " out of envy and strife." He resembles that planet which revolves nearest the sun, which makes only very moderate excursions from the luminary round which it rolls, and is generally lost in his beams.

It is not surprising that from the strange history of Paul, from the impossibility of accounting for his conduct by any ordinary motives—of reducing it either to enthusiasm or imposture, or any modification of the two,—many should have thought that his character and achievements, even if there were no other evidence of the truth of Christianity, would afford irrefragable proof.   So thought Lord Lyttelton in his well-known essay.

Before concluding this lecture, I would reply to an *objection* sometimes brought against some of the Scripture narratives, which, when the subject is fairly considered, seems to me rather to tell the other way.   The objection is, that whatever beauties of narrative and poetry the Bible may contain,—whatever treasures of spiritual and moral wisdom,—it also contains much which is repulsive to taste, and which cannot be read without pain.   But if it be a " Revelation " in very deed, it could not but be so.   If it addresses itself to all men, even the most abandoned,—it ought not (and it does not) scruple to lay bare the secret pollutions, to probe the worst ulcers, of our moral nature.   It professedly carries the "candle of the Lord" into the deepest and most tortuous recesses of the human heart.   In performing this necessary office of " holding the mirror up to nature," there is, no doubt, much in its history and biography, in its descriptions of human life, in its anatomy of character, in its exposure of sin and vice, which not merely grates on the ear, but is positively painful and repulsive.   The only question is, in what *spirit* and for what *purpose* is such matter introduced. For the matter itself, it makes no apology; it is discharging an obligation which, however unwelcome, is imperious; one which even specially belongs to it as designed to reach the very lowest outcasts of human kind, in the uttermost depths of pollution and misery, and exhibit to them a clear image of the moral evil from which it would rescue them.   But the mode in which, with all plain-spoken simplicity, it does this, deserves to be mentioned as one of the most striking peculiarities of the Bible, and which alone would contrast it with all human literature. Treatises of morality hardly dare to approach those dark spots of human nature which Scripture so fearlessly exposes, and still less to illustrate them by such appalling accuracy of moral anatomy. Satire, indeed (as that of Juvenal), is often as plain-spoken, and far coarser; but it is easy to see, in general, that indignation and contempt are the predominant emotions expressed and awakened; sometimes it is but the vehicle of misanthropic cynicism. As for all lesser forms of human infirmity, and many which are by no means to be counted such, comedy eagerly seizes on them as the legitimate food for mirth and laughter. Infinitely different is the tone of the Bible! In consistency with that universal aim which characterises it throughout, as asserting everywhere the paramount claims of religion and virtue,—it never approaches guilty man with less than the gravity and compassion with which a humane judge looks upon the criminal. It acts up to its maxim, that it is "fools" alone who "make a mock at sin," for sin is not a thing for mockery. It exposes it, indeed, unsparingly; but the light it sheds on it is as little contaminated by it, as the sun by the material pollutions it discovers to us. It denounces it also, but still with a yearning pity to the victims of it; to warn them by the "terrors of the Lord," to "flee from it as from the face of a serpent;" and to "beseech them by the mercies of God" to "repent and live." So clear is all this, that of all those who have complained of the plain-dealing of the Bible in this matter, —the repulsive and distressing details into which it sometimes enters,—probably no one ever taxed it with gloating on such things either with cynical malevolence or cynical levity,—far less with that pruriency which must so often be charged on satirists and comedians.[1]

---

[1] In mitigation of an objection sometimes made, that the *public* reading of some of the chapters of the Bible is a painful ordeal to a promiscuous audience, it may be allowed to ask, "Whose fault is that?" It may well

It may be remarked, as another peculiarity in the manner of Scripture in general, that, so far from being chargeable with this fault, it never seems even to glance at the comic side of life and the world at all,—as little as though, in its apprehension, there were no such thing. It cannot be that those who wrote the book did not feel there was plenty of scope for ridicule. No satire was ever more powerful than that in which Isaiah denounces the folly of the idolater; never sarcasm more bitter than that with which Elijah taunts the worshippers of Baal; nor invective so withering as that with which the Saviour unmasks

be a question, whether every part of the Bible is *intended* for "public" perusal in "a promiscuous audience,"—any more than the genealogies and lists of mere names, which are also found there, but are never so read.

As to some gross vulgarisms in our English version (the original equivalents of which passed without notice in countries and ages less artificially refined than ours), they are the result of translating idioms *literally*, instead of into corresponding idioms; and the same folly would make many phrases in our own or any other language sound almost equally uncouth to the ear of a foreigner. They will doubtless disappear from that "revised version" which, considering what immense accumulations have been made in every department of Biblical study since the authorized version was made, cannot but be of immense value. Let the learned "revisers" only guard against spoiling the racy *English* of that version, and for the rest they cannot but earn our thanks.

But the *topics* of the Bible, however painful occasionally, require no apology, if they are not wantonly intruded on "a promiscuous audience." If the book indeed speaks to *every* man, as well as to all men; if it says what is strictly appropriate to the individual as well as to the species; if the reader, whoever he be, is to feel, as Robert Hall says, "that it is impossible for him to escape by losing himself in the crowd," it must sometimes talk with us as a parent with a child, as a guardian with his ward, as a friend with an erring brother, as a clergyman with a condemned criminal, as a kind physician with his patient; that is, in confidential secrecy. As we are commanded to "enter into our chamber" for private prayer, and not "stand at the corners of the streets," so the Bible, which is to be the "man of our counsel," will have some things for our ear alone. If it has given needless offence in this matter to modesty, it is not because it has spoken plainly (for while human nature is capable of the evils it condemns, these must be exposed and denounced); but because men have unwisely proclaimed that which is intended "for the ear and the secret chamber" in "the market-place" and "from the house-tops."

the hypocrisy of the scribes and Pharisees. The Christian, of course, will be disposed to think that this trait arises from the very function which the Bible everywhere assumes ; that its object being so transcendently grave and solemn,—to assert the claims of God, and to reclaim " a lost world to Him,"—mirth, in the ordinary sense, however innocent, would have been as unnatural in these writers as laughter, though equally innocent, in the " Man of sorrows ; " and that as He, though the most perfect type of human nature, felt (under the perpetual weight of that burden which oppressed Him) no temptation to exhibit this phase of it, so for similar reasons the airy tones of wit and humour in the pages of the Bible would be as unnatural as a jocular vein in a judge on the bench of criminal justice, or a physician by the bedside of patients in their mortal agony. Doubtless this is sufficient reason for the peculiarity ; but still, it *is* a peculiarity, which distinguishes the Bible from every other growth of human literature. If it had been the product of mere human genius, it might not have been very easy to account, among so many different writers, for the absence of what is so large an element in other literature; and in this point of view, perhaps the feature in question might have been added to those in which it is argued that the Bible is not a book that man *would* have produced. But it is more natural to mention it here, as one of the characteristic traits in the structure of the Bible, and which discriminate it from human literature in general.

LECTURE VII.

THE SAME SUBJECT CONTINUED.

LECTURE VII.

AT the revival of letters, keen controversies arose, and long raged, with regard to the literary capabilities of the languages in which the Bible was written, and its consequent qualities of style. There were not wanting those, of more piety than wisdom, who contended for perfections of diction and of eloquence, which the sacred writers themselves resolutely disown. They declared that the Hebrew, being the original language (which they took for granted), must be as copious and expressive as any of later derivation; and that the New Testament,—in spite of its being in that "common Greek" which was formed after the Macedonian conquests, and in the formation of which, as is usual in such cases, the language had undergone great changes of structure; in spite, too, of its being full of grammatical idioms which would have shocked an Attic ear, and of Syriac, Hebrew, and Chaldee barbarisms, which would have shocked it still more,—wanted little of Attic purity, and could match in force and grace the periods of Demosthenes or Plato.[1]

They much mistook the matter. While contending that the Bible had a force and grace of its own, which would more than justify comparison with the classic writers, they should have owned that it is palpably destitute, and proclaims its destitution, of the elaborate polish and artificial beauty of the eloquence

---

[1] There is an excellent dissertation of Werenfels, entitled *De Stylo Scriptorum Novi Testamenti*, in which many of these follies are exposed and rebuked in a spirit of criticism far in advance of the time.

which " man's wisdom teacheth."   As truth and candour should have compelled them to acknowledge so much, so they should have gladly accepted the position, and made their argumentative gain of it.   They should have shown, in the first place, as Michaelis does, that the very style of the New Testament, with its strong tincture of Hebrew and oriental thought and idiom, is itself a voucher for its antiquity and genuineness; that none but Jewish Christians could have written it; that after the destruction of Jerusalem it was as incredible that impostors could have written in so peculiar a dialect, as that they should have been able to weave a contexture of narrative which, like that of the New Testament, is so minutely in harmony with the events and customs of the preceding period as known from profane history.   Next, they should have argued that, willingly admitting the imperfections of the vehicle which the writers of the Bible employed,—the ruggedness and restricted compass of the Hebrew,—the barbarisms, the solecisms, uncouthness, and deformity of the Greek,—it is all the more wonderful that, in spite of all this, the writings of the Bible have *somehow* been imbued with a force, grandeur, and beauty of their own, which have procured for them a name and place in the forefront even of the world's literature, and extorted the highest admiration even of those who denied them all other than a literary claim to it.

That the Bible possesses many qualities of style, which, like so many other things touched in this volume, make it *unique* among books, and fit it for being cosmopolitan, is what I am about to endeavour to show.   It is only a few of these properties that I have space to touch; but they will be sufficient, I think, to prove what has been just said.   Of course, though I have said the Bible is generally characterised by its own peculiarities, there are large portions of it—consisting of dry statements of the barest fact, genealogical catalogues, juridical matter—which, however conducive to some of the many ends enumerated in a preceding lecture, do not admit of any beauty or grace of composition; or any excellence, indeed, beyond that (not a very common one) of saying the thing that is meant to be said in the plainest way and in the simplest words. But large as is the amount of matter to be deducted on this account, even in the *residuum* there is more than enough to test the justice of what I have said,—or to confute it.

Speaking generally, I venture to say that the style of the Bible is very distinguishable from that of all other literature. It is neither oriental nor occidental; its writers were, indeed, of the East, and as they speak *naturally*, they have a tinge of oriental thought and imagery sufficient to remind us perpetually of their origin ; but it is *not* such as to prevent their readily making themselves denizens among any people, and being heartily appreciated by the western world,—a privilege which Asiatic writers in general, Hindoo, Chinese, Arabic, Persian, scarcely ever attain.

Into some of the causes of this curious phenomenon I shall briefly enter by-and-by, when I come to speak of the facility with which the Bible can be translated as compared with books in general. Here it is sufficient to point out that, tested by the fact of general appreciation, its position is unique. One has but to compare it with ninety-nine out of every hundred orien- tal books, translated into the western languages, to see how widely different it is ; how free from the peculiarities that dis- gust us with them—the excess and extravagance of imagery, the meretricious and florid ornament, the diffuseness, the bombast and fustian, which are so repulsive to western taste and intellect. It may be said, and justly, that only a thorough knowledge of oriental languages, manners, and customs, can enable a critic to see how far a work *has* been adequately translated. I admit it, and the more willingly, as it makes for my argument. Doubtless only a competent knowledge of the original language will enable us to judge of the merits of any translation. But here is the remarkable difference between the Bible and other oriental books ; that while the oriental style in general cannot be so translated as to overcome the disgust of the western nations, the Bible is everywhere capable of it. My point is, that whereas *they* cannot be naturalized, the Bible can. Nay, the more literally *they* are translated, they become (like the translations of the classics) less attractive ; the more literally the Bible is translated, the better, for the most part, it appears. Oriental compositions in general, like many imported articles, require to be adapted to the European market. There are comparatively few books of the East that can vie in popularity with the "Arabian Nights ;" and yet it may be questioned whether the literal translation of Mr. Lane, generally acknowledged by competent judges to be excellent, is, after all, so much relished by the English reader in general as the "translation of a translation" with which we were long contented in the version from the French of M. Galland ; and that precisely because the translation of Mr. Lane is more *literal.*[1]

Few men have been of more catholic taste in literature than Sir W. Jones, and certainly as few whose familiarity with oriental literature could better enable them to appreciate its merits ; merits which he sets forth with no stint or grudging in those "Commentaries on Eastern Poetry" which he wrote in imitation of Lowth's Prelections. But though, as an excellent critic has said, he had "an exceptional power of assimilating the exotic beauty of Eastern poetry," he everywhere admits the superiority of the Hebrew bards, and of the Scriptures generally, as compared with all other literature. He has left an emphatic eulogium of them in his Eighth Discourse : "Theological inquiries are no part of my present subject; but I cannot refrain from adding that the collection of tracts, which we call from their excellence the Scriptures, contain (independently of a Divine origin) more true sublimity, more exquisite beauty, purer morality, more important history, and finer strains both of poetry

---

[1] Sir W. Jones, in his translations from the Persian and Arabian poets, freely admits the necessity of adapting them to western taste. Where he has given us a literal version, he rarely succeeds in abating their repulsiveness.

and eloquence, than could be collected within the same compass from all other books that were ever composed in any age or in any idiom. The two parts of which the Scriptures consist are connected by a chain of compositions which bear no resemblance in form or style to any that can be produced from the stores of Grecian, Indian, Persian, or even Arabian learning."[1]

The Bible, in general, belongs to no school of literature. A similar remark may be made on the peculiarities which characterise its several compositions as compared with their analogues in other literatures. As literature has various species of composition addressed to those principles of human nature which inspired them, so the Bible has compositions in analogy with these, yet specifically different. They bear but a very general resemblance to similar productions in other literatures. Nor can one now read with patience many of the pedantic disquisitions of our elder critics (and even of some of more recent date), who, borrowing all their measuring-lines from classical standards, disputed whether any creations of the Hebrew poets comply with the conditions of the true epic or the genuine drama. Even Lowth has a long discussion (Prelect. xxxiii.) as to whether the book of Job be or be not a regular drama— whether it complies with the rules laid down by the Father of Criticism; and he justly decides that it does not. But the discussion is about as much to the purpose as those older disputes as to whether the New Testament Greek was such as Attic taste would have approved. The true answer is that, though the Bible has compositions which approximate to various species of composition in other literatures,—didactic, narrative, poetical,—they refuse to come under any strict canons of criticism, and differ from other compositions of the same name, almost as much in form as in substance.

A marked peculiarity in the style of Scripture, as compared with other books, is the prodigious extent to which what is called *parallelism* prevails in it; that is, a mode of speech by

[1] Sir W. Jones's Works. Eighth Discourse. Vol. iii. p. 183. Ed. 1807.

which similar or contrasted ideas, and, indeed, ideas related in many other ways, are expressed in various forms of antithesis. Though not exclusively found in the Bible (in fact, it is a favourite form of speech in oriental style generally), it may be justly said that the *degree* in which it prevails there is so enormous, and the functions it performs so important, as to constitute it a distinguishing feature. The " parallelism " has been copiously treated by Lowth in his Introduction to his Translation of Isaiah, and in his Lectures on Hebrew Poetry; as also by Herder, by Jebb, by Ewald, and numberless other writers. They have treated it chiefly in relation to the *poetry* of the Hebrews,—in the form and expression of which it is an essential element; in fact seems to be the sole substitute for the metres which are such essential adjuncts of poetry in general. But though chiefly of importance in poetry, it is in fact a prevalent characteristic of the Scriptures throughout,—of the New Testament in a considerable degree, as well as of the Old.

Of the various *species* of the parallelism, critics have endeavoured to give an exhaustive analysis; but refined, and often over-refined, as their classifications have been, they have not succeeded in reducing them all within the circle of formal definition. As the compositions of Scripture are *sui generis*, and have only a general analogy with those of similar character in ordinary literatures, so it may be said of this prevalent *modus loquendi*, that it does not submit to the artificial classifications of rhetorical criticism. So ample is the range, so elastic is the nature of this one expedient of expression that though it might be imagined that nothing but monotony could ensue from its predominant use, it is far otherwise; and not even the most copious analysis suffices to exhaust all its varieties. The believer in the Bible can hardly help suspecting that that same wisdom which knows how to give infinite variety to the few features of the " human face divine," has so subordinated the language to the thought, the instrument to its end, as to secure boundless diversity in the modifications of this one form. No doubt its

principal varieties, as Lowth states, may in gross be ranged
under " synonymous," "antithetic," " constructive," and so on ;
but there are manifold modifications either of idea or form
which cannot be reduced to such Procrustean tests.   It has
been well said that " there is *rhythm* in all poetry, and in that
of the Hebrew it is prominent enough."   But it cannot be
fettered by artificial rules ; it is free, untrammelled, as the spirit
which moulds it ; no more capable of being reduced to precise
scale and measure than the music of the Æolian harp to the
laws of artificial melody.

By this one generic form, infinitely varied in its applications,
the Hebrew poets, though destitute of those regular metres
which so many critics, with such waste of subtilty, have endeavoured to discover in their compositions,[1] have given expression to what the whole world recognises and confesses to be
poetry of the very highest order, and in a form worthy of the
substance ; poetry exhibiting wonderful rhythm and music,
though not metrical in the ordinary sense of the term ; in fact,
poetry that in its *form* is more nearly allied to *prose* than verse.

Here, then, is another striking anomaly in the style of Scripture ; that whereas in other literature there is nothing so intolerable, so offensive to a pure taste, as those hybrid compositions
which attempt to express poetry in the forms of prose, the Bible,
by a strange felicity, seems to have conciliated the seemingly
incompatible claims of both.

A form so very prevalent as the *parallelism* suggests that

---

[1] After finding all sorts of classic metres in the Hebrew poetry—hexame-
ters, pentameters, trimeters, and many more,—critics by general consent
are agreed that there are none.   An amusing summary of the controversy,
from Jerome to Jebb, may be seen in Smith's " Dictionary of the Bible,"
under the article Poetry.   Marcus Meibomius, in the seventeenth century,
professed to have discovered, by aid of Divine revelation, the true metrical
system of the Hebrews ; but he was prudent, and proposed to let the world
have the secret for thirty thousand pounds !   It was a high price to pay for
—nothing ; for such his scheme was found to be when, in compassion to
mankind, he gave some glimpses of the secret *gratis.*

there may have been other reasons for so generally resorting to it.   At all events, we see that it *is* conducive to other ends, which, if the Bible be what it professes to be, are of great importance.   No doubt its principal use may be found in the various functions it performs in relation to Hebrew poetry. But it is not difficult to see that if the Bible was designed for the use of all mankind, facilities must be given for perpetual transmission and universal translation ; and this peculiarity of style is of great importance in relation to both objects.   As to the first ;—it conduces in a variety of ways to preserve the text incorrupt, as well as to assist the critic in the attempt to restore it where it has been accidentally vitiated.   It is true that neither this, nor any other expedient of composition, can perfectly exempt the Bible, any more than other books, from the influ- ence of those innumerable causes of minute error which subjec- tion to the ordinary laws of transmission implies, and which must produce, in the course of successive transcription from age to age, appreciable results : but there can be little doubt that the integrity of the text of the Bible is in part to be attri- buted to that form of *parallelism* which so generally characterises it.   The way in which it operates as a check on the corruption of the text is obvious.   The duplicate expression of thought makes each member of the parallelism a guard and key to the other.   It acts as a perpetual admonition to the transcriber,— forewarning him by the form of expression when he has gone or is going wrong, and recalling him, in the revision of his copy, to any erroneous substitute of one word for another ; or, if it has *not* prevented his going astray, it has in many cases assisted the critics of after times in the recovery of the text, or, at all events, of the meaning.   Too great caution cannot be exercised before actually admitting into the text of any author emenda- tions opposed to the weight of manuscript authority ; still, in the case of not a few " parallelisms " of the Bible (even though the critic may not feel justified in substituting his conjecture for the text), we are enabled to see there *has* been error, and to feel morally certain in what sense, if not by what word, the true text is to be recovered. Thus, though every sober critic must condemn that license of conjectural criticism in which Bishop Lowth was wont to indulge, it must be allowed that he has given some felicitous examples of corrections suggested by the parallelism, and the same may be said of many other critics.[1]

Some critics have compared the "parallelisms" of Scripture in this respect with the beneficent arrangement by which (as the wise man says) God has made many "things double;" thus giving us a twofold security for our senses of sight and hearing, and many other important organs and functions of our physical nature.

The parallelism also facilitates the translation of the Bible into other languages, especially its poetry. This one simple, though flexible form, being the chief vehicle of it, it is released from all bondage to the highly complex and artificial metres in which poetry is usually expressed; and is assimilated, though without losing its rhythm, to the character of prose. The comparative ease with which the Scripture is transfused, with the least possible sacrifice of grace or strength, into other languages, is in a considerable degree due to this.

But it is only one of many causes which conduce to that

[1] "Ihr Parallelismus," says Herder's imaginary objector, "ist eintönig: eine ewige tautologie, dazu ohne Mass der Worte und Sylben, das sich nur einigermassen dem Ohr empföhle. 'Aures perpetuis tautologiis lædunt,' sagt einer der grössten Kenner derselben, 'Orienti jucundis, *Europæ invisis*, prudentioribus stomachaturis, dormitaturis reliquis,' und das ist Wahr." Whether the *Latinist* might not have improved his own style in the two last uncouth antitheses, by imitating the " parallelism " a little better, I will not stay to ask; but, however " hateful to Europe " the oriental form in general may be, the mystery is (as I have already urged) that in the exceptional case of the Bible it has *not* proved hateful. The Bible has been a greater " success," as Carlyle says, " than any Paternoster Row in the world ever heard of."

The squeamishness of the above critic reminds one of the Ciceronian cardinal, who said he had once read the Bible (in the Vulgate, of course), but that he should never read it again, lest it should ruin his Latinity!

facility of translation which characterises the Bible, and which forms, as I think, another *unique* peculiarity of it. This, of course, is not proved by the unprecedented number of languages into which it has been actually translated; for though that fact gives it a solitary pre-eminence over all other books, sacred or profane, it may be accounted for by the profound conviction the book has somehow wrought in so many different communities, during so many ages, that it is the duty of those who receive it to make its contents known to all mankind, and therefore to give it a voice in every language. This conviction, indeed (as I have elsewhere said), is a curious phenomenon, which itself requires to be accounted for; but it will not account for the fact I am now considering—namely, that the book has not only inspired men with an intense desire to give it a diffusion commensurate with human speech, but has itself, by peculiarities of structure, diction, and style, given peculiar facilities for the task it has imposed.

Of course, every book must in some degree suffer from translation, and therefore the Bible. No one can compare even the best translations of the great works of human genius with the originals—of Homer, for example, or Virgil, or Milton, or Dante, or Goethe, and, above all, Shakespeare—without feeling that the sacrifice is great, and that to give anything approaching a perfect translation is (what it has been represented) an insoluble problem. To turn to a translation after perusing the original has been well compared to looking on the wrong side of a piece of tapestry, from which the brightness of the colouring and the sharpness of the figures are gone; or looking at a scene by moonlight after gazing on it by the sunlight. Somehow the energy of the diction is weakened, the imagery paled, the grace of manner, the " curiosa felicitas," to a great extent vanished. The connection between the thoughts and words was so vital, that to tear them asunder was to touch the life.

Now, it is a great merit in the works of human genius when the divorce of thought from language is thus nearly fatal; it is a test of excellence; so much so, that it is no paradox to say that the more perfect a work of genius, the less capable it is of adequate translation.   But this cannot be said of the Scriptures.

It may be urged, perhaps, that if the Bible be more easily translated than other books, then the application of the preceding canon may account for it; and that since a book, the more perfect it is, is less transfusible into other languages, the Bible, if it indeed possesses this unrivalled quality of assuming a multiform garb, must possess it from its having less literary merit than any other!   But this, I fancy, will be said by few who recall the homage it has exacted from so many of the greatest of the sons of men, by the eulogiums pronounced upon it by such an array of genius and intellect, and the qualities conceded to it by so many to whom it has no special merit beyond its literary excellence.   Moreover, the argument is met by this simple *reductio ad absurdum:* that even if it were true that a book is more easily translated in proportion as it has little merit (which, however, is far enough from being without exceptions), it would be, in the same proportion, less likely to get itself translated.   Now as the Bible is found in two hundred languages, it can hardly be its inferiority to all other books which has given it so many voices.

However, let the fact be accounted for as we will, I believe none ever inspected a number of translations of the Bible, of even tolerable execution, without feeling that though they no doubt differ in merit, yet that in all the elevated passages, *where there is no doubt about the meaning,* the rendering in one and all is closer, and sounds more idiomatic, than translations of equally lucid passages of other books into the same languages. I say, "where there is no doubt about the meaning," because this is essential to the comparison.   No doubt there are passages in the Bible (as there are in Plato and Pindar) which are difficult enough;—in the prophets for example.   They are difficult partly from their intrinsic, perhaps sometimes designed, obscurity; partly from their lyric character, and the consequent brevity, elliptical constructions, and rapid transitions of thought proper to that species of poetry.[1]   Such passages, whether in the Bible or profane authors, are obscure in the translation, rather from inadequate comprehension of the sense, or insufficient means of ascertaining the true text, than from any difficulties proper to translation ; that is, of *conveying* the meaning when once ascertained.   The real comparison, of course, must be between passages well understood of the one, and passages well understood of the other; between, for example, Isaiah's magnificent apostrophe to the crowned phantom of Babylon, when all Hades is moved at his coming, and Homer's sublime description of Apollo's descent on Mount Ida.   The difficulty of *adequately* translating an ode of Pindar, or a chorus in Æschylus, is all but insuperable, though a translator may understand the meaning perfectly ; while, on the other hand, the Bible—wherever there is no difficulty in ascertaining its meaning -may in general be translated almost without the loss of either energy or beauty ; and viewed in almost any translation, seems to do little violence to the foreign idiom.

The causes of this are partly disclosed in some of those peculiarities of style to which reference has been already made. Among the chief is the parallelism ; to which may be added the great simplicity of construction which ordinarily obtains, the *character* of the metaphors, and not least, the *specific* character of its language—a quality which distinguishes the Bible

---

[1] The number of these passages will no doubt be much diminished in the " Revised Version."   The learned investigations of nearly three centuries cannot be without effect.   Admirable as our authorized version is, there are many passages of Job and the prophets, in which the worthy translators, perplexed to find the meaning, have been content to put down words without any.   Such has always seemed to me the last verse in Job xxxvi., on which the previous verse, in spite of the liberal use of interpolated italics, sheds no light.

32 With clouds He covereth the light ; and commandeth it *not to shine* by *the cloud* that cometh betwixt :

33 The noise thereof showeth concerning it, the cattle also concerning the vapour.

more than any other book equally occupied with moral subjects
and abstract thought, and which is itself more conducive to
perspicuity and force than any other quality whatsoever.[1]   In
numberless passages, again, of great energy, the effect is due in
the smallest possible degree to the felicities of *language;* it is
due to the majesty of the *thought,* and hence is equally preserved
in any language.   The terms in many of these passages,—
wonderful for compressed force and strong imagery—are often
of the most common, homely, and even trivial character.   It is
the ideas suggested and placed in juxta-position by them, not
any rare excellence of diction or construction, that produces
the effect.   To take two or three brief illustrations.   Isaiah
asks, in his magnificent challenge to find the "equal" of
Jehovah,—"Who hath measured the waters in the hollow of
his hand, and meted out heaven with the span, and compre-

---

[1]   "The ox knoweth his owner and the ass his master's crib, but Israel doth
not know—My people doth not consider."   Let this be translated into its
philosophic equivalent : "The lower animals recognise and are grateful for
kind treatment, but My rational creatures are insensible to it;" and it is
easy to see that the pathos and energy are gone.   Campbell has admirably
illustrated this subject in his Philosophy of Rhetoric, in which he applies the
same refrigerating process to a part of the Sermon on the Mount.   There is
a little gentle satire, I fancy, directed against Doddridge's paraphrase,
which on the same portion of the New Testament is hardly less preposterous
than Campbell's caricature.   Campbell, as we have seen, abhorred paraphrase, one of the most insipid expedients of which is the translation of the
specific into the *general*—of the picturesque into the *soi-disant* philosophical.
The dependence of definiteness and vividness of conception on the speciality
of language has been copiously and admirably illustrated both by Campbell
and Whately.   *Individuals* alone have an objective existence ; *species* and
genus are intellectual creations.   The former are the source of our most
vivid states of mind—of our perceptions ; and our conceptions being
definite and vivid in proportion as they approach these, and hazy in proportion as they recede from them, expression will follow the same law, and
the energy of terms be in inverse ratio to their generality.   "The more
general the terms are," says Campbell, "the picture is the fainter ; the
more special they are, the brighter."

hended the dust of the earth in a measure, and weighed the mountains in scales, and the hills in a balance?"[1]

Jeremiah promises the easy conquest of Egypt to the King of Babylon in these terms—"He shall burn their gods with fire, and shall carry them away captives; and he shall array himself with the land of Egypt, as a shepherd putteth on his garment, and he shall go forth from thence in peace."[2]

The utter overthrow of Jerusalem is predicted to Manasseh in that contemptuous image—"And I will wipe Jerusalem as a man wipeth a dish,—wiping it, and turning it upside down."[3]

Such passages as these, energetic though they be, produce their effect by means of metaphors borrowed from the most common objects, expressed in the most undisguised literality. No language, however meagre, in which such vulgar things as scales, weights, dishes, and shepherds' plaids are to be found, can fail to render them perfectly; nothing depends on felicity of language or construction. Whether, therefore, we compare the translation of such passages in the Septuagint, Vulgate, French, German, or English, every reader feels that there is hardly any difference worth noting; in one and all, the rendering assumes a most natural and idiomatic dress. By these and other artifices (Divine artifices, the Christian will say; unaccountable freaks of accident, the unbeliever will call them, as he well may if the Bible be purely of human origin), this book is capable of being more perfectly translated into every human language than any other. I believe the former theory to be the true one; and that hence the difficulties of a problem which human genius cannot solve,—that of combining the highest literary excellences, with aptitude for transfusion into all languages—has been solved in the construction of the Bible; and that the old saying is true in another sense than the one originally meant by it,—that while "Mortals speak many tongues, the Immortals have but one."

πολλαι μεν θνητοις γλωτται, μια δ'αθανατοισιν.

Another peculiarity in connection with Scripture style is this; that while, for the reasons just stated, the Bible, on the whole, is more easy to translate than any other book, and suffers less injury in the process, it is perhaps more than any other susceptible of injury if it be cast in any mould but its own. It will submit to no fetters of metre or rhyme; it is impatient of the yoke, and rebels against it. Take the very best metrical versions of the Psalms, for example. There is hardly one of them—I know of none—that does not palpably fall below the level, both of the original and of any simple *prose translation* in which the original may be rendered. This is another of the paradoxes of the Bible. It easily accommodates itself to a dress like its own in *any* language, but will not submit to foreign costume. The Hebrew, in the strict sense, has no *metres;* at least in the modern sense,—as the infinite controversies on the subject suffice to show. Yet the rhythm, the music, ot these compositions is generally far beyond that of the *metrical* and *rhymed* translations of them, whether in Greek, Latin, or English. It is just the contrary with renderings from Greek, Latin, or any other poetry,—of which no prose version can be endured.

It cannot be said that it is because none but inferior men have set themselves to the task. They have not always been Sternholds and Hopkinses, Bradys and Tates. No less men than Bacon, Milton, Barrow, Buchanan, Parnell, Cowper, Sandys, Herrick, Davies, Heber, Milman, Watts, Keble, have tried their hands at it. Dryden asked Milton's leave to turn his majestic blank verse into rhyme. The poet replied that he was welcome to "tag" them if he liked. It was a thankless task; but the attempt is still more hopeless to improve the poetry of Scripture by running it in any mould but its own. To a man of any taste and sensibility, with an ear for the true music of language, and a soul capable of feeling the majesty and sublimity of the Hebrew poetry when reproduced in its own simple forms, the difference is hardly to be expressed. Whatever the powers of the imitator, and however qualified by sympathy of spirit with the sacred writers to express religious sentiment and devotional feeling, it is impossible, I think, not to feel that a simple prose translation is better.[1]

I had hoped to illustrate this at some length, and had collected a variety of examples for the purpose. But my space fails me, and I must be content with two or three brief illustrations. Let us take the simple, yet exquisite image in the very first Psalm, which describes the happy condition of him who " meditates in the law of the Lord day and night."

> " And he shall be like a tree,
> Planted by the rivers of water ;
> That bringeth forth his fruit in his season ;
> His leaf also shall not wither ;
> And whatsoever he doeth shall prosper."

It is surprising to see that Bacon,—whose genius may perhaps be said to have rivalled Shakespeare's, and who "took all knowledge for his patrimony,"—could have been content with

---

[1] The following observations of Lowth illustrate this point :—" Duo hic occurrunt adnotanda, quæ ex jam dictis quasi consectaria quædam enascuntur. Primo quidem, Poema ex Hebræa in aliam linguam conversum, et oratione soluta ad verbum expressum, cum sententiarum formæ eædem permaneant, multum adhuc, etiam quod ad numeros attinet, pristinæ dignitatis retinebit, et adumbratam quandam carminis imaginem. Hoc itaque in vernacula sacrorum poematum interpretatione cernitur, ubi plerumque

' Invenias etiam disjecti membra poetæ :'

quod in Græcis aut Latinis eodem modo conversis longe aliter eveniret. Alterum est, quod poema Hebræum Græcis aut Latinis versibus redditum, sententiarum formis ad peregrini sermonis indolem jam accommodatis, id est, confusis, perditisque, nativi ornatus et propriæ venustatis non exiguam faciet jacturam. Nam in exprimendis alia lingua egregiorum poetarum operibus, multum in eo positum est, ut non tantum iidem sint intimi sensus, par in sensibus explicandis vis et venustas, sed ut quantum fieri potest externa etiam oris lineamenta effingantur, ut suus cuique color atque habitus, suus etiam motus et incessus tribuatur. Qui itaque sacros vates Græco vel Latino carmine exprimere, adeoque eorum veluti personam sustinere conati sunt, fieri non potuit quin toto genere et forma, si non inferiores, multum certe, ab iis dissimiles essent : an ex altera parte ad eorum vim, majestatem, spiritum propius accesserint, non est hujus loci quærere." Prælect. iii.

Lowth cites a single sentence from Rabbi Azarias to the same effect. " Is

a version not much better than that of Sternhold and Hopkins.
But it is the exigencies of artificial metre and rhyme that
plainly baffled him.

> " He shall be like a fruitful tree
>   Planted along a running spring,
> Which in due season constantly
>   A goodly yield of fruit doth bring ;
> Whose leaves continue always green,
>   And are no prey to winter's power ,
> So shall that man not once be seen
>   Surprisèd in an evil hour."

But if it be said that Bacon was a philosopher and no poet
(though he certainly had imagination enough to make a score
of ordinary poets), let us see how it fares with Milton.   It is no
better with him, and for the same reason.   He has kept almost
the very terms of the simple prose translation ; but he has so
shuffled and transposed them, to meet the exigencies of his
metre, that we hardly recognise them again.

> " He shall be as a tree which planted grows
>   By watery streams, and in his season knows
>   To yield his fruit : and his leaf shall not fall,
>   And what he takes in hand shall prosper all."

Buchanan's Latin is no real version at all, but a free paraphrase : the secondary images with which he has adorned it are
wholly unauthorised by the original, and "Sirius" jars upon
the ear almost as much as Phœbus Apollo would do.

> " Ille, velut riguæ quæ margine consita ripæ est
>   Arbor, erit : quam non violento Sirius æstu
>   Exurit, non torret hiems, sed prodiga læto
>   Proventu beat agricolam : nec flore caduco
>   Arridens, blanda dominum spe lactat inanem."

---

it not plain that if you translate the Hebrew poems into another language,
they retain their own rhythmical construction, if not wholly, yet in a great
degree ; which cannot be the case with those poems whose measure consists
of a certain number and quantity of syllables." See also Pareau's *Principles
of Interpretation.* Vol. i. p. 241. Vol. ii. p. 185 (Clark's Biblical Cabinet),
for some judicious remarks on the points here touched.

Watts, who, in spite of all his defects, is one of our greatest hymn writers, is as bald as any :—

> " He like a plant of generous kind,
>   By living waters set,
> Safe from the storms and blasting wind,
>   Enjoys a peaceful state.

> " Green as the leaf, and ever fair
>   Shall his profession shine,
> While fruits of holiness appear
>   Like clusters on the vine."·

Take again the forty-sixth Psalm :—

> " God is our refuge and strength,
> A very present help in trouble.
> Therefore will not we fear,
> Though the earth be removed,
> And though the mountains be carried into the midst of the sea :
> Though the waters thereof roar and be troubled,
> And the mountains shake with the swelling thereof."

Here it is impossible not to feel that the grand march and rhythm of this *poetical prose* is infinitely better than anything that exact metrical arrangement could give us. It is impossible to imagine anything much tamer than Watts's version :—

> " God is the refuge of His saints,
>   When storms of sharp distress invade ;
> Ere we can offer our complaints,
>   Behold Him present with His aid.

---

¹ Watts's translation of the seventy-second Psalm is one of his most beautiful effusions. But on inspection it confirms what I am saying. It is no translation at all, or even a paraphrase : it is an independent poem, in which in fact he declines the task of rendering the Psalm, and contents himself with applying its general spirit, and retaining two or three of its images. For like reasons it is that so many sacred poems, *founded* on passages of Scripture—some of those of George Herbert, Habingdon, Cowper, and Keble, for example—are so much better than any metrical versions. Buchanan has successfully imitated the various Horatian metres. But he necessarily reminds one of Horace as much as of David ; or rather he is like Horace turned Christian, with the Geneva bands and gown on, and his Latin a little rusty with time.

> "Let mountains from their seats be hurled
>   Down to the deep, and buried there ;
> Convulsions shake the solid world,
>   Our faith shall never yield to fear."

His failure is equally conspicuous in the close of the Psalm. The English version is as follows :—

> "He maketh wars to cease unto the ends of the earth,
> He breaketh the bow,
> And cutteth the spear in sunder ;
> He burneth the chariot in the fire.
> Be still, and know that I am God ;
> I will be exalted among the heathen,
> I will be exalted in the earth.
> The Lord of hosts is with us,
> The God of Jacob is our refuge."

Watts's version reads thus :—

> "He breaks the bow, He cuts the spear,
>   Chariots He burns with heavenly flame ;
> Keep silence all the earth, and hear
>   The sound and glory of His name.

> "Be still, and know that I am God,
>   I'll be exalted o'er the lands ;
> I will be known and feared abroad,
>   But still My throne in Sion stands ! "[1]

He has done better in *one* of his three versions of the nine-tieth Psalm,—the others have the usual faults of the metrical translators :—

> "Our God, our help in ages past,
>   Our hope for years to come,
> Our shelter from the stormy blast,
>   And our eternal home.

> "Under the shadow of Thy throne
>   Thy saints have dwelt secure ;
> Sufficient is Thine arm alone,
>   And our defence is sure.

---

[1] Even Luther's celebrated metrical rendering of this Psalm will not bear comparison with the poetic prose in his own admirable version.

> " Before the hills in order stood,
>   Or earth received her frame,
> From everlasting Thou art God,
>   To endless years the same.
>
> " Thy word commands our flesh to dust,
>   ' Return, ye sons of men ; '
> All nations rose from earth at first,
>   And turn to earth again.
>
> " A thousand ages in Thy sight
>   Are like an evening gone ;
> Short as the watch that ends the night,
>   Before the rising sun."

Still, compared with the original, it is as the tinkling of a lute to the majestic roll of an organ, or (to use a grand Scripture image) the " voice of many waters."

> " Lord, Thou hast been our dwelling-place in all generations.
>   Before the mountains were brought forth,
> Or ever Thou hadst formed the earth and the world,
> Even from everlasting to everlasting Thou art God.
> Thou turnest man to destruction, and sayest, Return, ye children of
>   men :
> For a thousand years in Thy sight are but as yesterday when it is past,
> And as a watch in the night."

Here any one who has the slightest tincture of taste, or any ear for the music of language, will see the immense interval between the simple prose translation and the metrical imitation ; in simplicity, in condensation, in the solemn march and cadence of the rhythm.[1]

[1] D'Alembert, whose exquisite simplicity of taste, like that of Pascal, seems to have derived additional severity from his geometry, has some remarks in his " Reflexions sur l'Elocution oratoire et sur le Style en général," which show that he felt, sceptic as he was, the vast superiority of the Scripture *poetic prose* to the best metrical versions of his countrymen.   The constraint, the feeble expletives, the redundant phrases, the stuck-on ornaments of these, justly offended him.   He says : " L'éloquence ne consiste donc point, comme quelques anciens l'ont dit, et comme tant d'échos l'ont répétés, à dire les grands choses d'un style sublime, mais d'un style simple. C'est affaiblir une grande idée que de chercher à la relever par la pompe

One of the most successful of close metrical translations of
Scripture is that of the passage in the last chapter of Habbakuk,

des paroles.   Le Psalmiste à dit, 'Les cieux racontent la gloire de Dieu,
et le firmament annonce l'ouvrage de ses mains :' voyez comment un de nos
plus grands poëtes a défiguré cette pensée sublime, en voulant l'étendre et
l'orner.

> Les cieux instruisent la terre
>   A révérer leur Auteur ;
> Tout ce que leur globe enserre
>   Célebre un Dieu Créateur.
> Quel plus sublime cantique
>   Que ce concert magnifique
> De tous les célestes corps ?
>   Quelle grandeur infinie,
> Quelle divine harmonie
>   Résulte de leurs accords ?

L'exemple, dira-t-on peut-être, est mal choisi ; cettes trophe presque toute
entiere est mauvaise en elle même, et indigne d'être comparée à son modele.
Prênons-en donc une autre dont on ne puisse contester la beauté, la pre-
miere du Cantique d'Ezechias, traduit par la même poëte, et rapprochons-la
de l'original.

> J'ai vu mes tristes journées
>   Décliner vers leur penchant ;
> Au midi de mes années
>   Je touchais à mon couchant ;
> La mort déployant ses ailes,
>   Couvrait d'ombres éternelles
> La clarté dont je jouis,
>   Et dans cette nuit funeste
> Je cherchais en vain le reste
>   De mes jours évanouis.

Quelqu' admirables que soient ces vers, on y reconnait encore le Poëte :
'Le midi et le couchant des années, les journées qui déclinent vers leur pen-
chant, les ailes de la mort déployées.' Ces images, belles à la vérité, mais
l'ouvrage de l'esprit *qui cherche à peindre, et non du sentiment qui ne veut
qu'exprimer*, peuvent-elles être comparées à la simplicité touchante de l'Ecri-
ture, à la tristesse profonde et vraie avec laquelle le prince, jeune et mour-
ant, se représente aux portes de la mort ?   'J'ais dit au milieu de mes jours,
je vais mourir : et j'ais cherché le reste de mes ans.'"---*Mélanges.* Tom. ii.
pp. 326-8.

by Cowper.   It is elegant (as Cowper ever is, no matter what he touches), but there are few who will not prefer the original.

> " Though vine nor fig-tree neither,
>   Their wonted fruit shall bear ;
> Though all the field should wither,
>   Nor flocks nor herds be there ;
> Yet, God the same abiding,
>   His praise shall tune my voice ;
> For, while in Him confiding,
>   I cannot but rejoice."

> " Although the fig-tree shall not blossom,
> Neither shall fruit be in the vine ;
> The labour of the olive shall fail,
> And the fields shall yield no food ;
> The flock shall be cut off from the fold,
> And there shall be no herd in the stalls :
> Yet I will rejoice in the Lord,
> I will joy in the God of my salvation."

Another peculiarity of the style of Scripture worthy of notice —a peculiarity which has arrested the attention of many who doubt its Divine claims—is its unique power of adequately expressing devotional sentiment and emotion.[1]   It not only gives us the most copious, but by far the noblest, specimens of this language that can be found in all extant literature ; and so uncontested is its superiority in this respect, that the most celebrated compositions of the kind,—the liturgies by which the Jewish and the Christian Church have endeavoured to kindle or sustain the flame of devotion in their public assemblies,— are close imitations of the models which the Bible furnishes ; and, indeed, their most effective portions are little else than appropriations from this treasury of devotion,—tesselations of the Scripture phraseology itself.[2]

[1] See Appendix No. VII.

[2] " It is but feebly, and as afar off, that the ancient liturgies (except so far as they merely copied their originals) come up to the majesty and the wide compass of the Hebrew worship ; such as is indicated in Psalm cxlviii. Neither Ambrose, nor Gregory, nor the Greeks, have reached or approached this level."—Isaac Taylor *On the Spirit of the Hebrew Poetry*, p. 157.

Take, for example, the English liturgy.   Most justly admired it is, no doubt, for the propriety and fulness of its matter, and for the majesty and rhythm of its style.   And it may well be ; for not only has it incorporated many of the best specimens of liturgical composition which the ancient Church has handed down to us, and wisely enriched itself with the spoils of ages, but its most impressive and beautiful portions (as was the case also with the ancient liturgies it has laid under tribute) are derived directly from Scripture itself.   This is its chief excellence, as it was theirs.   If any one will analyse the contents of the Book of Common Prayer, and deduct, not only the larger portions of Scripture, but all the minute scripture phrases and clauses which it has most judiciously interwoven, he will find that at least five-sixths of the whole book is simply extracted from the Bible.   I am far from saying this in derogation ; rather it is, in my view, the highest eulogium that can be pronounced upon it.

From the extreme rarity of the choicer specimens of this species of composition, we may infer its immense difficulty. How is it then that the Bible has almost a monopoly of it ? How is it that there, and there alone, we find language so expressive of the loftier and deeper moods of devotion, that we are continually tempted, not to say compelled, to borrow from Scripture, and uniformly fail when we attempt to do long without it ?   How is it that so few attempts are made to compete with it in original compositions of the same kind, or the results so poor when they are made ?   Of course *if* the Bible be a book of Divine origin, if it be a manual designed by celestial wisdom to instruct men in the offices of religion, to inspire and express devotional thought and feeling, we need not wonder that it should so immeasurably outstrip mere human composi- tions of the same class.   If not, this is one more paradoxical feature of the Bible, for which it is difficult to account, and which compels us to ask whence came it ?

The chief object of the present lecture is to point out certain peculiarities of style which discriminate Scripture from other books.   I shall therefore say but little on the *degree* in which it possesses those qualities which, if it is to answer the purpose of books in general, it must have in common with them.   But there are three—of chief importance for all purposes of *impression*—energy, sublimity, and pathos, which it possesses in so pre-eminent a degree, that it may well make us wonder how the Jews, who did so little, except in this one book, to distinguish themselves in literature, thus immeasurably surpassed themselves.   As it has been asked how they came " to be men in religion, and children in everything else "? so it may be asked how it is that their almost solitary literary relic should be marked by such prodigious excellence in the three most important qualities of all composition?

I have already said that there are huge portions of the volume which (however rendered necessary by its complexity of design and purpose) do not admit either of much force or of any ornament of style ;—portions in which the highest merit is a natural and unadorned simplicity.   Nor does it, in *any* part, affect that uniform elegance or fastidious refinement which may be looked for in more homogeneous writings,—still less those elaborate artifices of human rhetoric which itself most vehemently disclaims.   Yet in those parts of Scripture in which alone the above three qualities can be rationally looked for, I think it may be safely said that they exist in greater copiousness than in any equal amount of written matter in the world.

Of all the qualities of style on which the effect of writing principally turns, that which rhetoricians indifferently call energy or vivacity is the most important; and of its chief elements, philosophical writers on rhetoric, like Campbell and Whately, have given a careful enumeration.   It principally depends on what I have already mentioned as a perpetual quality of Scripture,—the suppression, as far as possible, of all general and abstract, and the use of the most specific, terms ; on the selection of characteristic incidents or objects in narrative or description, rather than on full enumeration of them, or of one or two salient points as representative of a whole group of associated circumstances; on metaphors marked rather by strength than beauty; and sometimes on the iteration of the same idea under various forms, though more frequently on brevity and condensation of expression.

A very general characteristic of Scripture style is undoubtedly a pregnant brevity in its separate utterances : in no book can we find so many weighty sentences expressed in fewer words.   Yet in many parts (in Deuteronomy and Ezekiel, for example) we see, however brief each single expression, an amount of repetition which has often been taxed with diffuseness.   How then shall we reconcile the conflicting claims of energy as usually dependent on paucity of words, and yet as sometimes demanding iteration of statement?   In the way that nature and the critics teach us to reconcile them.[1]   The true remedy for a too stringent brevity, which proverbially becomes "obscure," is not a diffuse copiousness, but a varied exhibition of the same thought.[2]   Sometimes this is absolutely necessary to produce the due effect, for the mind must be *detained* on the same thought for a certain time to insure its impression ; the work cannot be done by a simple stroke, but by a number of them, as by the repeated touches of the sculptor's mallet. We see this continually exemplified in Shakespeare.

[1] Lowth has beautifully described both these characteristics of energy in the Hebrew poetry.   Speaking of the song of triumph at the Red Sea, he says :—" Unum tantum adnotabo, quod et in *universa Hebræorum Poesi* locum habet, et in hoc poemate præcipua cernitur : nimirum dictionis brevitatem unum esse maximum subsidium sublimitatis.   Rerum ponderi plerumque officit diffusa et exuberans oratio : quantum sano corpori carnium et obesitatis addideris, tantum detraxeris de vigore et viribus.   Hebræi, *si universa spectes,* sunt largi, copiosi, uberes ; *si singula,* parci, restricti, pressique : variando, repetendo, subinde addendo amplificant : tota quidem res fuse interdum tractatur, sed iteratis crebrisque, et per omnia brevibus et nervosis sententiis ; ita ut nec copia, nec vis desit."—Prælect. xxvii. p. 362. Ed. Oxon. 1810.

[2] Whately's Rhetoric.   Part iii. ch. 2.

Now Scripture, full (so to speak) of negligent and scattered graces, but never fastidious about continuous beauty or elegance, nor solicitous about them at all in comparison with *strength* of expression, profusely exemplifies all the above characteristics of energy. Its narrative style, as I have already had occasion to remark, is exquisitely dramatic, but as bare as possible, not only of all general reflections, but of all words of general and abstract import. It is for the most part the naked presentation of individual facts in the most appropriate and most specific terms by which they can be expressed. Agents and actions are there, but the reader himself must fully interpret them. The representation is like that of sculpture or painting, where the mute action, the *pose* of a figure, a gesture, an incidental adjunct, is the symbol of a whole group of associated ideas. The eyes look on it, but intuition is the commentator. Thus the effect of the whole preceding train of incident, and all the variety of emotion which it inspired in the actors, is conveyed in that simple passage in which Joseph, overmastered by the pathetic speech of Judah, and surprised out of his mask of assumed austerity, makes himself known to his brethren. Even the apparently irrelevant question about his father, "Is he yet alive?" of which his previous inquiries had left him without a doubt, is a natural expression of that tumult of joy and grief in which the perturbed soul hardly knows what it says, and yet, in its confusion, instinctively turns to the object nearest the heart, and therefore nearest the lips.

Everywhere we see indications of the graphic suppression of all needless generality. A feature which to some extent may be natural (for it is found more or less in the laws of many ancient nations) is wonderfully characteristic of the laws of Moses. A great part, even where we cannot doubt that general principles of duty and humanity are inculcated, are expressed by individual specifications: "Thou shalt not curse the deaf;" "Thou shalt not lay a stumbling-block before the blind;" "Thou shalt not wholly reap the corners of thy land;

thou shalt not glean thy vineyard, neither shalt thou gather every grape of thy vineyard; thou shalt leave them for the poor and the stranger. I am the Lord your God." "Thou shalt not muzzle the ox that treadeth out the corn,"—where the comment of Paul shows that the precept is not intended for the benefit of "oxen" alone, or chiefly. Similarly, a great part of the gnomic wisdom of Scripture is expressed (as is usual indeed with proverbs) by the specification of a particular case.

Examples, again, in which some specific circumstance is selected as the representative of a whole class of associated ideas, and the picture is completed at a stroke, might be cited by hundreds. The utter panic of soul which makes a man start at everything, and (as Scripture has it) "flee when none pursueth," is wonderfully expressed in that image, "The sound of a shaken leaf shall chase them;" as is also that contrasted spirit of heroic daring which a good conscience and a sense of Divine protection can inspire—"And five of you shall chase a hundred, and a hundred put ten thousand to flight."[1] That utter weariness of heart, which vainly seeks relief (like the fever-stricken patient) in mere change and tossing to and fro, is comprehensively depicted in the single trait, "In the evening thou shalt say, Would God it were morning; and in the morning, Would God it were evening." Nor can anything better express the helplessness of a mind dazed and stunned by overwhelming calamity, than the words, "Thou shalt grope for the door as the blind." No length of description could possibly convey a more forcible picture of the utter degradation that was to overtake the Israelites after the doom of their dispersion, than the threat that they should be exposed in "the slave mart," and even then be regarded with such contempt "that no man should buy them." Devastation, whether of war or of locusts, was never more vividly suggested by any amount of details than by the simple expression, "The land is

---

[1] Levit. xxvi. 8. The hyperbole is varied in Deut. xxxii. 30.

as the Garden of Eden before them, and behind them a desolate wilderness ; " nor benevolence more graphically painted than
in the words, " I was eyes to the blind, and feet was I to the
lame ; the blessing of him that was ready to perish came upon
me, and I caused the widow's heart to sing for joy."

In conformity with the same preference for *energy* as the great
instrument of impression, most of the tropical terms of Scripture are chiefly characterised by *force*.   Where beauty is not
incompatible with it, they are often exquisitely poetical and
elegant, as in those plaintive expressions of Job, when thinking
of his past prosperity, " When the ear heard me, then it blessed
me ; and when the eye saw me, it gave witness unto me : my
root was spread out by the waters, and the dew lay all night
upon my branch."   But as a rule, the metaphors and other
figures are principally marked by the quality on which I am
insisting ; often homely, sometimes even to coarseness ; but in
admirable conformity with the true canons of criticism adopted
by the *earnest* writer, whose object is not elegance, but *strength* ;
and whose end is not to charm, but to convince and to persuade.

How contemptuous but expressive is that image in which God
threatens the great Behemoth of despotism, Sennacherib, " I
will put my hook in thy nose and my bridle in thy lips, and I
will turn thee back by the way by which thou camest."   Is it
possible to imagine the condition of the " wicked," torn and
distracted by their own passions, and the tumults and terrors
of an evil conscience, more aptly described than by comparing
them with the " troubled sea, when it cannot rest, whose waters
cast up mire and dirt "? or can the condition of a conscience
which has at last lost all sensitiveness to sin, be more terribly
denoted than by saying that it is " seared as with a hot iron ; "
implying that, as in the eschar produced by actual cautery, no
nerve thrills and no life-blood circulates there ?   But examples
of this prevailing quality of its metaphors abound in every part
of Scripture.

The energy of our Lord's language is usually very remarkable, especially from its condensed brevity. Never was more meaning expressed in fewer words than in many parts of the Sermon on the Mount ; in many of His parables, as in those of the Prodigal Son and the Good Samaritan ; and in that wonderful description of the Last Judgment in Matt. xxv., where He expounds the *principles* on which the decisions of that day will be based. The energy of the passage is gradually enhanced, as it proceeds, by the perpetual condensation of the expression. There is, in truth, everything—even to the adjuncts of cadence and rhythm—to give solemnity and impressiveness to the description. In whatever language translated, Latin, German, Italian, French, English, it reads with nearly equal force as in the Greek. In brief, I have no scruple in saying that neither in Demosthenes nor in Shakespeare (and if not in them, certainly in no other author) is this cardinal property of style more prodigally exemplified than in many parts of the Pentateuch (especially Deuteronomy) and of the Prophets [1]—in the parables and discourses of Christ, and in the more impassioned parts of Paul's Epistles.

[1] The bitter taunts of Elijah, addressed to the prophets of Baal, and the still more wonderful passages of Isaiah xliv. 9–20, are fair specimens. The folly of idolatry was surely never more vividly expressed than in this passage. After describing the devotee as warily choosing a tree worthy of becoming a god, the main *desideratum* of which (as expressed in another passage) is that it shall not soon " rot," the prophet represents him as economically using the superfluous wood his axe has lopped from the embryo Divinity, to kindle his fire and to cook his food ; and then proceeding with strenuous toil and infinite cost of thirst and "sweat," and lavish skill of all that art of carver and gilder can do, to make the residue of his "log" into " a god, that it may remain in the house." "And the residue he maketh a god,—his graven image ; he falleth down unto it, and worshippeth it, and prayeth unto it, and saith, Deliver me, for thou art my God ! . . . . And none considereth in his heart, nor is there knowledge or understanding to say, I have burnt part of it in the fire ; yea, also I have baked bread upon the coals thereof ; I have roasted flesh, and eaten it ; and shall I make the residue thereof an idol ? Shall I fall down to the stock of a tree ? He feedeth on ashes : a deceived heart hath perverted him, that he cannot deliver his own soul nor say, Is there not a lie in my right hand ? "

Of the *sublimity* of Scripture, I need say nothing; for it is universally admitted to possess this quality in at least as large a measure as any equal portion of written matter in the world, and, as critics in general agree, sublimity of a far higher order. Few, I think, will doubt it who will duly examine the volume itself, or the copious proofs and illustrations given in the Lectures of Lowth, or the Dialogues of Herder on Hebrew Poetry. In Deuteronomy,[1] in Job, in the Psalms, in the Prophets, in almost every part, we are struck with this characteristic. From that utterance in the commencement of Genesis - "Let there be light, and there was light" which evoked the admiration of the heathen Longinus, to that "sevenfold chorus of hallelujahs and harping symphonies" in the Apocalypse, which moved the congenial soul of Milton, examples of the "true sublime" meet us at every step. But when we reflect on all else the Jews have done in literature, can we fail to ask whence had this one book of theirs such an exceptional majesty of thought and diction?

But the *third* quality, *pathos*, exists in so large a measure in the Bible, and fulfils such important functions, that it requires somewhat more to be said of it. Deducting that large portion of Scripture in which this quality could not be expected, a candid inquirer will be astonished at the excess of this element in the remainder, as compared with what is found elsewhere, in an equal compass, and especially in any so called "sacred" books. It is a remark (if I do not mistake of Principal Campbell) no less ingenious than just, that there is perhaps not a single passage of genuine pathos in the whole Koran; scarcely one which can be imagined to extort a tear even from a Moslem himself, notwithstanding all his associations in its favour!

Now, pathos of the highest character is perhaps the rarest of

---

[1] It is not without reason that Dean Milman says of the latter portions of Deuteronomy: "The sublimity" (and assuredly the energy) "of the denunciation surpasses anything in the oratory or poetry of the whole world."—*History of Jews.* Vol. i. p. 211. Ed. 1866.

all the excellences of composition; the most potent spell by which great historic or poetic imaginations hold the human mind in thraldom. It is one to which all yield. Profound reasoning is for the few; didactic wisdom raises no emotion; even beautiful and sublime fancies require a correspondent sensibility and culture to appreciate them; but "one touch of nature makes the whole world kin." [1]

It is also the most powerful vehicle in which moral wisdom can convey its lessons; and hence, as Aristotle remarked, the force with which these may be embodied in tragedy. Moral truth is there steeped in human emotion, and "the heart," as he expresses it, "is purified by pity and terror."

Now of this most insinuating and persuasive element, this chief instrument of touching the soul, the Bible (in proportion to the matter in which this quality is possible) not only avails itself more frequently, but more powerfully, than any other single volume in the world. It abounds in pathetic incidents and passages which do not become stale, though so often read; which make the eye glisten and the heart throb even on the hundredth perusal.

I am now only speaking of the higher exhibitions of this quality, and these in literature generally have ever been rare. If any one, whose reading is tolerably extensive, were called upon to name those examples of pathos which he would consider *worthy* to rank in the very first order of excellence, for example, with the parting of Hector and Andromache, the meeting of Priam and Achilles, the farewell of Medea to her children, the description of the death of Desdemona, or of the sorrows of Ophelia, he would, I think, be surprised to find how slender the catalogue with which all his reading could

[1] "La raison," says Pascal, "agit avec lenteur, et avec tant de vues sur tant de principes lesquels il faut qu'ils soient toujours présents, qu'à toute heure elle s'assoupit et s'égare, manque d'avoir tous ses principes présents. Le sentiment n'agit pas ainsi; il agit en un instant, et toujours est prêt à agir. Il faut donc mettre notre foi dans le *sentiment*; autrement elle sera toujours vacillante." *Pensées de Pascal.* Faugère. Vol. ii. p. 176.

furnish him.   Plenty of touches of pathos of a slighter kind, and plenty more spoiled by overdoing and affectation, he could no doubt recall; but those in the very first rank—those which are read again and again with unabated feeling, exact our tears for the fiftieth time, and defy familiarity to deaden their charm, are comparatively few.[1]

[1] It may be remarked that many of the most touching specimens of pathos in modern literature derive their chief effect from the Bible sentiments and associations which suggested them, often even from the Scriptural incidents and phraseology by which they are illustrated and expressed.   This is not seldom the case with Shakespeare, and far more frequently with Walter Scott.   Many of the more affecting examples of pathos in his masterpieces, the "Antiquary," "Guy Mannering," the "Heart of Midlothian," the "Bride of Lammermuir,"—owe the greater part of their power to the consummate way in which he conjures with the incidents and phraseology of Scripture, and applies them to his purpose.   Thus the scene in which the faithful Dominie Sampson devotes his life to the orphan child of his old patron, derives its chief charm from the "affectionate creature's" beautiful application of the language of Ruth to Naomi.—"The Dominie laid the money on the table.   'It is certainly inadequate,' said McMorlan, mistaking his meaning, 'but the circumstances——'   Mr. Sampson waved his hand impatiently.   'It is not the lucre—it is not the lucre—but that I, that have ate of her father's loaf, and drank of his cup, for twenty years and more, to think that I am going to leave her—and to leave her in distress and dolour. No, Miss Lucy, you need never think it!   You would not consent to put forth your father's poor dog, and would you use me waur than a messan?   No, Miss Lucy Bertram, while I live, I will not separate from you.   I'll be no burden to you.   I have thought how to prevent that.   But, as Ruth said unto Naomi, Entreat me not to leave thee, nor to depart from thee; for whither thou goest I will go, and where thou dwellest I will dwell; thy people shall be my people, and thy God shall be my God.   Where thou diest will I die, and there will I be buried.   The Lord do so to me, and more also, if aught but death do part thee and me.'"

The same observation applies still more strongly to the "Heart of Midlothian."   In numberless instances the intense pathos of that incomparable novel is derived from Scripture allusions; as for example in the last dying prayer of Douce Davie Deans for his "puir lost Effie."   "He prayed in the most affecting manner for Jeanie, her husband, and her family, and that her affectionate duty to the 'puir auld man' might purchase her length of days here, and happiness hereafter.   Then, in a pathetic petition, too well understood by those who knew his family circumstances, he besought the Shepherd of souls, while gathering His flock, not to forget the little one.

And this element in Scripture, frequent as it is, and whether of a higher or lower intensity, is expressed with the most inimitable simplicity. It is nature herself speaking to us, in that severely simple style in which the narrative of Scripture is generally clothed. Pathos there, is equally free from that exaggeration which too often spoils it in the hands of inferior writers, and of that highly-coloured poetic imagery in which even genius sometimes mistakenly arrays it ; and which, though we may pardon it for the sake of that light of genius that plays about it, we feel to be after all a trespass on nature ; a language in which the soul of grief, under the given conditions, never would or could have expressed itself.

This element in Scripture (and that too of the highest order) is so profuse, that it would not be easy to exhaust the catalogue of examples. It will suffice to remind the reader of such scenes as that between Abraham and Isaac on the mournful journey to Moriah, and especially the question with which the unconscious Isaac rends his father's heart : " My father, here is the fire and the wood, but where is the lamb for a burnt-offering ? " —of the scenes between Joseph and his brethren in Egypt, and especially the passionate intercession of Judah, to be allowed to take the place of Benjamin ;—of the lament of Jacob over Joseph, when he refused " to be comforted " by his sons, and suppressed the suspicions which had evidently made his anguish so much more bitter ; his equally passionate refusal to let Benjamin " go down with his brethren," and that heart-rending explosion of his long pent-up thoughts—" Me ye have bereaved of my children ; " [1]—of the meeting between the patriarch and

that had strayed from the fold, and even then might be in the paw of the ravening wolf."

In a word, the higher examples of Scott's pathos are felt to be so, not only because they are so true to nature, but because they are so bound up with the incidents, sentiments, and emotions with which the Bible had made him familiar, and are so deeply tinctured even by its phraseology.

[1] The spark which kindled that explosion was evidently the ominous discovery of the money which his sons had taken to Egypt to pay for their

his long-lost son ; the pleading of Joseph's brethren in deprecation of his anger after Jacob's death, and that touching
argument of their father's last wish, the very appeal to which
dissolved him in tears;—·of the scene in which Pharaoh's
daughter discovers the ark among the bulrushes, and is melted
into compassion by the infant wail of Moses ; the interview of
Ruth and Naomi ; the parting of David and Jonathan ; David's
lament over his friend ; the death of the Shunammite's child, and
her passionate expostulation with the prophet ;—of the tragic
scenes at the siege of Samaria ; of the judgment of Solomon, with
its thrilling revelation of the unfathomable depths of a mother's
love ; of David's lamentation over Absalom, in which nature
herself speaks to us in the accents of that desperate sorrow
which can do little but iterate in varied tones the name of the
lost object of its love :—these and many other passages in the
Old Testament are full of pathos.[1]   It equally pervades the

corn, but which was found returned in their sacks, when they came to un-
load. This, coupled with the *absence* of their brother Simeon, seems to
have reawakened suspicions which had no doubt often perplexed Jacob about
Joseph's fate, and to have suggested that Simeon might have been similarly
made away with. This would readily account both for their bringing back
the corn without *payment* for it, and for Simeon's mysterious abduction ;
and seemed to point to a like fate for Benjamin, if he should leave his
fond father's side. The whole transaction, exquisitely natural, affords, on
analysis, an instance of two things of which, as I have said, Scripture is
full : undesigned coincidences—recondite correspondences—between different
statements, which it is left to the sagacity of the reader to detect ; and that
purely dramatic style in which the history of Scripture is told ;—bare incidents being given, most graphic, indeed, but without comment on the
causes which connect them. Nothing is here said to account for the sudden
transport of suspicion into which Jacob was surprised, and which for so
many years he must have suppressed. But the facts of the narrative show
how natural that suspicion was, how deeply it had rankled, and how poig-
nantly it had been felt.

[1] Numberless brief passages might easily be added, which irresistibly
awaken sympathy, both as appealing immediately to the heart, and as representative of ten thousand analogous scenes in human life. They are
often compressed into a verse or two—sometimes into a sentence ; and are
as often, like some intaglios and medallions, masterpieces of artistic skill on

New. The parable of the Prodigal Son; the incident at the gate of Nain; the scenes connected with the resurrection of Lazarus; the fall and repentance of Peter; the institution of the Last Supper; the entire history of the crucifixion; the scene at the cross between Christ and the "beloved disciple;" that between Christ and Mary Magdalene at the sepulchre; Christ's prayer for His persecutors; His compassion to the dying malefactor; His last tender reproof of Peter; many passages of Paul's Epistles, especially to the Corinthians, to Timothy, and Philemon; suffice to show the frequency and intensity with which this element enters into the composition of the New Testament.

And human genius has shown its appreciation of this quality in the Scriptures by the enormous extent to which poetry, painting, and sculpture have resorted to this class of Biblical incidents and descriptions as subjects for art.

But the book is not only marked by its large infusion of the pathetic element in its ordinary narrative, in scenes which correspond to analogous scenes in ordinary life : it has a yet

a field of microscopic dimensions. Such is the description of the dying patriarch in Egypt (an exile in a strange land), yearning "for the sepulchre of his fathers." "There they buried Abraham and Sarah his wife; there they buried Isaac and Rebecca his wife; and there I buried Leah." There he desired his own dust to be laid,—not without a pang, probably, to think that the best beloved of all lay in her lonely tomb "on the way to Ephrath." Such is the description of Rachel's death, when her "departing soul" called the name of the "child of her sorrow," Benoni, but which he who had loved her so fondly, and for whom seven years' servitude appeared but as a day, exchanged for a name of happier omen. Such is the scene between Jacob and Joseph, in which the dying patriarch adopts, as his very own, Manasseh and Ephraim (born in Joseph's exile, and named in allusion to it), and blessed them, saying, "The angel that redeemed me from all evil, bless the lads." The whole scene, indeed, including the little contest between Jacob and his son in reference to the privileges of the first-born, and that touching last memorial of the patriarch's affection for him whom he had loved so much and lost so long,—"Moreover, I have given to thee one portion above thy brethren, which I took out of the hands of the Amorite with my sword and my bow,"—is one of the most graphic, as well as most affecting, in Genesis.

higher excellence. It has invested with the deepest pathos subjects to which that quality never belonged before,—in those numberless pictures in which Deity, with infinite condescension, and infinite knowledge of the fountains of human feeling, is represented as pleading with His wayward creatures and soliciting their love.

D'Alembert said that Pascal had illustrated the supremacy of his genius in his " Provincial Letters " by *theologising* two things that seemed not made for theology—wit and pleasantry. It may be said of the Bible that it has made susceptible of pathos, and brought within the range of human emotion, subjects which had hitherto dwelt in the region of remote abstractions, or, if they ever came nearer, came in forms which awakened only awe or terror. To familiarise, to endear, the thought of God, without degrading the conception; to bring Him within the sphere of human affections, without impairing His majesty, is the triumph of the Bible.

Viewed in this light, the scriptural representations of God, appealing as they do to all the deepest analogies of our own nature, far transcend those given by the most enlightened theism as elsewhere expounded. They are not only in the plane of human thought ; what is far more important to give them force, they are in the plane of human affection. This may be illustrated more particularly by the mode and degree in which Scripture dwells on the *paternal* character of God. Vivid indeed is the contrast in this respect between its tone and that which generally prevails, whether in the current religions or the current philosophies of the world. And no wonder ; for, on the one hand, superstition has troubled and deformed men's conceptions of God, and invested Him with terrors, naturally ascribed, indeed, by a heart that is more prompt to dread Him as the Governor than to love Him as the Father of His creatures,—but which, so far as they prevail, naturally repel and alienate affection. On the other hand, philosophic theism has almost exclusively dwelt on His abstract perfections, and placed Him in inaccessible remoteness from human sympathies ; He is not only incapable of being adequately conceived, which must be always true, but so secluded and shrouded in the mysteries of His own nature, that all that can kindle the emotions of childlike love and trust is obliterated from His character. We " stand afar off," and gaze in silent awe ; paying mute homage, indeed, to such Infinite Perfections, but feeling that if any Being possesses them, He is so completely beyond the sphere of our affections, that all emotion must be faint, and at best more akin to fear than to love. In the contemplation of such a Being, we feel utterly unable to echo the words of the Psalmist, " As the hart panteth after the water brooks, so panteth my soul after Thee, O God :" " This God is *our* God for ever and ever ; He will be our guide even unto death."[1]

[1] The following eloquent remarks of Dr. Mozley I believe to be profoundly just :—" The vulgar believed in many gods, the philosopher believed in a Universal Cause ; but neither believed in God. The philosopher only regarded the Universal Cause as the spring of the universal machine, which was necessary to the working of all the parts, but was not thereby raised to a separate order of being from them. Theism was discussed as a philosophical, not as a religious question ; as one rationale among others of the origin of the material universe, but as no more affecting practice than any great scientific hypothesis does now. Theism was not a test which separated the orthodox philosopher from the heterodox, which distinguished belief from disbelief ; it established no breach between the two opposing theorists ; it was discussed amicably as an open question ; and well it might be, for of all questions there was not one which could make less practical difference to the philosopher, or, upon his view, to anybody, than whether there was, or was not, a God. Nothing would have astonished him more than, when he had proved in the lecture-hall the existence of a God, to have been told to worship Him. ' Worship whom ? ' he would have exclaimed. ' Worship what ? ' ' Worship how ? ' Would you picture him indignant at the polytheistic superstition of the crowd, and manifesting some spark of the fire of St. Paul, ' when he saw the city wholly given to idolatry,' you could not be more mistaken. He would have said that you did not see a plain distinction ; that the crowd was right on the religious question, and the philosopher right on the philosophical ; that however men might uphold in argument an infinite abstraction, they could not worship it ; and that the hero was much better fitted for worship than the Universal Cause ; fitted for it, not in spite of, but in consequence of his want of, true divinity. The

Even the Israelites, in spite of the more benignant aspects under which God had already revealed, and was even then revealing Himself, are represented as palsied with terror in front of the burning mount, at the momentary manifestation of those austerer aspects of the Divine character which it was important for them, as it is for us, not to forget. In vain did He proclaim that He was " the Lord, the Lord God, merciful and gracious, long-suffering, and abundant in goodness and truth, forgiving iniquity, transgression, and sin." That He also proclaimed Himself, amidst such awful scenes, to be the righteous Governor of the world, who would not suffer His laws to be broken with impunity, and who, therefore, would "not clear the guilty," was too much for them. They naturally " stood afar off," and found no heart within them to approach a Being who made " the thick darkness His pavilion," and revealed Himself in " earthquake, tempest, and fire." " Let not God speak to us any more, lest we die," was their cry; and God Himself bore witness both to the naturalness and reasonableness of their emotion in contemplating *such* aspects of Himself;— " They have well said all that they have spoken."

And if the philosophic representation of the Deity as an infi-

same question was decided in the same way in the speculations of the Brahmans. There the Supreme Being figures as a characterless, impersonal essence ; the mere residuum of intellectual analysis, pure unity, pure simplicity. No temple is raised to Him, no knee is bended to Him. Without action, without will, without affection, without thought, He is the substratum of everything, Himself a nothing. . . . Thus the idea of God, so far from calling forth in the ancient world the idea of worship, ever stood in antagonism with it. The idol was worshipped because he was not God ; God was not worshipped because He was. One small nation alone of all antiquity worshipped God, believed the Universal Being to be a Personal Being. That nation was looked upon as a most eccentric and unintelligible specimen of humanity for doing so ; but this whimsical fancy, as it appeared in the eyes of the rest, was cherished by it as the most sacred deposit ; it was the foundation of its laws and polity ; and from this narrow stock this conception was engrafted upon the human race."—*Mozley's Bampton Lectures. Miracles.* Pp. 76-78.

nite abstraction creates, from its very remoteness from all our
sympathies, no terrors, it kindles as little love, and exerts no
attractive force. If not from conscious moral alienation, yet
from intellectual apathy, arising from the impossibility of being
en rapport with such a Being, man, in his impotence and ignorance, is apt to say to *this* God also, "Depart from us, for we
desire not the knowledge of Thy ways."

The Bible takes a different and more effectual way. In the
frequent assertion and iteration of those aspects of the Divine
character which are most likely to allure us, it constantly and
unfalteringly appeals to the analogy of the deepest and most
familiar emotions of our own nature. It does not scruple to
resort to the most naked anthropopathic images and expressions ; either secure, according to the already quoted saying of
Coleridge, that it *could* not be misconstrued, amidst such clear
and copious assertions of the Divine spirituality ; or else as
careless, even *though* it were, in some degree, misunderstood,
if it could but win us from our fears and our distrust.[1]

[1] It is impossible, I think, to imagine anything more intensely pathetic
than the daring anthropopathic imagery by which the prophets often
represent God as chiding, upbraiding, threatening, and, anon, relentingly
beseeching His perverse and ungrateful creatures. There is a free assumption of all the passions, and, if the reader will, even some of the infirmities
of our nature : all that tumult and conflict of contradictory and tempestuous
passions—indignation, anger, sorrow, love—by which a father's heart is
torn as he sees some unthankful and rebellious child proof against all
chiding, chastisement, and affection. See particularly Isaiah i. 2, 3, 18;
Jeremiah xxxi. 18-21 ; xxxii. 36-40; Ezekiel xvi. 3 ; Hosea vi. 4; vii.
13-16 ; xi. 7, 8; xiii. 4-10, and a host of other passages.

The symbolic lesson which God instructs Jeremiah to read to the Israelites from the conduct of the Rechabites, whom no temptations — no presentation of "wine cup and flagon"—could induce to swerve from their
"father's commandment," while Israel so easily forgot and trampled upon
His, is wonderfully touching : "Thus saith the Lord of hosts, Go and tell
the men of Judah and the inhabitants of Jerusalem, Will ye not receive
instruction to hearken unto my words? saith the Lord. The words of
Jonadab the son of Rechab, that he commanded his sons not to drink wine,
are performed ; for unto this day they drink no wine, but obey their father's
commandment : yet I have spoken unto you, but ye hearkened not unto Me.

It may be said without hesitation, that in this point of view, no religious book ever written, no professed revelation ever propounded, comes within appreciable distance of the Bible, and especially the New Testament ; above all, in the teaching of Him who expressly "came to reveal to us the Father." Nothing in the mythologies of Greece or Rome ever reminds us of the tone of the Scriptures in this respect ; none of the religious systems formed in the *absence* of the Bible (and these, after all, are the true tests of what man's unaided powers can do), no, nor any of the religious theories which philosophic theism has propounded, even *when* aided by the Bible, approach the Bible in the purely human interest, the intense pathos which it has infused into its modes of exhibiting the relations between man and his Maker.   As to the few and cold expressions which are met with in heathen poets, it is perfectly ludicrous to compare them with those constantly recurring passages of Scripture in which God speaks to the heart of man in the language of its own emotions.

The purest and best instincts of our nature are freely resorted to for illustration.   That parental compassion, to which the spectacle of helpless weakness, cast on its protection, gives such tenderness,—such as is felt by a mother for the infant hushed on her bosom, or a father for the child whose tiny fingers confidingly clasp him by the hand ;—that yearning of soul which views with indulgence every error and failing in the objects of its inextinguishable love ; which inflicts chastisement with more sorrow than the culprit suffers it ; which thinks of the pang it

I have also sent unto you all My servants the prophets, rising up early and sending them, saying, Return ye now every man from his evil way, and amend your doings, and go not after other gods to serve them, and ye shall dwell in the land which I have given to you and to your fathers : but ye have not inclined your ear, nor hearkened unto Me."   Nor is it the least instructive part of the lesson, that though "the children" He had "nourished and brought up had rebelled" against Him, He declares He would signally honour and reward the filial obedience even of the inferior type; and commissions Jeremiah to assure the Rechabites of it.

has inflicted almost with self-reproach; which asks for recon-
ciliation with a passionate desire, which no sullenness and no
obstinacy can overcome; which not only smiles with benignant
complacency upon every effort to obey, but exaggerates every
symptom of affection which it fancies it still sees in the ungrateful child who has cast off the yoke of authority, and
wandered forth from his father's house; which cannot cast him
off when the world, wearied out at last with his falsehood and
his vices, has closed every door to him; which, on the slightest
symptom of returning sense of duty and affection, impatiently
rushes to meet him, and will not hear those sobs of a broken
heart which it breaks a father's heart to listen to; which cuts
short even the short confession of error and guilt that sincere
penitence longs to utter, and seals the lips that would make it
with a kiss of all-forgetting love :—such traits as these are freely
attributed to God, "the Father of our spirits," in delineations
of Him drawn from the depths of the purest, profoundest,
sincerest, least corrupted font of human emotion.   In vain shall
we search for them, or anything approaching them, in the Vedas
or Koran, in the poetry or philosophy of ancient Greece or
Rome.   In vain shall we search for such texts as these :—
" Like as a father pitieth his children, so the Lord pitieth them
that fear Him."   " He knoweth our frame; He remembereth
that we are dust."   " Is Ephraim My dear son ? is he a pleasant
child ? for since I spake against him, I do earnestly remember
him still."   " Thou hast had compassion on the gourd for which
thou didst not labour, neither madest it grow ; and should not
I have compassion on this great city, in which are more than
three-score thousand persons who know not their right hand
from their left ? "   " Can a woman forget her sucking child,
that she should not have compassion on the son of her womb ?
Yea, she may forget : yet will not I forget thee."   " And while
he was yet a great way off, his father saw him, and had compassion, and ran, and fell on his neck, and kissed him ;" and
said, " Bring forth the best robe, and put it on him, and put a

ring on his hand and shoes on his feet; and kill the fatted calf, and let us eat and be merry; for this my son was dead, but is alive again; he was lost, and is found." "Son, thou art ever with me, and all that I have is thine. It was meet that we should make merry and be glad, for this thy brother was dead and is alive again; he was lost and is found." Such are a very few of the expressions which may serve to illustrate this point.

In our Lord's teaching, who came to make known to us the "Father," this free use of analogies is appropriately emphatic. As it was said of Socrates that he brought down philosophy from the skies, to dwell with men, it may be said with yet greater truth of Christ, that He brought God Himself down from cloudy abstractions into the sphere of human apprehension and human affection.

If He would have us trust in Divine Providence for the supply of our wants, it is because our heavenly Father "knoweth that we have need of such things;" if He would have us confide in that minute care which, like that of the human parent, thinks nothing little that affects the welfare of those who are its objects, He tells us that "the hairs of our heads are all numbered, and that not even "a sparrow can fall to the ground" without the cognizance and permission of our heavenly Father. If He would have us forgiving and forbearing, it is because our Father has compassion on the ungrateful and disobedient,—for He "makes His sun to shine on the evil and the good, and sends His rain upon the just and the unjust." If He would encourage us to ask boldly what we need from the all-bestowing bounty, He tells us that, "evil" as we are, we know by an unerring instinct how to "give good gifts to *our* children;" and how much more will our heavenly Father give them to His? "If the son of any of you that is a father, ask bread, will he give him a stone? or if he ask a fish, will he give him a scorpion? If ye then, being evil, know how to give good gifts unto your children, how much more will your heavenly Father give good gifts to them that ask Him?" In His comprehensive model of all prayer, the invocation is not to the Infinite, the Holy, the Just, the Wise, but to "our Father in heaven." When He rose from the dead, His first announcement to the disciples was the renewed recognition of the same relation: " I ascend to *my* Father and to *your* Father ; to *my* God and to *your* God."

In brief, no small portion of that pathos in which, as I have said, the Bible abounds above all other books, is found in the various manifestations of the paternal character of God, by which He would seem intent on subduing both that dread which results from our sense of guilt, and that intellectual apathy which is the equally certain effect of the bare contemplation of His abstract perfections. All these illustrations are drawn so freely from the depths of our own nature—from that parental heart which He Himself inspired with its passionate and unquenchable love,—that no self-despairing, forlorn child of pollution and misery, is without ample warrant to come in his rags and deep poverty—the effect and sign of his transgression—and, breaking through the cloud of doubt and distrust which the sense of in-finite purity and the awe of illimitable power and wisdom might interpose, to cast himself, though it be with burning shame and blinding tears, into those loving arms, which he is assured, in accents and by arguments so infinitely touching, are ever open to receive him.

LECTURE VIII.

ON THE EXCEPTIONAL POSITION OF THE BIBLE IN THE WORLD.

LECTURE VIII.

IT is not a little paradoxical that amidst the wreck of the many nations by which the Jews were surrounded—some of them incomparably mightier than themselves—they, and they alone, should have succeeded in preserving copious and continuous written memorials of themselves. The passion for durable monuments was certainly strong enough in Egypt and Assyria,—as the pyramids and gigantic wrecks of architecture prove; and not less perhaps those *mummies* of the former country, by which it was sought to make even " evanescence immortal." But the Hebrews, and they alone, seem to have learned the higher art of " embalming " the spirit, the thought, the laws, in a word, all that constitutes the life of a nation. While the Egyptian, Assyrian, and Babylonian monarchies have perished, so that their " memorials " for the most part have perished too, or are being reclaimed in tattered fragments, as the " huge drag " of the antiquary (casually, and at intervals of centuries) brings them up; while the hieroglyphics of Egypt, and the inscriptions of Nineveh and Persepolis, still provoke, and, for the most part, still baffle the sagacity of the most accomplished scholarship, which, with all its efforts, can but imperfectly explore the mystic characters, and often fails to convince the world that it has truly deciphered them ; the Jews, an utterly insignificant nation compared with those just named—insignificant in arts and arms, in wealth and population, in civilisation and refinement—have handed down a record of the history and fortunes of their race from remote ages ;—not in vague symbols, but by means of an alphabetic notation ; in characters clearly decipherable, and in a language, the grammar and syntax of which are as regular and intelligible as those of Greek and Latin.   Whether their annals contain truth or fable, or how much of either, is not now the question.   I am speaking merely of the *fact*, that they alone have consigned to us (what the far greater surrounding nations, nay, that whole ancient world with which their elder history is involved, either never had, or were never able to keep) their annals and their language.

It is certainly no abatement of the mystery that this nation would appear to have had very little literature, and has seemingly conserved nearly all that it had ; while the written records possessed by the other nations connected with their fortunes (and they certainly inscribed much on stone and metal, whether they had books or not) have as hopelessly gone into oblivion as the score of Roman authors who lived between Cato the Censor and Augustus, or even as the still earlier utterly unknown annalists, in whom the later Roman historians groped for the materials of their narrative.   If a fragment like that of the " Moabite Stone " comes to light once in a thousand years, it awakens the astonishment of the learned world.   Even this, however, is clearly read only by the light of the chronicles of the Jews,—to the antiquity of whose language it bears witness, and the credibility of whose history it in some measure confirms. But it exhibits still more conspicuously, by *contrast*, the difference between the copious and well-preserved records of which the Jews can boast and the scanty relics of the surrounding nations.   The little ark of the Jewish literature still floats above the surges of time, while mere fragments of the wrecked archives of the huge Oriental empires, as well as of the lesser kingdoms that surrounded Judæa—mere "flotsam and jetsam"—are now and then cast on our distant shores.   "Time sadly overcometh all things," says one who has happily imitated Sir Thomas Browne, "and is now dominant, and sitteth upon a sphinx, and looketh unto Memphis and old Thebes; while his sister Oblivion reclineth semi-somnous on a pyramid, gloriously triumphing, making puzzles of Titanian inscriptions, and turning old glories into dreams. History sinketh beneath her cloud. The traveller, as he paceth amazedly through those deserts, asketh of her who builded them, and she mumbleth something, but what it is he heareth not."

This paradox of the exceptional superiority of the Jews in this matter is certainly not diminished by their alleged insignificance and comparative obscurity. It is a theme on which their enemies have been fond of dilating, though surely not wisely; for the greater their obscurity and insignificance, the more difficult is it to account for the *rôle* they have played in the world. It would seem that they have done, and done effectually, a work their far greater neighbours, more enterprising, more populous, more civilized, either never attempted or could not achieve,—that of inscribing, on more durable forms than brass or marble, a continuous narrative of their history and fortunes, which "Time and Oblivion" should *not* be able to " overcome."

If these records really contain a contemporary or nearly contemporary account of the events they describe, this singular nation has anticipated, without knowing it, that canon which modern criticism has established as the true condition of all *reliable* history. Niebuhr, indeed, while contending for the fabulous quality of so much ancient history, and perhaps in his iconoclastic zeal using the sponge too freely, flattered himself that it was possible for critical sagacity to divine to a great extent what the past has been, and, by cautiously treading in the footsteps of tradition, to ascertain what no contemporary documents vouch for. Too many of his countrymen have essayed this perilous task of manufacturing history, or interpreting what ancient tradition " drowsily mumbles;" but one cannot but feel with Dean Milman in this matter. Speaking of the too common modern fashion of making history without historic materials, this author says : " I confess that I have not much sympathy for this—not making bricks *without* straw—but making bricks entirely *of* straw, and offering them as solid materials."[1]   That accomplished scholar, Sir George Cornewall Lewis, in his great work on the credibility of the early Roman history, has sufficiently confuted the error of these historical diviners, and shown that for distant periods there can be no authentic history without written documents.   The Jews would seem to have acted (ignorant as they were) on that condition ; and whether their books be proved ancient and authentic, or comparatively modern, they at least come before the bar of criticism with books of their own.   They have composed and preserved records which time could not destroy, and which the whole world is now resolved " not willingly to let die."

What still adds to the singularity of the case is, that if the Jews can thus point to their written treasures, while time has confiscated those of contemporary antiquity, those records also contain express declarations that the great nations immediately surrounding them should thus be " overcome of time and oblivion," and pass away without a history.   Of the great monarchies whose history is more or less connected with that of the Jews, it is declared that they should be destroyed, and their memorials and monuments perish.   A few passages to this effect have been already alluded to in a previous lecture for another purpose, and it is not necessary to repeat them, or to add to them, for they are familiar to all.   I do not appeal to these declarations as *prophecy*, for that would depend on when they were written ; but few critics would deny that they were written some time before the *final* desolation of the countries and cities to which they apply.   They are here mentioned merely as illustrating the exceptional destiny of the Jewish people ; that they not only had memorials which the above-named nations had not, but ventured to declare that these other and often greater nations should have none !

[1] "History of the Jews." *Preface to New Edition.* 1866. p. 25.   See also p. 23.

On the hypothesis that the Hebrew records had more than a human origin; that they were designed to embody, in gradual and successive disclosures, a Divine revelation to the world, accommodated to the various stages of its history, and illustrative of the great principles of God's moral government; that the Jews were to be the depositaries of the elementary truths and principles which were elsewhere and everywhere buried under superstition and idolatry; it is not of course surprising that this nation should thus possess, and so wonderfully preserve, their national history and its written records; or that Scripture has conformed, without its authors being aware of it, to the conditions on which, by a law of necessity (as modern criticism declares), the safe transmission of facts to distant epochs is suspended. This would *account*, indeed, for the anomalous fact on which I am commenting; but I must not take such solution for granted. Let the fact then simply pass for one of the many curious facts on which I am insisting—one of the innumerable proofs of the unique character and position of the Bible.

It does not diminish the singularity of which I am here speaking—it merely shifts it—to suppose, after the favourite method of modern rationalism, that the historic records of the Jews were not contemporary with the events described, nor compiled from trustworthy annals that were so; but late compilations of unknown authors. It has been not unreasonably surmised that this theory would not have been suggested, except by considerations altogether foreign to the evidence, whether external or internal; for the stress of both is the other way. But it does not abate the singularity of the fact now insisted on, though it transfers the paradox to another point. For (as already insisted on in a previous lecture) is it credible that a bundle of fictions thrust wholesale into the middle of the history of a nation, could or would be accepted by that nation as its true history? Could it receive a *rationale* of its national existence— of its laws and institutions—of which their fathers had no consciousness and left no record; and all, too, without a murmur, denial, or remonstrance?   Could a series of romances pass into the most intense historic belief, and the whole nation be so profoundly ignorant or so unanimous in fraud as not to mutter a word of doubt or suspicion?   And, lastly, and above all, would it so act in favour of fictions, which so far from flattering the humour or exalting the character of the nation, are, if fictions, terrible libels upon it?   But on this I have said enough in a previous lecture.[1]

Thus this theory is beset with difficulties; but even if it were true, it admits that paradoxical position of the Jewish records of which I am here speaking.   For even supposing the earliest of these records was unknown till the days of Solomon (and few rationalists would go so far down), and the latest extant four hundred years before the Christian era, the Jews would still have had a series of national memoirs and a national literature which the other countries about them—Moab and Edom, Assyria and Babylon—never had or always lost.

We are struck with another anomaly, or rather a knot of anomalies, when we come to consider the various modes and the extraordinary degree in which the Bible, as compared with any other book sacred or profane, has stimulated the intellect and energy, and attracted the love and veneration of men.   It will be seen, I think, as we follow the argument into its details, that on the supposition that this book is a fortuitous collection of tracts, composed by men who belonged to a nation in many respects among the most insignificant, and certainly among the most despised, on the face of the earth—a nation that is chiefly distinguished by the degree in which these writings have extorted the homage of mankind—their prodigious influence is not a little curious.   It adds to the difficulty, that all subsequent literary productions of this nation have been characterized by no special excellence; in fact, are rather below than above the average merit of other literatures.   Indeed, the productions of Jewish

Rabbis are generally such as to engender a natural suspicion that, since they did no better, even with such models for imitation before them, no such powers as theirs unaided could have produced books which have so arrested the attention of an alien world. Nearly all else that the Jews have written men willingly leave in obscurity. On these books alone they concentrate their regards.

These books make a volume of no very great size. In hundreds of cases the "Opera Omnia" of single authors have contained many times the bulk of all the tractates of this book put together, and have not seldom included among them works which rank among the choicest productions of human genius— genius that had deserved and secured the applause of mankind. But in no one of these cases can the influence exerted on the world be for a moment compared with that of this volume, as measured by the facts to which I am about to refer.

Among these facts, I will not insist on the absolute self-surrender, the passionate love, this book has inspired in the thousands and tens of thousands who have laid down their lives, or been ready to lay them down, rather than consent to renounce it, or abjure the faith it has taught them. I will not insist on the long array of martyrs who have sealed their testimony to their vehement zeal for it, and intense belief in it, with their blood. I am persuaded, indeed, that the influence of the Bible (or, which comes to much the same thing), of the religion it teaches and enjoins, is, even in this point of view, *unique*, whether we consider among how many different nations and communities, and through what a long succession of ages, this self-sacrifice has been demanded and repeated, or contemplate the *character* of the martyrs themselves. The phenomenon is quite independent of race, culture, tradition, national characteristics ; while the character of the martyrs the Bible has so often inspired, has been the same,—of a type wholly different from that of the devotees of other religions. To suffer in majestic patience, in silent meekness, with forgiveness on their lips, and, as far as can be discerned, in their hearts, has been the characteristic of thousands of Christian martyrs since that hour in which their Great Exemplar prayed on the cross for His murderers. The style of such a martyr differs from that of the soldier-martyr of Islam, who died for his prophet with all those impetuous passions which, in the fierce eagerness of battle, quench fear and deaden pain, as much as " the lamb led to the slaughter" differs from the lion who casts himself in rage on the spear of the hunter. Polycarp and Huss, the martyrs of Lyons, of the Vaudois, of the Malagasy in our own day, are no more like the Fakirs of India swinging on their hook, or devotees casting themselves under the wheels of Juggernaut, than Howard dying of prison fever resembles the vulgar suicide.

But I will not insist on this. Such is undoubtedly the strength even of the *perverted* spirit of religion in human nature, and such also the power of human passion, that it is too possible even for the most degrading superstitions to point to those who have been willing martyrs for them. And in this respect, the worst, as well as the best of religions, bear witness to the depth and indomitable energy of those principles of our nature on which religion is founded; principles far mightier than any which usually prompt men to attach themselves to any schools of politics or philosophy. This is a fact which, if duly dwelt upon, would make men despair of uprooting these principles of our nature, and, instead of attempting it, render them solely intent on discovering what religion is the true. There is scarcely a religion, however " beggarly " its " elements," that cannot point to more willing martyrs for it, simply because it is a *religion*, than philosophy or science could ever boast.

Without, therefore, conceding that the various manifestations and characteristics of the martyr-spirit the Bible has inspired, furnish no argument in favour of the perfectly unique influence it has exerted, or might not be enumerated among the many paradoxes involved in the theory of its purely human origin,— I waive it. For the same reason, I as little insist upon the mere numbers it has succeeded in persuading of its Divine claims to attention. It cannot be doubted that the adherents of other religions, those who have sworn by the Vedas or the Koran, may have been equally or more numerous; mere nominal suffrages are of no avail for any system. Let this argument, therefore, be also waived as precarious; though here, too, I am persuaded that there is no other "sacred book" in the world that can pretend to the suffrages of so many men of great genius, of so many intelligent and educated adherents, from so many different races and nationalities, as those which the Bible has extorted; and these, moreover, in numberless cases, in spite of previous prejudices, and after prolonged and patient examination. In truth, the difficulty is to find, in the otiose reception or rejection of *other* sacred books, the traces of any severe criticism or examination at all.

But the following *facts*, which show the peculiar position the Bible occupies among books, and the paramount influence it has exerted, cannot be disputed.

1. It is curious to see how wonderfully independent of race has been the welcome given to this book. It has been spontaneously received (by spontaneously, I mean as the fruit of persuasion only, and to the exclusion of all political influence or military violence) by men of far more various races and nations than any other religious books ever have been. I have already conceded that, unhappily for the Bible, those who have misunderstood it, and therefore wronged it, have not always refrained from the above methods (though prohibited by itself) of extending its influence.[1] But still, during the three first

---

[1] It must be added that the Bible, so far from authorising these proceedings, has itself too often been the victim of them, and has been imprisoned, exiled, burnt, like its own confessors and martyrs. Not the heathen Diocletian alone hunted down for destruction the copies of the Scriptures. In the worst times of *Christian*, or rather Antichristian persecution, the Bible has had to suffer its full share : whoever might be chargeable with heresy, that was still the heretic of heretics; and this fact is a sufficient compurgation from the charge, sometimes made, of being an accomplice with the Alvas and the Bonners.

centuries, the religion it teaches and the book which embodies it made their way, without any such questionable allies, into almost every part of the "Orbis Romanus;" and since that time, with similar independence of all such aid, have made similar impressions on various heathen communities in all quarters of the world, from Greenland to the Cape of Good Hope, and from Otaheite to Madagascar.

Now history shows us that the progress of a religion, apart from the fanaticism or ambition which leads men to fight for its diffusion, is almost uniformly circumscribed by race and nationality; and also how impassable is the barrier which these—fortified by old superstitions and the customs which they consecrate—oppose to it.   It is almost impossible, in ordinary cases, to get people to pay any attention at all to an alien religion, except as a subject of curious or learned investigation; and we should be as much astonished at any European becoming a worshipper of Brahma by poring over the Hindoo mythology, as at a student of Homer becoming a devotee of Jupiter.

How is it, then, that the Bible has had so little difficulty in transcending the bounds of race and nationality?   By what gift has it been capable of breaking through the barriers which, in general, so obstinately enclose each variety of religious belief?   An objector may, perhaps, say it was not so with the Hebrew Scriptures—the greater half of the volume.   Why, no; but that rather increases the wonder.   The addition of the lesser half altered the complexion and the properties of the whole.   *That* is so buoyant, that it bears up itself and the mass which is attached to it, and which had been almost as little known to the world in general as the contents of other sacred books usually are.   Those who received the Old Testament, and accounted it to be the inspiration of the Most High, yet followed the law of other religionists, or nearly so; and, for the most part, kept their oracles to themselves.   The rest of the world followed *their* own law, in caring nothing about alien oracles at all.   I have had occasion to observe in a previous lecture that the Jews, though not required to reject proselytes—far from it—yet in general did little to make them : they seem to have been only too well pleased to think themselves the exclusive possessors of a Divine revelation, and to hug themselves on that superiority.   If they received proselytes from among the heathen, it was with no very genial welcome; they acquiesced in their occupying an inferior place in the "Court of the Gentiles," but would have vehemently protested against the "middle wall of partition," which shut them off from the more sacred enclosure, being broken down.[1]   On the other hand, the Gentiles recoiled as strongly from the Jews as the Jews from them.   Both mutually repelled, instead of attracting one another.

It is, therefore, not a little wonderful that the Bible, though with its larger half in this sense a dead weight upon it, and as little likely to pass, by spontaneous reception, from race to race and from people to people, as any other collection of so-called sacred books, has found it *comparatively* easy to break through the barriers; and, as the ages have rolled on, to migrate without violence into new regions, and find a home among tribes, separated by every conceivable difference of climate, government, customs, culture, and religion, from those which had previously accepted it; among the various nationalities which acknowledged the Roman sway, and among modern nationalities which succeeded it; among the conquering Goths and other barbarians of the early centuries, and in the South Seas, in Africa, and in Madagascar, in our own time.

Will it be said that it is because this book, alone among sacred books, teaches a religion which is worthy of universal reception, enjoins its universal diffusion, and is alone capable of forming a succession of men heroically bent on *making* it universal?   Doubtless, if this be granted, the mystery is solved.   This concedes the special characteristics of

[1] See "Davison on Prophecy," pp. 280-82.

the book, for which I am contending. It is indeed unlike all *other* sacred books, if so much can be said for it !

It is true, however, that this strange volume has the power, wheresoever it got it, of prompting men to proclaim and to propagate its contents. Whether we look at the ancient or the modern converts to it, they are somehow instantly bent on proselytism.

2. Among other singularities of this book, if it be a mere production of human genius, like any other book or collection of books of the same size, may be mentioned the prodigious *literature* which it has evoked. Either it must have claims to attention altogether transcendent to those of any other,—even the greatest compositions of human genius,—in order to account for men's ceaseless activity in translating, illustrating, explaining, interpreting, propagating, impugning, and defending it ; or we must conclude that, on this one subject, no inconsiderable portion of mankind has virtually gone mad ; or, rather, that each successive portion of the race, each new community or nation, that comes under the fascination of this book, is smitten with this same incurable bibliomania, and proceeds to do in behalf of it, or *against* it, what it would never dream of doing for or against any other books in the world, sacred or profane ! This mysterious book (the whole or parts of it) speaks no less than two hundred languages, and is daily learning to speak more ; that is, probably speaks as many as any ten of the very chiefest classics of human genius, however widely translated, put together ; more than Homer, Virgil, Dante, Shakespeare, Milton, Goethe, Walter Scott, put together ; very far more than the Vedas and Koran put together. In numberless cases, again, it has allured men to do what, so far as we know, was never done on behalf of any other book, howsoever counted " sacred," before. It has induced them, not only to encounter every form of peril and the most enormous self-sacrifices, to get the mere chance of proclaiming the substance of its contents, but to undergo the most gigantic labours, in

order to translate it into barbarous and uncouth languages. Nay, more; in a score of cases it has impelled them to submit to the more arduous preliminary drudgery of giving a notation and visible shape to languages which were previously but a "wandering voice," and nothing else. This book it is that first conferred on many a barbarous nation the wondrous art of condensing the volatile vapour of human thought into a visible form, taught them the first elements of those arts which are the necessary condition of all progress and civilisation, and opened to them the road which leads on to all the triumphs of human intellect and national greatness. Many such nations —perhaps hereafter to be graced by a muster-roll of names as illustrious, and achievements as great as adorn the history of our own country—may say, as *she* in great part must say also: "These things we owe to some obscure missionaries, who, like the birds that carry the seeds of forests to desert islands, brought us the germs of all these blessings in giving us the Bible. They first made language *visible* to us; they analysed the sounds which it represents, expressed them in an alphabet, reduced them to grammatical forms, compiled a lexicon for us, opened to us the intellectual treasures of all literature and science, and made it possible to have a literature and science of our own."

Meantime its translators wrought, not for the sake of these vast collateral and adventitious benefits (however much they may have rejoiced in them), but simply for the book's sake itself; and would have done the work, all the same, if they had been sure that no literature but that one book would ever be known to the people for whom it was translated. Such is the strange enthusiasm it is capable of inspiring!

Similarly, this book has probably done more to fix and preserve the languages into which it has been translated, to retard the progress of change and corruption, than any other single cause whatever. This has been conspicuousiy a result of our own English version.

And it is only just to remember that many languages, which

already had a written character indeed, but were still so incrusted with barbarism as to make them wholly unfit for the purposes of literature, have been largely indebted to the toil of those who sought to transfuse the contents of this book into these uncouth vehicles for it. This has often done more to purify and polish them, to mould them into forms which science and poetry could deign to use, than any other single cause. This was to a good extent the case with the early translations into our own language and the German. The " Körnige Sprache " of Luther's translation, as a German critic calls it, played no mean part in the development of that language.

The passion for translating the Bible into other tongues has been intense from the very commencement of the Christian era, and may probably be said to have *created* the taste for translation in general. The ancients seem to have had little that was worthy of the name. Cicero and Quintilian, indeed, speak of the signal benefits the rhetorical student and youthful orator may derive from frequent translation of fine passages from the Greek into their own tongue,—just as Lord Chatham commends the same exercise to his son, William Pitt. But the practice of systematically endeavouring to import the masterpieces of Greek literature into the Latin, or *vice versâ*, seems not to have been adopted in the ancient world. Nor, in days when printing was unknown, and there was such infinite toil and cost in making even *original* manuscripts public, is it any wonder that this sort of literary labour was generally declined. But no such difficulties depressed the energies of men where the Bible was concerned. By about the middle of the second century, there were no less than three Greek versions of the Old Testament, in addition to the Septuagint,—those of Aquila, Theodotion, and Symmachus. Still earlier, the Peshito-Syriac version, including Old and New Testaments, was completed. About the same time it appeared in Latin (the old Italic). It was translated again into that language by Jerome. By the end of the fourth century, the Scriptures were translated in whole or in

part,—but certainly nearly the whole of the New Testament,—
into Coptic, Sahidic, Armenian, Ethiopic, and Gothic.   Nor
were the darker ages without their like triumphs.   In the sixth
century it was translated into Georgian ; in the ninth into the
Sclavonic; and various translations of the Gospels and other
parts of Scripture into Anglo-Saxon, and several other Teutonic
languages, were executed at intermediate dates.   If it be said
that reverence for a supposed " sacred " book will account for
all this, we must reply ;—first, reverence for *other* supposed
" sacred " books has never produced anything like it ; and
secondly, that if, in this case, reverence was so exceptionally
powerful, what inspired it ?

One of the most interesting books in the world to *look* at,—
few, perhaps, except Professor Max Müller, and two or three
other accomplished linguists like him, can *read* more than
a few pages, of it,—is the handsome quarto volume entitled
" The Bible of every Land ; " in which beautifully printed typo-
graphical specimens are given of the multitudinous versions of
the Bible in all their variety of alphabetic characters.   It is impossible to inspect it without feeling what stupendous (and if the
Bible be not more to the world than the Koran or the Vedas,
Homer or Plato), what utterly disproportionate and wasteful toil
man has foolishly expended on this one volume !

How much more must we feel this in contemplating the
enormous masses of literature to which it has given birth!
This one book, not more than the three-hundredth part of the
extant Greek and Roman literature, has probably attracted to
it, and concentrated upon it, more thought, and probably produced more works, explanatory, illustrative, apologetic,—upon
its text, its exegesis, its doctrines, its history, its geography,
ethnology, chronology, and evidences,—than all the Greek and
Roman literature put together.   There is scarcely a tractate in
it, however short, that has not had more pains expended upon
it than many even of the more voluminous ancient writers.   In
walking through any great library, in inspecting any large cata-

logue (as that of the British Museum, or the Bodleian), one is astonished at the immense bulk of literature which, either directly or indirectly, owes its origin to this one book. It is surprising to see how large a portion of the huge London Catalogue is made up of books which, had it not been for this one, would never have had an existence !

And now, endeavouring for a moment to place myself in the point of view of those who regard this book as a simple collection of tractates, written by a number of obscure men, of no greater actual endowments than those possessed by many others (often their equals, sometimes their superiors), and all of them, with perhaps one exception,[1] belonging to one of the most despised of human communities, I am lost in amazement at that insanity (I can call it, on *that* hypothesis, by no other name) which has kept the most diverse nations, but always those in the very van of all science, learning, and civilisation, thus everlastingly poring over this book; illustrating, interpreting, attacking, defending it ; thinking no pains too great to be bestowed even on its least significant parts, and deeming it of more importance to prosecute this task than to give themselves to the like labours on the very *chef-d'œuvres* of human genius.

The " Propaganda " for this book is a phenomenon we should in vain seek in the case of any other books, sacred or profane. The Bible Society, for example, may be a fanatical organisation ; but fanaticism never evoked anything like it in behalf of any other book, however revered as presumed to be inspired, or admired as pre-eminently instinct with human genius. I observe that during the year 1872–73 no less than 2,592,936 copies of the whole Bible, or large portions of it, were issued by the Society. Now, the " Publishers' Circular " tells us that last year (1872) 4814 works of all kinds, including pamphlets (not sermons), and reprints, were published in London; and if we suppose each impression to average 1000 copies (rather a

---

[1] I refer to Luke; but even that is doubtful.

liberal allowance, and perhaps only too flattering to most authors), then the copies of this one old book issued in London, exceeded the half of all the copies of the new and old books of the year put together![1]

A library made up of all the books which have been written solely in *defence* of the Bible, would be an imposing spectacle. About a century and a half ago the great Fabricius gave a *Catalogue Raisonné* of all the books that had been, directly or indirectly, evoked in defence of Christianity down to his time. Though not exhaustive (some pages, however, are occupied with other subjects), it forms a quarto of more than seven hundred pages. I apprehend that, by this time, a similar work would extend to at least three times the bulk.[2]

Equally striking, in some respects, would be the spectacle of all those works which have been written, more or less, *against* the book ;—in general confutation of its claims, or against some of its principal facts and evidences. The volumes thus written for the purpose of correcting men's eccentric love and veneration for it (eccentric on the hypothesis of its merely human origin), showing either that it is substantially incredible, or, like other books, a mixture of wisdom and folly, would form a library of no inconsiderable bulk. If collected from the earliest times (beginning with the fragments of Celsus and Porphyry) to the present day, they would occupy far more than a thousand times the space of the one volume against which they are directed ; and would certainly be much more numerous than all

---

[1] One does not readily imagine Euclid to be, in any sense, more popular than Homer or Virgil ; or that his Geometry has had a larger circulation than the Iliad or Æneid. Yet it was certainly the fact for some generations after the revival of letters. So De Morgan assures us in his admirable Life of the old Greek Geometer, inserted in the Dictionary of Greek and Roman Biography. But as he truly says, if all other books may be challenged to rival Euclid in circulation, the Bible must still be excepted.

[2] "Jo. Alberti Fabricii Delectus Argumentorum et Syllabus Scriptorum Veterum Recentiumque qui Veritatem Religionis Christianæ asseruerunt." 4to. Hamburg. 1725.

the works that all other "sacred" books ever had the honour of provoking either *for* or *against* them.

If all these books were placed in one library, and this single one set on a table in the middle of it, and a stranger were told that this book, affirmed to be, for the most part, the work of a number of unlearned and obscure men belonging to a despised nation called the Jews, had drawn upon itself, for its exposure, confutation, and destruction, this multitude of volumes, I imagine he would be inclined to say : " Then, I presume this little book was annihilated long ago ; though how it could be *needful* to write a thousandth part so much, for any such purpose, I cannot comprehend. For if the book be what these authors *say*, surely it should not be very difficult to show it to be so ; and if so, what wonderful madness to write all these volumes ! " [1] How surprised would he then be to learn that they were felt not to be *enough ;* that similar works were being multiplied every day, and never more actively than at the present time ; and still to no purpose in disabusing mankind of this same phrenzy ! He would learn, indeed, that so far from accomplishing their object, the new volumes are little more than necessary to replace those of this fruitful, yet fruitless literature, which are continually sinking into oblivion ; [2] a fate which may be said, perhaps, with almost

---

[1] If he were asked, " Do you find, then, that error and prejudice are so easily dispelled ? Do not men cling with inexpressible tenacity to any system consecrated by custom? " He would probably say, " Yes ; but then such systems have never had a thousandth part of the same energies directed against them which this prodigious array of controversial volumes implies. Usually we have otiose assent on one side, and laws prohibiting all discussion on the other ! "

[2] " Who," said Burke, nearly a century ago, of a whole library of this literature, " who, born within the last forty years, has read one word of Collins, and Toland, and Tindal, and Chubb, and Morgan, and that whole race who called themselves Freethinkers ? Who now reads Bolingbroke ? Who ever read him through ? Ask the booksellers of London what has become of all these lights of the world."—Burke's Reflections. Works. Vol. v. p. 172.

equal truth, to await the new works written in its defence. A large mass of these, too, pass every age out of sight, or are known only to the literary student.

But the volume itself survives both friends and foes. Without being able to speak one word on its own behalf, but what it has already said ; without any power of explanation or rejoinder, in deprecation of the attacks made upon it, or to assist those who defend it ; it passes along the ages in majestic silence. Impassive amidst all this tumult of controversy, in which it takes no part, it might be likened to some great ship floating down a mighty river like the Amazon or Orinoco, the shores of which are inhabited by various savage tribes. From every little creek or inlet, from every petty port or bay, sally flotillas of canoes, some seemingly friendly and some seemingly hostile, filled with warriors in all the terrors ot war paint, and their artillery of bows and arrows. They are hostile tribes, and soon turning their weapons against one another, assail each other with great fury and mutual loss. Mean time the noble vessel silently moves on through the scene of confusion, without deigning to alter its course or to fire a shot : perhaps here and there a seaman casts a compassionate glance from the lofty bulwarks, and wonders at the hardihood of those who come to assail his leviathan.

In spite, and perhaps, indeed, in consequence of these attacks (M. Rénan's " Vie de Jésus " in particular is said to have had this effect in France), the book is more and more widely diffused, every year multiplies its copies, and every year speaks some new language.

3. It may be said, further, that there is no other book, and I think I might say no other ten books, that have left so many or so deep traces on human literature ; none that are so often cited or alluded to ; none which have supplied so much matter for apt illustration, or been so often resorted to for vivid imagery and energetic diction. It has lived on the page, not merely of great divines such as Barrow or Jeremy Taylor ;—in such cases, though genius might be stimulated by the literary

beauties of the book, reverence for it, and familiarity with it, might be thought to account for so frequent and spontaneous a use of it. But the remark is applicable to modern literature generally, on which the traces of the influence of this book are incomparably deeper and more legible than those left by any other single volume.

None but those who have been in the habit of inspecting the best portions of modern literature, with the express view of tracing the influence of the Bible upon it, can have any adequate idea of the extent to which it has moulded thought and sentiment, or given strength or grace to expression. Its literary excellences in general have insensibly extorted the homage and tinged the style of the greatest masters of eloquence and poetry, with little reference to the degree in which they yielded tc its claims on their reverence, and in many cases though they rejected those claims altogether. Its apophthegms, its examples, its historic illustrations of human life and character, its moral maxims, its lessons of conduct, its vivid and intense imagery, come spontaneously to the lips, as more exactly or forcibly expressing thought and feeling than anything found elsewhere. [1]

In reperusing lately some of the greatest masters of prose,—Bacon, Milton, Cowper, Burke, Macaulay,—expressly with a view to this subject, I have been surprised to note how often, when struggling to give emphasis to their thought, or to inten-

---

[1] Such, indeed, is its comprehensiveness of meaning, and so various its susceptibility of application, that it perpetually tempts wit and humour (by no means always or generally with a profane intent) to resort to it for illustration, albeit the occasions on which its language comes so pat to the lips may often seem light and trivial. The religious mind, which regards the book as the book of God, may be somewhat scandalised (not without reason) by this too familiar use of it ; but it at all events bears testimony to the force, aptness, and plasticity of the language of Scripture. In reading some of our principal daily papers, during my preparation of these lectures, I have been much struck with the frequency with which the writers have quoted clauses or sentences of the Bible—its historic parallels or its proverbial wisdom—not lightly or irreverently or in mockery, but evidently as the most apt and expressive for the purpose.

sify a feebler expression of it, they have laid hold unconsciously, as it were, of Scripture phrase or metaphor.

In Bacon's Essays, in his " Novum Organum " and his " De Augmentis," one is perpetually struck with the felicity with which passages of Scripture are introduced, and, in the two last works, where one would little expect them. As to Shakespeare, no less than three works have been expressly written to trace the influence of the Bible on his genius and writings. The matchless energy[1] of Milton's diction in many parts of his prose writings is in no slight degree due to the use he has made of Scripture. In that lofty passage in the "Animadversions on the Remonstrant's Defence," conceived in the very spirit of the Hebrew poetry,—in which, pledging himself for his immortal Epic, he says, " And he that now for haste snatches up a plain ungarnished present as a thank - offering to Thee, may then perhaps take up a harp and sing Thee an elaborate song to generations,"—in that most splendid passage, some phrase or clause of the Scripture adds energy to almost every line. It is a wonderful mosaic indeed, but a mosaic still.

Carlyle's book on the French revolution—even were its defects as a history all that the most unfriendly critic would make them out to be—will be confessed by all to be one of the most graphic in our own or any other language. Now it is curious to see how often, in describing the scenes of his tremendous " Trilogy

---

[1] In this quality of style, many single passages of Milton's prose writings are unrivalled in English literature. In spite of his long involved periods, which, though Coleridge might admire them for their " majestic march and complex harmony," are certainly a solecism in our language, and in spite of his pedantic coinage of Latinized words, which made Hobbes profanely call his style " a Babylonish jargon," he has often risen to an energy which is only to be paralleled in Demosthenes—or the Bible. Redundant as are his Latinisms, he had an absolute mastery of the raciest and most sinewy Saxon English. It has been said of Shakespeare that had he not been the Prince of Dramatists, he might have been the Prince of Orators. Perhaps it might be said of Milton with equal justice, that if he had not rivalled Homer, he might, if he had cultivated his oratorical powers, not have fallen far short of Demosthenes ; at all events, in energy.

of Tragedies," fragments of Scripture language come unbidden to his pen, as the best and most forcible he can employ. In reperusing the work recently, for the very purpose of ascertaining the degree in which phrases are interwoven, and examples and illustrations cited, from the Bible, I could not help being struck with their frequency. In truth, however, it is no wonder; for it is not possible to imagine any phraseology more exactly adapted to express the lurid sublimity, or point the terrible moral, of the scenes he describes, than that which the " Law and the Prophets " often launch against communities that have " sown the wind, and shall reap the whirlwind;" that, being incurably corrupt, are threatened with being " swept away with the besom of destruction ;" and yet, deaf to warning and chastisement, persist in " treasuring up wrath against the day of wrath." There is no book in the world in which the inevitable doom which waits on guilt, let its seeming security be what it may, is so vividly set forth as in the Bible ; none that so energetically proclaims that " thrones are established only in righteousness," and that nothing else can permanently " exalt a nation."

" There never was," says Carlyle somewhere,—or to this effect, for I quote from memory,—" any book like the Bible, and there never will be such another."—" Read to me," said the dying Scott to his son-in-law. " What book shall I read to you ?" said Lockhart. " Can you ask me ?" Scott replied. " There is but *one;*" and bade him read a chapter in the Gospel of John. " This collection of books," says Theodore Parker, in a passage of great eloquence, " has taken such hold of the world as no other. The literature of Greece, which goes up like incense from that land of temples and heroic deeds, has not half the influence of this book from a nation despised alike in ancient and in modern times. . . . It goes equally to the cottage of the plain man and the palace of the king. It is woven into the literature of the scholar, and colours the talk of the streets. It enters men's closets, mingles in all the grief and cheerfulness of life.   The Bible attends men in sickness, when the fever of the world is on them. . . . It is the better part of our sermons; it lifts man above himself.   Our best of uttered prayers are in its storied speech, wherewith our fathers and the patriarchs prayed.   The timid man, about to wake from his dream of life, looks through the glass of Scripture, and his eye grows bright; he does not fear to stand alone, to tread the way unknown and distant, to take the death angel by the hand, and bid farewell to wife and babes and home. . . . Some thousand famous writers come up in this century to be forgotten in the next.   But the silver cord of the Bible is not loosed, nor its golden bowl broken, as Time chronicles his tens of centuries passed by." [1]

[1] The following striking admissions of Professor Huxley, which I read with equal surprise and pleasure, as to the marvellous qualities of the Bible, show what impressions it is capable of making on a candid mind, however sceptical of its Divine origin; and many similar testimonies might be added to his.   But surely all who think with him ought to enter deeply into the question—*Whence* had this one volume this singular, and altogether exceptional ascendency, over the human mind?   "I have always," says Professor Huxley, "been strongly in favour of secular education, in the sense of education without theology; but I must confess I have been no less seriously perplexed to know by what practical measures the religious feeling, which is the essential basis of conduct, was to be kept up, in the present utterly chaotic state of opinion on these matters, without the use of the Bible.   The pagan moralists lack life and colour, and even the noble Stoic, Marcus Antoninus, is too high and refined for an ordinary child.   Take the Bible as a whole; make the severest deductions which fair criticism can dictate for shortcomings and positive errors; eliminate, as a sensible lay teacher would do, if left to himself, all that it is not desirable for children to occupy themselves with; and there still remains in this old literature a vast residuum of moral beauty and grandeur.   And then consider the great historical fact that, for three centuries, this book has been woven into the life of all that is best and noblest in English history; that it has become the national epic of Britain, and is familiar to noble and simple, from John o' Groat's house to Land's End, as Dante and Tasso were once to the Italians; that it is written in the noblest and purest English, and abounds in exquisite beauties of a merely literary form; and, finally, that it forbids the veriest hind who never left his village to be ignorant of the existence of other countries and other civilizations, and of a great past, stretching back

To these testimonies it were easy to add many more—some of them from men wholly sceptical as to any superhuman claims of the Bible on our reverence or belief.   I am far from charging them with any insincerity, either in what they admit or in what they deny ; but I would fain ask, What must be the qualities of the Bible, coming " from a nation alike despised in ancient and modern times," and whence did it get them, that could prevail on men like these,—men of capacious minds, the acutest reason, adorned with all that culture and taste could bestow,—to speak of the Bible in terms they never would dream of applying to any other book or books whatsoever ?

I would not be misunderstood.   I can easily fancy the derisive smile with which those who will not be at the trouble of con-

to the furthest limits of the oldest nations in the world. By the study of what other book could children be so much humanized, and made to feel that each figure in that vast historical procession fills, like themselves, but a momentary space in the interval between two eternities ; and earns the blessings or the curses of all time, according to its efforts to do good and hate evil, even as they also are earning their payment for their work ?

" And if Bible reading is not accompanied by constraint and solemnity, as if it were a sacramental operation, I do not believe there is anything in which children take more pleasure. At least, I know that some of the pleasantest recollections of my childhood are connected with the voluntary study of an ancient Bible which belonged to my grandmother. There were splendid pictures in it, to be sure ; but I recollect little or nothing about them, save a portrait of the high priest in his vestments. What comes vividly back on my mind are remembrances of my delight in the histories of Joseph and of David ; and of my keen appreciation of the chivalrous kindness of Abraham in his dealings with Lot. Like a sudden flash there returns back upon me my utter scorn of the pettifogging meanness of Jacob, and my sympathetic grief over the heartbreaking lamentation of the cheated Esau, ' Hast thou not a blessing for me also, O my father?' And I see, as in a cloud, pictures of the grand phantasmagoria of the book of Revelation.

" I enumerate, as they issue, the childish impressions which come crowding out of the pigeon-holes in my brain, in which they have lain almost un-disturbed for forty years. I prize them as an evidence that a child of five or six years old, left to his own devices, may be deeply interested in the Bible, and draw sound moral sustenance from it."—*Contemporary Review*, Dec. 1870 (pp. 14, 15).

sidering what degree of importance is attributable to each variable element in a complex argument like the present, may say: "This writer seems to think that because great authors have used the Bible for purposes of illustration more frequently than other books; because it has, no doubt, deeply tinctured the literature of the ages and nations familiar with it, that *therefore* it must be inspired, and of supernatural origin!" Not so. I mention the fact merely as one of the "thousand and one" paradoxical facts insisted upon in these lectures. It *is*, I think, a strange thing, that one moderately-sized book (if it be no more than the hypothesis of a purely human, and that a Jewish, origin assumes it to be) should have left wider and deeper traces of itself on modern literature than any dozen of the *chef-d'œuvres* of human genius which grace that literature, and pre-eminently on many of those *chef-d'œuvres* themselves. Surely it is a curious phenomenon; but it is only one of many which beset us in considering the peculiarities and the exceptional character and fortunes of this singular volume.

Should it be said again, "All this is accounted for by the *reverence* which it has somehow inspired;" in part, I grant it. But on the hypothesis I am proceeding upon, the purely *human*, and that, too, the *Jewish*-human, origin of the book, whence this profound reverence? How should the book have inspired it, and why should the world feel it? Either the Bible is invested with the properties which give it this pre-eminence, or it is not. If it is, whence, considering its source, did it get them? If not, how came the world to invest it with them?

I say then it is *curious* that, supposing the book to be the unaided product of man, far less endowed by nature than many writers of Greece, Rome, France, England, or Germany, and inferior in culture and education, it should have exerted greater influence, and left deeper traces on literature than any one, or any five, or any ten writers of all these countries put together. It is a *curious* phenomenon; curious, I say;—not a proof that the Bible may not be purely human, but one of the many paradoxes which, on that hypothesis, compel us to ask, as the Jews concerning Christ, " Whence hath this book all this wisdom ? "

4. Similar observations, with similar cautions as to the precise argumentative value attached to it, will apply to the inordinate influence of this book, as compared with any other, on the imaginations of men,—especially as seen in poetry, sculpture, painting, and music. Though genius has had all the resources of Greek and Roman story to resort to (and has profusely used them), to say nothing of that far ampler field which the annals of the last eighteen centuries have opened to it, no cycle of incidents and events, equally limited with that of the Bible, has stimulated genius in anything approaching the degree in which the scenes of the Bible have stimulated it. Every event of any importance in its records has been again and again the theme of painting or music. The greatest masters in each of these arts seem never weary of embodying ideas which have been thus suggested to them. The inimitable word-painting of Scripture, its graphic narratives, its poetry and pathos, seem an in-exhaustible fount of inspiration to the painter; while every group of events of importance has been made the subject of some great oratorio, on which Handel, Haydn, Mozart, Beethoven, and Mendelssohn have lavished all the gifts of their genius. Not only has this book been resorted to more *frequently* than any other book, as furnishing themes to pictorial, poetical, and musical genius; but, in general, the *chef-d'œuvres* of modern art are those which this book has inspired. The greatest paintings of Raphael and Michael Angelo are to be traced to it ; the greatest modern epic, the only one that is worthy to be compared with those of Homer and Virgil, and the greatest musical creation by many degrees—the " Messiah "—both have for their theme the great theme of the Bible. Which work of the two is the greater effort of genius it is hard to say. They are so akin, that whether Milton be called the Handel of poetry, or Handel the Milton of music, little matters. But each, supreme in his

own art, has identified his genius with the Bible, and drawn his inspiration from it.

Now, this class of facts again constitutes a curious phenomenon (I mention it as no more), one of the many which swarm about the Bible ; — which either must have properties which will account for them all, and if so, suggests the question how it came by them? or if it have them not, suggests another, why mankind should have been so infatuated as to surround it with this halo of glory, and allow it thus "in all things to have the pre-eminence"?

5. Proceeding on the same supposition of the purely human origin of the Scriptures, I think it might fairly have been anticipated that in some ages of the world, and especially within the last eighteen hundred years (during which the human mind has made such prodigious progress and exhibited such intense activity), some quasi-*sacred* books, or *other* works of human genius, would have been produced, which might in general estimate have vied with the Bible, if not supplanted it ; and which, in the various influence they exerted, and the enthusiasm for their diffusion which they voked, might have had a history in some faint degree like that of the Bible, as proved in the *facts* already pointed out. Yet nothing of the kind is seen; the Bible still has an exceptional destiny. Its superiority to other quasi-sacred books is universally admitted by those who can make the comparison, even though they reject its peculiar claims. Nor are there, among the immense variety of theological works which itself has created (hundreds of them the fruit of the richest genius and the most various learning), any that have concentrated upon themselves a tithe of the interest which mankind (with strange servility, if all stand on the same level of a purely human origin) have attached to this one volume. Amidst all the schools of religious thought, and the manifold types of religious character it has itself originated, we search in vain for any author, though it be a Luther or a Bossuet, a Pascal or a Butler, whose pretensions (and *least of*

all in the estimate of the authors themselves) can be placed on a par with those of the Bible, or whose works have provoked anything like the same interest or a similar solicitude for their preservation and diffusion. To the illustration of this subject, and some others related to it, I propose to devote a page or two.

As to the superiority of the Bible to all the so-called *sacred* books, I need not insist; all with whom I am arguing would at once grant their intrinsic inferiority. They would admit that the Bible, in its views of the Deity, in its spiritual elevation, in its moral wisdom, in the grace of its narrative, in sublimity and force of imagery, diction, and style, transcends them all. But there is one of them, perhaps, which may be supposed to demand a few words more: I mean the Koran. It is the most celebrated, and perhaps the most widely diffused among the nations, of these so-called sacred books. Its author had all the advantages of some acquaintance with the Bible, which he assumed to contain a true revelation. He freely borrowed from its matter, and seems to have closely imitated its style. Yet the difference is immense. It is not, perhaps, easy, and certainly not necessary, to determine the character of the Arabian prophet; whether he was a fanatic or an impostor, or first one and then the other, or even at times both together. This is of no consequence to the argument; of his great powers none can doubt.

Now one would imagine there ought not to be so great a contrast between the Bible and the Koran, if each was the mere composition of unassisted human genius. Nay, one would even think that the advantage would have been, in some signal respects, on the side of the later work. If the one was the production of many minds, of very unequal power, writing without concert (as they must, for ages separate them), one would suppose the advantage, in point of unity of character and continuous elevation, would be with that book which was the effusion of one master mind. As such, it might have been expected to be marked by many qualities which could not belong to the varying and casual productions of the authors of the Bible. Yet, though Mahomet had this model to work by, was able to borrow its light and avoid its presumed errors, this new product of religious genius is immeasurably below the old. The doctrines, indeed, so far as they are coincident with those of the Bible,—the doctrines which declare the unity and attributes of the Supreme Being, and affirm His universal government of the world,—are excellent. But then, if they be not plagiarisms from the Bible, the Bible, *ex confesso*, had pre-occupied the ground, and expressed the same thoughts incomparably better; and where the imitation of the Bible is palpable, the inferiority to it is equally so. A candid reader can in some measure put the matter to the test by comparing the sublimest passages from the *best* translation of the Koran with corresponding passages—I will not say from the best—but from *any* translation of the Bible.

If there be anything in the Koran capable of being confronted with what may be found in the Bible, one would imagine, from the frequency and applause with which it has been cited, it would be the following : " God ! there is no God but He ; the living, the self-subsisting ; neither slumber nor sleep seizeth Him ; to Him belong all, whatsoever is in heaven and on the earth. Who is he that can intercede with Him, but through His good pleasure ? He knoweth that which is past, and that which is to come. His throne is extended over heaven and earth, and the preservation of both is to Him no burden. He is the high, the mighty."—Yet any one can see that this is little more than a *cento* of Scripture phrases[1] strung together, and that not very coherently ; for it is not easy to perceive the relevancy of the question in the fifth clause to the rest, while the whole falls far below many passages of Scripture in energy and majesty of expression. It has been so often cited, however, that one cannot help feeling that such passages in the Koran must be

[1] Compare Isaiah xliii. 10 ; xliv. 6 ; xlv. 5-12 ; Psalm cxxi.

rather rare,—as indeed they are. It figures in White's Bampton Lectures, is repeated in Möhler, is cited from him by Castenove in his article on Mahomedanism,[1] and is one of the three passages of the Koran which Gibbon has thought it worth while to signalise by his encomium.

But it would be futile to dwell longer on this subject. Probably none but a Mahometan would challenge any comparison of merit between the Koran and the Bible, in respect of either *matter* or *manner*. Even those who think both to be equally the product of human genius, would as little hesitate to affirm the superiority of the latter as the most devout Christian ; and in manner no less than matter. Every one knows, of course, that the *plenary proof* of the inspiration of the Koran,—a proof to which Mahomet himself appealed,—is said to be its incomparable style ; in fact, in the lack of all other miracles, and in reply to the demand for them on the part of the "faithless" among the "faithful," Mahomet affirmed that this was in itself a " miracle."

"This argument," says Gibbon, with eloquent irony, "is most powerfully addressed to a devout Arabian, whose mind is attuned to faith and rapture, whose ear is delighted by the music of sounds, and whose ignorance is incapable of comparing the productions of human genius. The harmony and copiousness of style will not reach, in a version, the European infidel : he will peruse with impatience the endless incoherent rhapsody of fable, and precept, and declamation, which seldom excites a sentiment or an idea, which sometimes crawls in the dust, and is sometimes lost in the clouds. The Divine attributes exalt the fancy of the Arabian missionary, but his loftiest strains must yield to the sublime simplicity of the book of Job, composed in a remote age, in the same country, and in

---

[1] " We feel the justice," says Castenove, "of Möhler's dictum, 'That without Moses, and the prophets, and Christ, Mahomet is simply inconceivable—for the essential purport of the Koran is derived from the Old and New Testaments.'"—*Encyclopædia Britannica. Art. on Mahomedanism.*

the same language.   If the composition of the Koran exceed
the faculties of a man, to what superior intelligence should we
ascribe the Iliad of Homer, or the Philippics of Demosthenes?"[1]

If Mahomet had reflected how very questionable *that* test
of a *universal* revelation must be, which only an Arabian can
fully understand and appreciate, he would, perhaps, have laid
less stress upon it.   Surely it were better that the subject-matter
and contents of the volume should attest its Divinity, than the
language in which these are expressed.   It must be one of the
disadvantages of a *universal* revelation, to have the thought so
tied to the words, that the very *test* of its Divine origin, the
celestial aroma of its force and beauty, must exhale and vanish
when it is translated into another tongue.   Its chief excellences, in that case, are intransferrible.   It is certainly a much
more rational ground which the apologist for Scripture takes,
when he endeavours to show that, though its language is
admirably adapted to the subject-matter, yet it is so subordinated to it, that its merit is as nothing in the comparison ; and
that, *therefore,* the book is eminently fitted for transfusion into
every language with the smallest possible diminution of energy
or grace.   While the Mahometan affirms that none but an
accomplished Arabic scholar, or rather none but a born Arab
(for he alone is fully competent), can judge of those intransmis-
sible felicities of style which, to those who *can* discern them,
are, it seems, the best proofs of the inspiration of the Koran,
no Christian contends that the Hebrew is essential to the force
or beauty of the Old Testament (though some minor graces
may be better seen by those who are acquainted with the
original language), or that the Greek of the New Testament,—
its enemies themselves being judges,—at all approximates to
the classic elegances of Sophocles or Plato.   As a universal
revelation, the Koran would have more to say for its pretensions
if it readily fell into the idiomatic forms of any language
whatsoever ; it would be the better in proportion as it lost *little,*

Gibbon's Decline and Fall.   Chap. 50.

not *much*, of its force or beauty in the process. As the matter stands, the evidence, *par excellence*, which is to prove its Divine origin, which is even to take the place of all "miracles," is that very incommunicable excellence of which a foreigner cannot judge ; and which therefore must, *ipso facto*, prevent the great bulk of those for whom it was designed from comprehending its chief claim to inspiration !

But let the mysterious merit of the Arabic be what it may, the world in general is obliged to submit Koran and Bible to the equal test of translation ; and judged by that, the interval is seen to be enormous, even if we take the *worst* English translation of the Bible and the *best* English translation of the Koran.

But I repeat that, on the supposition that both are on the same level, as products of mere human intelligence, it is hard to say why there should have been either so great an intrinsic difference, or that it should appear so great in the translation.

The facts of the history of both correspond. The Koran has not, like the Bible, been spontaneously sent to the most various races and nationalities,—differing by every conceivable diversity of religion, customs, laws, and language,—or been spontaneously received by them. It has, indeed, gone wherever the sword went before it ; and any book would go where so potent a missionary led the way. It has not, like the Bible, prompted to ceaseless efforts to translate, to multiply, to diffuse it. Some of the principal translations of it have been made by Christian scholars ; and even including these, it probably does not speak a tenth part of the languages in which the Bible speaks.

There is one point, indeed, in which there can be no comparison between them, but it serves to make the position of the Bible more singular. The Koran has never been subjected to the ordeal of hostile criticism among its own votaries to which the Bible has been subjected, nor seen growing up about it that enormous harvest of general literature which can only be produced on the soil of freedom. We cannot, therefore, judge how it would have fared under such conditions; whether something might not have appeared to rival, supplant,—or destroy it. The Bible has stood this test. It may be said indeed of both, that the reputation of *quasi*-sacred books has been their protection. This may in part be true; but if the Bible be a book only *quasi*-sacred, if it be really only human, it would not seem unlikely that, amidst the freest examination of its claims, and full liberty to accept or reject it, something might have appeared in the immense and varied literature of so many centuries which would, by self-evident equality or superiority, have tended to dissipate this illusion,—especially when aided by the multitudinous books which, during so many ages, and in the very communities among which it has been received, have been written expressly to show the world that this exceptional reverence for the Bible *is* an illusion. The thing is still more remarkable when we consider how various are the schools of thought and types of religious character reflected in the literature produced by it; showing us that, whatever the reverence for the Bible, it has not destroyed the independence of the human mind, nor prevented the natural growth and expression of the most diversified modes of thought.

6. Nevertheless, in all this immense succession and variety of literature, we cannot find any books which, in the estimate of men in general, or perhaps in the estimate of the fondest admirers of the authors themselves, will admit of comparison with the Bible.

As to the *Hebrew* Scriptures, no other writings of Jews, ancient or modern, come near them. *That* is equally affirmed by Jew and Gentile. As I have already remarked, it is curious that a single volume should contain almost all the extant *ancient* literature of the Jewish nation; and that so exceptionally superior to all their other productions, whether ancient or modern, that the nation not only acquiesces in its superiority,

but venerates it as sacred and inspired. It does not diminish
the singularity that the popular tendencies of the nation were in
perpetual revolt against the doctrines and institutions which
it was the chief object of this book to maintain. Thus the
chief literature they possess, instead of reflecting (as is usually
the case) the spirit of the people, was for the most part diametrically opposed to it. When that spirit (which had warped
the Old Testament, just as Christians afterwards warped the
New) embodied itself in a literature of its own, we see what it
produced: wide indeed is the interval between the Scriptures
and the Talmud. A strenuous attempt, it is true, has been
made in recent times to rescue the Talmud from neglect and
contempt. But it is in vain. That a work of so many folios
(even if it were put together by the dullest compilers) must
contain many passages of force and beauty, may be admitted.
A few of those passages are so similar to parallel passages of
the Gospels, as to suggest the idea of being plagiarisms, or, at
all events, imitations, though of inferior workmanship. It has
been pretty well proved that the date of the Gospels must have
been prior to the compilation of the traditions of the Talmud;
but even if this were more doubtful than it is, one has but to
compare the rare flowerets in question with the general products
of the soil, to feel that they are not indigenous; that foreign as
they are to the whole tone and spirit of the genuine genius of
Rabbinism, they are either the reflection of some parallel passages from the Old Testament, or borrowed from the New.
If such passages be abstracted, it is impossible to imagine a
more arid desert of words than the bulk of the Talmud; and
even if they be admitted to be genuine, they are in such
infinitesimal ratio to the mountain-loads of superstitious folly
and fable, that it is still impossible to imagine how people that
could only compile Talmuds could ever have composed the
Old Testament. But at all events, even the Jews themselves
loudly proclaim the immense chasm between them.

If, again, we take any of the genuine and undoubted remains

of the Apostolic Fathers, one is absolutely struck dumb with the difference between them and the New Testament. As immediate disciples of the apostles, we might have expected that they would in some degree have approached the level of their teachers; and in their *moral* excellences they seem no unworthy disciples. The remains of Clement and Polycarp, and such fragments of Ignatius as criticism pronounces to be undoubtedly genuine, exhibit traits of Christian piety, simplicity, and sincerity, which reflect no dishonour on the religion the authors had embraced. But in everything else, in force and weight of thought, sentiment, and diction, infinite is the difference if we compare even these, the best of the Apostolic Fathers, with the writers of the New Testament. As I have elsewhere expressed it, "the Alps amidst the flats of Holland could not exhibit a greater contrast than we find between the writers of the New Testament and these Fathers."

Observations to the like purport, though for different reasons, apply to the Fathers of the second, third, and fourth centuries. It is no slight portion of their remains which has come down to us, though probably as much more has perished. More than a hundred times the bulk of the entire Bible itself has been saved from the wreck. Many of these Fathers were very extraordinary men; masters of all the erudition of their age, and gifted with great natural genius. Chrysostom, Augustine, Origen, Tertullian, and Jerome, will bear comparison, in natural and acquired endowments, with any men of their time, and with most men of any time. Their intellectual character, especially of these five (though, as usual, very various if we compare them with one another), is favourably contrasted with the mediocrity of mental power which is found in the Apostolic Fathers. Yet no reader of any discernment will affirm that there is any fear of their rivalling, much more eclipsing, the Bible. They are not to be compared with it either in the force or accuracy with which they express religious truth. Their eloquence indeed is often great, but their style is as distinct as possible from that of the Bible, and as plainly inferior to it. It is of a cast far removed from the severe simplicity, the force, the compression and brevity, which so largely characterise the Scriptures. The style is sometimes dry and barren as a profitless dialectic subtilty can make it, and, more often, ornate and florid as can be found in the worst specimens of Oriental rhetoric. But if they are inferior to the Scriptures in *expression*, they are still more so in *matter*. In the third century, that transforming power of human nature on primitive Christianity, of which I have already spoken, had plainly manifested itself. Christianity, brought into contact with human preconceptions and tendencies, was moulded and warped by them in various ways, and showed in this transfiguration what is the natural bent and ply of man's nature; for he therein followed the law which had ruled in the formation of religions which undoubtedly bear his "image and superscription." In reading the later Fathers, in spite of all their excellences, we cannot help feeling that we have got into a different atmosphere of religious thought and feeling from that of the Bible : breathe, as it were, the air of a hot-house, and gaze on exotic productions. In the exaggeration or mutilation of some Scripture doctrines, in the suppression or neglect of others, in the fanatical thirst for martyrdom, in the superstitious honours given to celibacy, in the excessive value attached to austerities and ceremonial, in the passion for allegorical inter-pretation, in the childish multiplication of grotesque marvels and the enormous credulity with which they were received, in the doting homage paid to shrines and relics ;—in one or other of these ways—the Fathers of the third century—and still more those of the fourth, show us how materially they had deranged the system which the New Testament delivers to us, and inno-vated on its spirit and doctrines.

To those who believe that the Bible is a divinely inspired volume, there is of course no difficulty in accounting for all this. They would naturally expect, on the one hand, that it would exhibit a perpetual superiority in its form and contents to those of mere human productions; on the other (in conformity, as they would say, with its own express *predictions*), that its system would probably be deteriorated, like so many other excellent gifts of God, when it came into contact with human nature, and was interpreted by its prejudices and passions. As the light of heaven is refracted and obscured when it enters into the atmosphere of earth, so (they would say) were the rays of celestial truth distorted and dimmed when they came into the sphere of the human intellect. Raw converts from gross superstitions or false philosophies would attempt, as they naturally did, to reconcile Christian truth with antecedent theories or inveterate prejudices, rather than simply abandon them. It was this very thing that led even to the extremest forms of Gnostic error; they were but attempts to adjust the gospel to those dreams of Alexandrine metaphysics or oriental theosophy in which some of the early converts to Christianity had been nurtured, and to which they clung with perverse tenacity. In various degrees, and in infinite ways, the old entered into affinity with the new, and modified it accordingly. If any think this strange, the answer of the Christian apologist would be that it was inevitable, unless the laws of human nature had been themselves subverted by some inconceivable miracle, —a miracle multiplied, too, indefinitely, for it must have been as manifold as the erratic tendencies of the human mind itself. Further, these apologists would perhaps say that the phenomenon has been often repeated, and that two instructive reflections are suggested by it; first, that it is curious that the Scripture maintains its superiority to the various systems of religious belief which different schools of thought have founded on it, so that none rival and none supplant it; and, secondly, that their perpetual divergences from Scripture show how little likely human nature was to frame such a book, and in what directions it naturally gravitates.

This representation of the apologists of Scripture may be just; I believe, indeed, that it is so; but into that I do not

enter.   I merely note the fact (universally admitted, and by the
Fathers themselves as readily as by any), that the Bible far
transcends them, both in matter and manner ; a conclusion
which even those who think they have only *developed*, and not
depraved, the Scriptures, also affirm with one voice.   These
say, with the rest of the world, that the Fathers have left
nothing which can be put on a par with it.   It may not be so
easy to say, on the hypothesis that they and the Biblical writers
are simply and equally human, why they should not.

But the practice of the world is in harmony with its judgment.
Of the hundred tomes of which patristic literature consists (all
evoked by the Bible), only a small portion is ever read, and
that chiefly by those who have a professional interest in it.
The greater part is consigned to oblivion ; not the hundredth
part has had even a thousandth part of the readers of the Bible.
The books take their chance with all other literature ; if they
perish, they perish, and no man seeks to lay an arrest on the
judgment; there is no *furore* to guard, to diffuse, to propagate
them ; though, on account of their *connection* with the Bible,
there has perhaps been more solicitude to preserve them than
has been displayed about the generality of ordinary authors.

The accuracy of the judgment is confirmed by the testimony
of many who do not receive the Bible as other than a purely
human production, for they would be very slow to bestow on
the Fathers the eulogiums they have not hesitated to lavish
on the Bible.

Similar observations may be made on the incontestable
supremacy conceded to the Bible over those modern schools
of theological writers, with their many forms of religious
thought, to which it has given birth.   Whatever eccentricities
the human intellect may exhibit in dealing with it (in virtue of
the tendencies of human nature to which I have so often adverted), or whatever divergences it may wander into, the pre-
eminence of the Bible is still granted.   If we take the period
of the Reformation, or that which immediately followed it, we

see illustrations of this. These periods are all the more striking, as there was an unusual amount of newly awakened intellectual activity exerted in the direction of theology; and never, probably, since the times of the apostles, has there been a more profound and earnest spirit of religion than was then awakened. One might have expected, in this disentombment of the human mind, that men, in studying the Bible, would have been disenchanted of their mere prejudices (for such they were, on the hypothesis on which I am now arguing) in its favour; that, reading it with fresh eyes, they would have detected, among so many other ancient illusions then laid bare, this illusion among the rest; and justified the judgment by giving the world works which, if they could not supplant, might at least rival the Bible. Yet it is impossible to consider the characteristics of even Luther and his contemporaries, or the schools of religious thought to which they gave rise, without feeling what Luther and his contemporaries unanimously affirmed,—the superiority of the Bible to them all.

Take, again, the Puritan writers. All candid minds will be impressed with the profound religious character of the more eminent among these men; none ever studied the Bible more intensely, or made it more perpetually their model. Yet it is impossible to read even the best and greatest of them without feeling, as in the case of the Fathers, that they have fallen infinitely below that model, both in matter and in manner; in the ideal of religious character they deduced from it, and the style in which they expressed religious truth. And, therefore, however impressed with the religious elevation and the wonderful fertility of thought which distinguished many of the greatest of these men, we cannot turn from the Bible to them without feeling that we are descending to a lower plane. Some of its doctrines they distort or exaggerate, and hence their unsymmetrical theology — a theology here stunted, there unnaturally developed. Large classes of them cherished disproportionate zeal for the Old Testament, without sufficiently considering how far the New Testament had avowedly abrogated it. This and other causes (among which, doubtless, must be reckoned the sombre circumstances of their own life, and the shadow which persecution threw upon it) generated a cast of religion which, however sincere and devout, was marked by a gloom and austerity, not to say grimace, which have no counterpart in the serene and cheerful spirit of apostolic Christianity, even when, as in the case of Paul, men were exposed to the most depressing influences, and might be said, like him, to "die daily."

But what can adequately express the difference between their *style* and that of the Bible? Homely as the latter often is,—as it *must* be, if it be the book for all men and for all time,—yet how free from the vulgarity of conception and expression, the wearisome prolixity, the metaphysical subtlety, the pedantic quaintness, the endless divisions, the word-splitting and common-place too often chargeable on these excellent men. In the gross familiarity, again, with which they too often treat the most solemn themes, one is astounded that they have not more successfully learned the lessons of the book which they so devoutly studied. It is a manner often grotesquely contrasted both with the austerity of their outward life and the severity of their theology. Not rarely, quips and puns, and every kind of quaintness and unseemly paronomasia, light up their sombre page, like a ghastly smile. In these and various other points we see at how great a distance these writers stand from their model. Yet many of them were men of the amplest powers, with a fertility of imagination and extent of learning very far beyond anything the generality of the writers of the Bible (according to the hypothesis I am combating) could make the smallest pretensions to. In the writings of men like Fuller, Bishop Hall, Adams, or Trapp (and many more might be added), eccentric as is their manner, intolerable as is their quaintness, there is more of original illustration,—more new thoughts, more novel applications of old thoughts, more sudden turns of fancy and unexpected applications of learning,—than can be found in hundreds of volumes written by ordinary men.[1]

Similar remarks apply to the greatest names of that or of the next age—to the " Dii majores " of English theology—to such men as Barrow, Jeremy Taylor, Howe, Leighton. Though distinguished by great genius and erudition, they still none of them originate anything which leaves the superiority of the Bible (to which they all pay homage) in peril. They are content to sit at its feet, and learn, but declare that they cannot approach it. This is the fountain-head that supplies all these conduits, and the water in them cannot rise above its level. If it be asked : " Who affirm this ? " I answer, men in general, but chiefly the men themselves; for thus they speak both of themselves and of one another. They, with one voice, proclaim the justness of the world's verdict. As it was said of Christ, " Never man spake like this man ;" so they say of this book, that never book was written like it. But why this should be so, considering the lofty endowments of so many of these sons of genius ; why the world in general should acquiesce in such a judgment, and why these men should, with such humility, not only admit, but loudly affirm its justice, is, I confess, to me a puzzle, on the supposition I am now arguing upon,—namely, that the writers of the Bible had no more than the ordinary endowments of men, and less, certainly, than those of many of *these* men.

Take, again, the best of the imaginative works which have been founded on the Bible ; for example, Bunyan's " Pilgrim's Progress," and which I the rather name, because in all probability the original position of its author was not very much below that of some of the men who record the life of Christ.

---

[1] Of Fuller, Coleridge was wont to say, that next to Shakespeare, he was not quite sure that Fuller did not most impress him with wonder and admiration at the perfection in which certain faculties were possessed in comparison with the like qualities in other men. Nothing ever seemed to enter the mind of Fuller that he could not immediately digest into aliment of the imagination.

Born in humble life, with little education beyond what he
bestowed on himself, with abundance of mother wit, but
with little culture of intellect, Bunyan may bear some comparison with those humble Jews whose Memoirs of Christ have
from that time to this kept the world in perpetual wonder; who
in a few brief pages (all of them together not half the bulk of
the "Pilgrim's Progress") have been able to fix on themselves,
or rather upon their Master, the continued gaze of the world.

No one can more ardently admire than I do that work of
the inspired tinker, which makes an equal impression on age
and childhood, on the learned and the unlearned; that book,
ignorance of which, in Bishop Percy's little child, made Dr.
Johnson put her from off his knee in splenetic contempt for her
stupidity or incuriosity.[1] Its merits must indeed be great,
when such different men as Macaulay and Southey—each with
strong, though different reasons for being prejudiced against
Bunyan, if his genius had not vanquished them all—vie with
each other in the language of eulogium. But if we compare
even this book with any one of the Gospels, everybody will
justify the world in the very different place it assigns them.
Transcendent as was the imagination which gave birth to many
portions of Bunyan's allegory; full as it is, in parts, of sublimity
and pathos, and especially in those concluding pages which
Dr. Arnold said he could never read without tears; yet, in the
first place, there is not an idea, not a sentiment of more than
common interest in it, that is not, directly or indirectly, derived
from the Bible. That book *made* Bunyan; first evoked, then
perpetually nourished his genius; supplied the continual
aliment of his thoughts, and entered both into the "web and
woof," the entire tissue, of his immortal allegory. Yet none
will challenge equality with those Gospels which have given

---

[1] " Not read the ' Pilgrim's Progress !'—then I would not give a farthing
for you."—*Boswell's Johnson*. A summary conviction, no doubt, of the
surly old critic ; but marking his sense, at all events (however unamiable
his mode of showing it), of the wonderful attractions of the book.

him nearly all his materials.   And then how superior are they to his defects !   With all his wonderful merits, how often does he drop plumb down into the merest vulgarity and common-place ! Quaint and ingenious as some of his coarser scenes may be, we cannot imagine them forming a part of any one of the Gospels, without the strongest sense of incongruity.   The effect would be as grotesque as a Dutch painter's essay to remodel a painting of Raphael.

In brief, the position the Bible has occupied, and still occupies,—amidst such various circumstances and through such distant ages, amidst such fluctuations of taste and revolutions of literature,—is a unique phenomenon.

It is not unworthy of remark that while the Bible thus retains its pre-eminent position in successive cycles of literature, multitudes of works of high merit, to which itself has directly given birth, often pass into comparative oblivion in a few generations. The world, perhaps, would not "willingly let them die," if the ceaseless flood of new and equally excellent literature did not overwhelm them.   No zealous efforts, however, are made to perpetuate their memory, to multiply, to translate, to diffuse them.   With all their merits, they are left to the usual fortune of all other literature ; to keep afloat on the waters if they can, and to sink beneath them if they cannot.

The book which has given them all their ephemeral renown seems alone untouched by time.   It is like some old oak which has seen the harvest of a thousand years spring, ripen, and fall beneath the sickle.

It is in vain to say, " We have many instances of so-called 'sacred books' regarded with extravagant admiration and reverence by this or that particular nation in a low stage of civilisation, or by the mass of ignorant people among them."   I have already replied in brief to this evasion.   But, to anticipate once for all any such mock analogies, I would remark that, to find a parallel to the case of the Bible, we must see a collection of many writings—all written by one of the most obscure and despised nations—spontaneously accepted as a unique repository of Divine and moral wisdom, not by one tribe or nation only, but among many, and these of the most diverse races, of every conceivable variety in local position, historic origin, religious belief, tradition and language ;—not during a period of barbarism only, but in ages of the greatest knowledge, learning, and refinement ;—not by the vulgar and ignorant only among these various nations and races, but by multitudes of the loftiest and most accomplished minds ;—not by such as are led by tradition merely, and who give an otiose assent accordingly, but by men who have come to their convictions after the most sifting scrutiny as to the evidence of that which has thus enthralled them ;— not where error is so consecrated by law, and so fenced from all opposition, that nothing can be said against it, but where hostile criticism has had full liberty to do its worst.

When I find *other* sacred books, of which the same can be truly said, I shall admit the force of the above objection, and withdraw this item of my argument.

LECTURE IX.

ON CERTAIN ANALOGIES BETWEEN THE BIBLE AND "THE CONSTITUTION AND COURSE OF NATURE."

LECTURE IX.

ON CERTAIN ANALOGIES BETWEEN THE BIBLE AND "THE
CONSTITUTION AND COURSE OF NATURE."

IF there are many peculiarities in the Bible which seem in
contrariety to what might be naturally expected of man,
there are also many peculiarities which seem in analogy with
the "works and ways of God;" and the concurrence of such
contrariety and analogy is not insignificant in this argument.

It has been generally and justly asserted that the chief use of
Analogy, and especially in relation to theology, is in the refutation of *objections;* and Butler's book shows what a powerful
solvent it is. But it is not without force on the *positive* side,
in proportion to the number, closeness, and subtlety of the
observed analogies.[1]

At first sight it may seem strange that an argument, the very
same in substance and direction, should appear to be so cogent
in one aspect, and so much less cogent, or even feeble, in
another. The reason is that, though the argument is the same
in itself in either case, it derives its principal force, as an
answer to objections, precisely from the objector's own *state of*

---

[1] In a passage, justly commended by Bishop Hampden, Dugald Stewart
observes : " I may be permitted to express my doubts whether both of these
ingenious writers (Reid and Campbell) have not somewhat underrated the
importance of analogy as a medium of proof and as a source of new information. I acknowledge, at the same time, that between the positive
and negative applications of this species of evidence there is an essential
difference. . . . . In some instances, however, the probability resulting
from a concurrence of different analogies may rise so high, as to produce an
effect on the belief scarcely distinguishable from moral certainty."

mind. So employed, it is strictly an *argumentum ad hominem.* An illustration or two will make this plain.

If it were contended that a man could *not* have written a certain letter, on account of some supposed *incompatibility* between its sentiment or expression, and some indications of the character of the writer otherwise known, then it would demonstrate the absolute futility of this conclusion if we could produce an undoubted letter of the same man, in which similar sentiments had been expressed, and in identical terms. On the other hand, if it were contended that the man *did* write the letter, merely because it was marked by modes of thought and expression which *harmonised* with what he was known to have thought and said, then the conclusion would at best be but probable, and in many cases precarious.

Similarly, if it were contended that a certain painting could *not* be by Raphael, from some supposed enormous incongruity of subject, or from the mode of treatment, then it would be sufficient to annul that objection, if we could produce a genuine work of that same artist to which the same objections might be made. But if it were argued that the work *was* a genuine painting of Raphael, because it had many characteristics of his style, then it would be but a probable conclusion, and in many cases open to much doubt.

Once more : if a being, happily ignorant of our own planet, and familiar only with worlds on which sin and sorrow had never cast their shadow, were to urge that a world *could not* be otherwise constituted under the government of omnipotent wisdom and love, he would be sadly, but irresistibly, refuted by visiting the earth, or receiving authentic accounts of its condition. He could not deny the *fact*, though it might be (as it undoubtedly is) an inexplicable difficulty that there should be such a world. On the other hand, if a philosopher were to argue (as many a philosopher has done), from the analogies among the members of our planetary system,—the physical resemblances observable amongst them,—that, since the earth

is inhabited, those other orbs, which roll round the same centre
of light and heat, must be inhabited also, the conclusion would
be but probable and precarious ; and, in fact, has been eagerly
disputed in one of the most ingeniously sustained and instructive controversies of our day.

Nevertheless, in this last case, could it be shown that a
second, a third, a fourth planet—and so of the rest, in proportion as they became known—were characterised by more and
more of the physical conditions which accompany life in our
world, then the argument, though still only founded on probabilities, would be strengthened at each step ; and, at last, in
spite of the great diversity of circumstances still subsisting
among the different orbs compared, might produce nearly the
conviction of a complete induction.   The argument, therefore,
would not be of little weight, though it could not possibly have
the absolute validity of Butler's " Analogy."   *That*, like the
first, third, and fifth cases given above by way of illustration, is
absolutely irrefragable.   It says in effect : " You deny that a
revelation can be true, because it contains such and such things
that could not be found in a book coming from God.   Survey
the world, which we both admit comes from Him.   See if the
same objections do not apply there, and whether God has not
done, or permitted to be done, the very things which you say
it is incredible that He should do or permit to be done, and for
which you reject this revelation."   He therefore shuts up his
opponents, so long as, like himself, they are theists, to one of
two courses—either to give up their theism, or to give up these
specific objections to Christianity ; and, therefore, as Butler
truly says—" Objections, which are *equally* applicable to both
natural and revealed religion, are, properly speaking, answered
by its being shown that they are so, *provided the former be
admitted to be true.*"

But now let us suppose that Butler has succeeded in showing
a man (as he happily has many) the futility of the objections
against which his argument is directed, does it follow that the

man must admit that Christianity is true? By no means, unless those objections be his sole objections. In that case, indeed, he has absolutely no logical alternative but to embrace Christianity or abandon his theism. And as, in thousands of cases, these are the *main* objections which stagger faith, so their removal has often happily issued in a surrender of the rest. But the chief force of the argument was no doubt spent in repelling the objections. The wind which may be irresistible while the ship meets it, may be hardly felt when she goes before it.

But is the argument of *no* force then in this case? This is not true either. The points of analogy between nature and a presumed revelation, between the professed word and the acknowledged works of God, may be numerous, varied, and subtle enough, to leave a very considerable impression on any candid mind, though no longer possessing that demonstrative force with which they may be used as an *argumentum ad hominem*. To this purpose — establishing a general similarity between nature and revelation, and a presumption of the identity of their origin—*all* the analogies on which Butler has insisted contribute their quota and have a legitimate influence. The resemblance in the characteristics of the Divine government, whether as exercised in relation to man's temporal interests or in relation to his moral probation; the seeming circuitousness of method by which the Divine wisdom attains its ends; the seeming inadequacy, or *a priori* unlikelihood, of the means employed; the *sort* of evidence on which man is called upon to act, whether as an inhabitant of this world or as a probationer for another; the obscurity or imperfection of that evidence in either case; the apparent inequality or partiality of the Divine administration; these, and many other considerations which suggest analogies between the "Constitution and Course of Nature" and "Divine Revelation," avail *pro tanto* on the positive side, as establishing *resemblance* between tne two,—though chiefly potent in refuting objections.

But as the force of the argument on this *positive* side depends on the number, variety, and concurrence of the "analogies," there are many others besides those insisted on by Butler, which, though it would have been irrelevant to dwell upon them in a work expressly constructed to neutralize objections, might be very properly added in any attempt fully to exhibit the positive side of the argument.[1]   On a few of these, I would now say a little.   It will, of course, be seen that I assume nothing as to the actual truth of the revelation.   I here reason only hypothetically.

I. *If* the Bible be what I have presumed to argue it,—if it be characterised by the unity which has been so generally ascribed to it,—then, in strong contrast with all the works of man, but in strong conformity with those of God, it is a very *gradual* development.   Man's plans are like himself; they must be circumscribed within very narrow limits, or they cannot be executed at all.   He must not count on distant ages, for he is an ephemeron.   To construct a machine, to excogitate a theory, to write half-a-dozen books, to fight twice as many battles, to found an empire or (which is more easy) to destroy one, is all that he can achieve.   His life in general is all too short even for *his* plans, and, limited as they may be, he cannot stay to finish them.   But if it be true, as it has been here argued, that this book is *one*, and yet the slow product of many and far distant ages; composed by writers neither conscious that they were co-operating, nor capable of it (which at all events is true, for centuries separated them); if it is embedded in the world's history, and forms part of it; if its disclosures are made piecemeal,—a fragment now and a fragment then,—and yet these constitute one whole, and are adjusted to one end ; then, though it neither is, nor conceivably could be, the work of man, it does

---

[1] Hampden, in his " Essay on the Philosophical Evidence of Christianity; or, the Credibility obtained to a Scriptural Revelation, from its coincidence with the facts of Nature," has successfully prosecuted a portion of this argument.

strikingly resemble the general manner of the works of God, in which we see results attained by slow evolution from the minutest beginnings, and by a prolonged application as well as stupendous complexity of means and instruments.

I shall not here insist on the proof that the supposed revelation *is* characterised by the features above mentioned, because that would be but to repeat the various arguments by which it has been attempted to establish the unity of the Bible. Whatever proves *that*, whatever tends to show that, though the writers be so various, and the times in which they lived so distant, yet that there is unity in the result; that the book possesses peculiarities of a unique character, which discriminate it from all human books; that it subordinates, in a way no other book ever did, everything to the claims of God, in relation to man and to the universe He has made and governs; that it develops from the beginning a plan for vindicating the Divine government and securing man's felicity; that it discloses this plan in minute fragments, in such a leisurely way, and by such gradual accessions of light, as to remind us of the process by which the day dawns or the bud opens;—in a word, whatever considerations (these and the many others before insisted upon) indicate the *unity* of the Bible, also show, *ipso facto*, that it has been, like the strata of the earth and the oak of the forest, marked by that slow continuous growth which is one of the signatures of the works of God.

His methods of procedure in general are notably impressed with the same characteristic. His plans work themselves out by the most deliberate processes, and long periods are required for tracing even a small segment of them. The index on the dial plate seems not to move at all, so slow and continuous is the motion. All this seems worthy of Him to whom a " thousand years are as one day, and one day as a thousand years ;" to whom Time, as we measure it, is nothing; who sees the future, present ; and the distant, near.

In every department of nature we see this note of the Divine

workmanship. Geologists tell us, and tell us with truth (however they may lose themselves in speculations as to the conjectural dates of their phenomena), of the enormous lapse of time
during which the earth has been slowly progressing to its present state ; of the immense periods required to condense it from
the condition of a fiery vapour into a solid sphere, to cool the
still glowing mass, and to give it, by revolution on its axis, like
a vessel on the potter's wheel, its present elliptical form ; of the
unknown ages, again, that passed before it assumed the condition which fitted it to be the abode of life, and during which
land and water seem often to have changed their seats ; and
of those other ages, equally unknown, during which it was pre-
paring, by successive forms of vegetable and animal life, for the
habitation of man.

But though it is in the phenomena of geology that we are most
forcibly struck with the inconceivably deliberate methods by
which the Divine Agent proceeds, we have but to open our
eyes to see that it is a general characteristic of all His workmanship and operations. He often *destroys*, indeed, in a
moment. The fierce fires of fever shall dissolve in a day the
wonderful fabric that has been slowly compacting for thirty
years, or a stroke of palsy shatter in a moment all the energies,
and with them all the schemes and activity, of the greatest of
human intellects ; the bolt of heaven shall shiver, in the
twinkling of an eye, the oak that has been growing for hundreds
of years, and an earthquake instantaneously reduce to ruin
cities that have outlived a millennium. But He brings things
into existence, and develops their powers and perfections after
a different method. The gradual continuous movement by
which the seasons change ; by which flowers and trees put
forth leaf and blossom ; by which the grain and fruit ripen ;
by which animals grow, from the minutest germs, to the perfection of their form, strength, and beauty ; all these are but
familiar examples of the same great law which pervades the
universe of God. The changes, however stupendous, are

effected by such imperceptible steps that they elude our observation. The oak is millions of times the bulk of the acorn, yet has it arrived at its majestic growth of many centuries by such infinitesimal increments, and by a law so strictly continuous, that no eye is keen enough to detect the advance from one stage to another.

It is by reference to this law of vegetable growth that our Lord illustrates the parallel law in the spiritual economy, and tells us that "the kingdom of God cometh not by observation," whether in the individual soul or in the history of mankind.

Similarly slow is the development of God's design in the government of the universe; of that final purpose of his providential administration which every devout theist must believe to be contemplated amidst all the fluctuations and apparent retrogradations of the world; and not only *in spite* of present distractions and confusion, but *by means* of them. All political changes, the rise and fall of races and empires,—in a word, all events,—each rational theist must believe are tending to some unknown result, some issue unspeakably glorious, though beyond our present comprehension. But if so, the movement is immeasurably slow. Man himself is "but of yesterday," though his race has existed for thousands of years; and probably only a small portion of his history,—and that seemingly strangely blurred and blotted,—has been yet written. For the *dénouement* we must wait. God's plan is so incomprehensibly vast, that partly from the contracted view which each generation, or even many generations, can take, and partly from the intricacy and complexity of the machinery by which the results are being wrought out, we can discern little or nothing of it as a whole. We must gain a knowledge of the designs of God (which, we are compelled to believe, must embrace the whole world He is governing) in the same way in which a great philosopher of a former age said we must gain a knowledge of His works. These, as they present themselves to our investigation, he compares to a huge piece of " rolled-up tapestry," or "scroll of writing," the significance of which can only be gathered as the cylinder which contains the figures or the characters is " slowly opened to our gaze."

Now it is certainly in conformity with this that the Bible, *supposing* it to be a revelation, is constructed. It is a very gradual development of Divine truth. Its disclosures, designed in part to illustrate the providential history of the world, run parallel with it, and, indeed, form part of it. And for the very same reason—however adapted to illumine some of that darkness which otherwise rests on the designs of God in the moral government of the world, and probably with increasing brightness as its pages " unroll,"—itself necessarily partakes in that obscurity which the gradual evolution of the Divine plan involves. That there is such a plan, some devout and thoughtful speculators among the heathen themselves seem to have guessed; but in the present scene of confusion it demanded something more than philosophical speculation to determine it. For though, as Butler shows, many things argue God's moral government of the world, not only are His designs very gradually unfolded, but His dispensations are often so inexplicably mysterious, and the events He permits so often in seeming conflict with equity and benevolence, that it requires the distinct and explicit assurance of Revelation to make us believe that the issues will be ultimately worthy of supreme power, wisdom, and goodness. Much, therefore, of the " cylinder " of the world's history as it is " unrolled " is found inscribed in hieroglyphics, on which speculation and conjecture exhaust themselves in vain; and the Bible, which without enabling us adequately to decipher them, gives, if it be true, a significance to some of these enigmatical characters, is involved in corresponding shadow. I say, *if* it be true, for I am not assuming its truth, but merely suggesting to the reader what are certain palpable features of it. Whether Scripture casts much or little light upon the darkness of the past, or projects strong or faint illumination on the future, its structure is in analogy with the general procedure of God in the slow development of all His purposes, and with the obscurity necessarily implied in a process so gradual; with that long array and succession of means by which He attains His ends and "perfects His work."

II.   And this suggests a *second* analogy between the structure of the Bible, as contrasted with other professed revelations, and "the constitution and course of nature."   The Divine plans, whatever they be, are being wrought out by the actions of moral agents, the sum of which constitutes human history; so that, when completed, the history of the world will also be the history of the Divine plan.   It is simply in analogy with this, that *if* the Bible be a genuine revelation,—whatever light it may cast from time to time on the Divine purposes, and however it may sustain faith by partially illumining what would be otherwise continuous darkness,—it is (and it cannot be said of any other professed revelation) thrown into an historic form, has an historic development, runs parallel, in its successive communications, with the great epochs of the world's history; and, as I have said elsewhere, is *let into it.*

Of the various ends to be answered in this form, I have already said something in the fifth lecture; more especially on the corroborations of the truth of the Bible, which this form insures, and which could belong to no other; the challenge which the book thus gives to detection, if it be false; the hostages which it gives to truth, if it be true; the impossibility that its unity, if there be unity, could be the result either of human contrivance or of any conceivable casualty.   But I am not here arguing its truth; I am merely pointing out that, *supposing* it a Revelation, it is in analogy with the *mode* in which God is fulfilling His designs (to use the expression of Bunsen) as "God in history."   This Revelation is imbedded in history.   It resembles the temple at Jerusalem, in which the masonry of the foundations not only rested on the natural rock, but in many places followed the line of it, and was let into it.

III.   *If* the Bible be a Revelation, the mode of giving it falls in with the method by which God usually operates on human destinies.   The progress of men, their advancement in knowledge, science, and civilisation, is brought about for the most part by His sending forth into the world from time to time, with special equipments for their task, certain transcendent geniuses,—the Bacons, the Newtons, the Shakespeares, the Miltons of our race,—who are the levers that move the world; who give a new stimulus and impulse to the human mind, and whose appearance constitutes the world's true epochs; who, bequeathing great discoveries or signal inventions, lift the intellect and imagination of man to a higher level, and become guiding lights of their species for many generations, or—some of them—even as long as the world shall last.   It is in analogy with this that God is represented in the Bible as raising up, from time to time, men who should impart continual accessions of spiritual light to the world; "speaking at sundry times and in divers manners by the prophets," till He at last consummated His Revelation "by speaking to us by His Son."

IV.   There is an analogy also in the material instruments by which the progress of man is in each case secured.   The development of the race, its advance in knowledge and civilisation, depends on garnering up the experience of the past and making it available for the future.   Without that, each man, each generation, is but a disjointed link.   Apart from some methods of conserving experience, there can be, in fact, no history; and accordingly of many ages and nations there is none. Until, therefore, men can secure and hand down the treasures of knowledge, fix volatile thought, and make it visible and permanent, there is, and can be, no progress.   Till that be done, the world must be in perpetual nonage.   Consequently all advance, all civilisation, waits on the discovery and application of—an alphabet.   Mechanical as it seems, pen and ink, or some equivalent, is the moving power of the world; the *sine quâ non*, without which it would be at an eternal standstill, or rather would be " ever learning," and never coming to a stable "knowledge " of any "truth." All the acquisitions of each generation would be but as "water spilt on the ground," or poured into a sieve. It is therefore in precise analogy that this Revelation—*if* it be a Revelation indeed—has taken the form for which so many have presumed to deride it,—the form of a "book," where all the successive communications it makes are durably registered. Ridicule the thing as we may, it is absolutely necessary in the very nature of things—each generation being ephemeral—that man's progress, whether in religion or philosophy or anything else, should be effected in this precise way. Nor is it a little curious (as I have remarked in a previous lecture) that the Bible would seem to have anticipated the conclusion to which just historic criticism leads us, and to have recognised most strongly the supreme importance of this condition of human progress. It alone gives us, in a plain written form and in intelligible language, any memorials at all of ages from which all other memorials have vanished.

Here, again, I am not assuming the *truth* of the book ; I am merely contending that the *form* in which it is addressed to us, and the continued augmentation and preservation of its successive communications by the pen, are in conformity with the laws and conditions on which alone all human progress is secured—or, rather, on which alone it is possible.

V. If this be a Revelation, it is submitted to us under conditions similar to those on which the works of God and His providential government of the world are submitted to us,— exacting profound study, investigation, and reflection. Man, in the physical world, is to be, as Bacon says, " the minister and interpreter of nature." If the Bible be from the same source, it is in analogy with this that he is summoned to similar functions here. The Bible has its difficulties and mysteries, as nature has ; and it requires, just as nature does, prolonged thought and effort to penetrate or decipher them. Both have their level plains, where the eye sees far and the feet travel softly ; but both also have lofty summits, which only persevering toil can scale, and deep abysses, which keen eyes and adventurous feet can alone explore.   And such things are probably found in both for the same reason,—to make ample provision for the moral and intellectual discipline of man. Some have said that if a revelation were to be given at all, it would be " written in the skies," and flash instantaneous and universal conviction.   No doubt, if man constructed one, he would endeavour at least to imitate such a " flash."   But on this point, all that need be said is, that if such a revelation were given, it would be in glaring contradiction to all the analogies of that natural revelation which God has given us in His works. There, as in relation to the Scripture, man is equipped, as Butler says, with apparently very inadequate instruments of investigation, to plod on his path to knowledge; and in each case his experience is analogous.   He has all along to wrestle with innumerable difficult problems, and in every direction finds that research terminates at last in insurmountable mysteries. He is often the victim of his own prejudices, and the dupe of his own imagination.   In both fields he is fond of generalising faster than his facts warrant, and is continually the slave of one or other of those seductive *idola* of the human mind which Bacon has so comprehensively sketched.   From the comparative rapidity with which, during the last few lustres, man has advanced the frontier of *physical* science, he is apt in the present day to forget what the real history of all science has been, and to become, from his very triumphs, the victim of one of the above illusions.   We are prone to fancy that, at least in this domain of science, we march on adamant, and along a plain and straight viaduct, reared on lofty and stately arches, far above the jungle and morass through which the pioneers of *other* truth have to toil their weary way.   No doubt a conclusion in this department, once established, is, from its peculiar nature, established for ever.   But it is forgotten through how many *errors* it has been attained,—how many lath and plaster tenements have usurped the site on which the solid edifice at last stands.   The structure, once reared, not only sweeps them away, but conceals and soon extinguishes the very memory of the numberless and often obstinate errors which preceded it.   The false views, the utterly inadequate and absurd theories which science once accepted, men are only too glad to cover with oblivion.   And thus the instructive, though humiliating history of man's past ignorance, and of his too often futile attempts to remedy it, is more apt to escape us in this department of science than in those in which, from the nature of the evidence and the complexity of the phenomena, the ultimate truth is established with less convincing certainty.   But we have only to explore the huge records (willingly thrown aside as so much lumber, or hidden away as with shame) of erroneous or imperfect science to see that here, too, as elsewhere, the path of knowledge is strewn with the wreck of vain speculations ; with hypotheses now utterly forgotten, or only recalled with wonder and derision that they could so long prevail, and so extensively impose on the human mind.   To these, not a few modern theories will, doubtless, hereafter be added, which now stand in imposing semblance of truth, or are even paraded as proofs of the accuracy and unfaltering course of human science; but which will be quoted hereafter as ignominious examples of man's proneness to hasty generalisation and overweening self-confidence.

And when truth, even in *this* department, is in part established, how slow is the advance to anything like a complete solution of all the phenomena it involves !   How many are the steps, and how gradual the process by which certain seemingly refractory facts, which a theory, true in the main, has not perfectly explained, are ultimately adjusted to it.   Of this, the enlargement and rectification of the Newtonian system by modern science, affords a conspicuous example.   But even the more fundamental truths of a correct theory, in any branch of physical science, are in general slowly verified, and through a succession of blunders.   As Butler truly remarks, the great objects and phenomena of the universe had been exposed to the gaze of men, and importunately invited the exercise of the human intellect, thousands of years before the true theory of the sublimest of the sciences presented itself. The heavens were as bright and the intellect of men as vigorous, three thousand years ago, as now. Yet a true astronomy is but of yesterday. Till within the last three hundred years, men in general, and philosophers among them, believed that the earth was stationary, and that the sun and stars revolved around it. Even when the Copernican theory was at last discovered, how slow were men to believe in it, and how tenacious of ancient error. Harvey's well-known saying, that "he could not get any man above forty to believe in the circulation of the blood," is instructive : it is a specimen of the difficulty with which even scientific truth breaks through the obstructions of ignorance and prejudice.

But this, as might be expected, is seen still more conspicuously in the history of all those sciences which are founded on moral evidence ; a result both of the greater obscurity of the evidence itself, and the more bewildering entanglement of the phenomena. But no matter what the department of study,—in all alike, though not in the same degree—man is so organised, and his condition such, that he can gain knowledge only by a tedious process, and through a labyrinth of errors and misconceptions.

If, therefore, the Bible has been constructed (as it certainly has been) in such way as to necessitate the perpetual activity of man's intellect, and to exercise industry, perseverance, and humility, in other words, to constitute a perpetual discipline for him ; it is in palpable analogy with his condition as a "minister" of the mysteries, and "interpreter" of the works, of nature. The rational, and, indeed, perhaps sufficient account of the fact in both cases, is suggested in the great truth that man is a creature who, to a great degree, must have "the making of himself ; " and that, presupposing such modicum of knowledge (whether of physical facts or of religious truth) as may be *essential* to him, placed within his reach, the strenuous exercise of all his powers, and its result in the formation of character, are of yet more importance to him than the absolute amount of knowledge he may acquire ; in a word, that the chase is to him of as much moment as the quarry.

No doubt it would be a serious objection to this view, if the things absolutely necessary to his being, or even to his *well*-being, were as difficult to attain as those which chiefly stimulate his curiosity, impel him to mental activity, or provide a discipline for patience and humility.   But this is not so.   The facts of the outward world, on which man's existence and sustenance depend, and on which the common arts of life are founded, are obvious to all.   And so, in the study of Scripture, are the truths that "belong to life and godliness."   But of the profounder "arcana," whether of nature or of Scripture, the same general analogy holds, that they necessitate and provoke the same diligent and persevering use of all the faculties of our nature.

Nor, in connection with this subject, ought the sagacious inference which Butler draws from the remark, last quoted from him, to be omitted ;—that if the true science of astronomy tarried so long and came so late, though the heavens had been ablaze for so many centuries with the bright hieroglyphics man was asked to decipher, there is no absurdity in supposing that the Bible may still contain undiscovered truths, which await the continued application of the human intellect to elicit them.   The remark has been verified by the progress made, since his time, in the interpretation and elucidation of Scripture, and especially in the construction of works founded on the evidence which the Scripture itself yields to the diligent investigation and collation of its own contents.   Several volumes have been written, for example, on the evidence supplied by "undesigned coincidences" which it "had not entered into the heart of man to conceive," though, like the phenomena of astronomy, they had been perpetually under man's eye for so many ages.

VI. There is another point, intimately connected with, and

indeed but a corollary from, the preceding, which suggests another analogy between the Bible (*if* it be indeed from God) and the Universe, which is incontestably His work. I mean that each seemingly affords, from its variety, ample scope for that study and reflection which each exacts. Not that the one can, in the same sense or to the same extent, afford such a field for investigation as the other. All I mean is, that, like the world, or even some very limited portion of it (as, for example, *man*), the book is apparently a theme of inexhaustible study and contemplation. I found this observation, not exclus. rely, or even principally, on the qualities on which I have insisted in previous pages,—the artificiality of its structure, or the varied character or complex relations of its contents, or the versatility of form in which these are presented to us,—though it is, in fact, by far the most varied book, both in contents and form, ever given to the world : I found it on that fact to which I have already adverted in a previous lecture and for another purpose, —namely, that though so many thousands of volumes have been written on this one, though it has been so familiarly known for so many ages, among widely different races, among nations speaking different languages, and differing also by every variety and degree of culture, men do not seem to come to a term of their curiosity or admiration or hostility; for their ceaseless efforts to refute its claims, as well as those to establish them, prove how profound and how constant is the impression it produces. And now, at the end of so many ages of unremitted study, the world still sees a never-ceasing flood of literature evoked by it, and the most gigantic efforts made for its elucidation, translation, and diffusion ! It is hardly possible, after such experience of unslaked interest in it, to avoid the conclusion that, in contemplating it, as in contemplating the works of God, the time will not soon come when the " eye will be" satisfied with seeing," or the " ear with hearing."

If, for extent and complexity, the book cannot—as all will confess—be compared with these last, it may at least be compared with many of the single objects which they present to us, and which, though small in compass, exhibit such marvels of design and structure, as to afford unbounded exercise for man's research and investigation.   Like man, the Bible is a "microcosm" of itself; and, as shown in a previous lecture, seems to have as great complexity of structure, and as great variety of contents—commensurate, however, with the variety of purposes it is designed to serve—as can possibly belong to a book; and which make it, as a book, as much *sui generis* as any of the works of God compared with the imitations of men.

VII. Another analogy suggested by the last topic (for it is one cause of that inexhaustible interest which both Nature and the Bible would seem capable of inspiring) is not unworthy of mention.   I allude to the seemingly unsystematic form in which the multifarious contents of the Bible are exhibited to us, and which, though in part a necessary consequence of its gradual formation, its complexity of structure, and its various matter, reminds us of the similar presentation of the phenomena of the universe, and involves similar effects on us.

Some, as we have seen in a previous lecture, have made this very characteristic a grave objection to it.   They have complained that its contents *are* delivered in so unsystematic a form, and have demanded that a true revelation should be marked by that orderly arrangement and classification of results which their logical propensities and habits of analysis best love.   In so doing, they bear witness to a certain tendency of human nature,—at least of *philosophical* human nature; in truth, one would expect that if man constructed the book, it would have been marked by less variety of form and complexity of structure, and far less apparent irregularity in the distribution of its contents; in a word, by more *seeming* method.   In the mean time, however incompetent we are (as must be admitted) to say in what form a Divine relation would be best given, it is incontestable that if the Bible be one, the mode in which its contents are presented is in palpable analogy with the mode in which the phenomena of nature are presented to us; that is, in glorious and seemingly bewildering confusion. In either case they are flung down, so to speak, before man, and invite him to employ his intellect upon them; to spell out the alphabet of that highly complex language in which the "manifold wisdom" of God speaks to us. Though science may be made out of the phenomena of nature thus submitted to us, they were not *primarily* made for science, but for immediately practical ends. The entire phenomena, indeed, constitute a *system*—though a system, as Butler says, so far beyond our comprehension, that " he must literally know nothing who does not confess his ignorance of it." We perceive also, for that is a visible fact, that the adjustments in this vast machinery, and the reciprocal influences at work in it, maintain a *stable* system,—a system in which even we may trace some of the relations which subsist between its most distant parts, and which connect by insensible gradations the sublimest phenomena of astronomy with the meanest phenomena of animated nature.[1] The more we study the phenomena, the more we perceive this mutual interdependence. But the aggregate of the phenomena are nevertheless in seeming utter confusion, and with an aspect the

[1] Exquisitely has Paley illustrated this in his "Natural Theology." "If," says he, "the relation of *sleep* to *night*, and, in some instances, its converse, be *real*, we cannot reflect without amazement upon the extent to which it carries us. Day and night are things close to us; the change applies immediately to our sensations. Of all the phenomena of nature, it is the most obvious and the most familiar to our experience; but in its cause, it belongs to the great motions which are passing in the heavens. Whilst the earth glides round her axis, she ministers to the alternate necessities of the animals dwelling upon her surface, at the same time that she obeys the influence of those attractions which regulate the order of many thousand worlds. The relation, therefore, of sleep to night, is the relation of the inhabitants of the earth to the rotation of their globe. Probably it is more: it is a relation of the system of which that globe is a part, and still further to the congregation of systems of which theirs is only one. If this account be true, it connects the meanest individual with the universe itself—a chicken roosting upon its perch with the spheres revolving in the firmament."—Paley's "Natural Theology," vol. i. p. 363.

very reverse of that of a well-arranged museum. Sun, moon, and planets; earth, air, and water; electricity and magnetism; inorganic and organic structures; countless tribes of vegetable and animal existence, are linked together by ten thousand relations of adaptation, and constitute a *system* only while they are so. All the laws of all the natural sciences, of astronomy, chemistry, anatomy, and a score more, are at work at once, and in infinite entanglement. To exhibit its elements apart, would be to take the universe to pieces, and destroy it by doing so. It would be to turn it into a collection of curiosities—the garden of Eden into a *hortus siccus*. It would be no more the universe, but the lamentable *débris* of a *post mortem* dissection; not a watch, but its various parts spread out on the watchmaker's board; the *elements* of a system, but a system no longer. Mean time it is given to man to exercise himself for ever about these objects—to take a survey of them, to trace their relations, analyse and classify them. To do this perfectly in any case, he must at least *imagine* the object on which his scientific curiosity is exercised no longer existing in reality, but reduced to its elements; and in many cases (for example, the system of a living organism) he must actually destroy it before he can attempt the work of analysis. That most marvellous of all, the human body, must cease to have that life, which alone makes it worth anything, before the scientific man can even lay the foundation of its anatomy and physiology. Man must cease to breathe before he can exist for the philosopher. He must die, that science may live.

But though the philosopher has plenty to do in his "interpretation" of the complex phenomena of nature, they are thus unsystematically exhibited because far other ends are contemplated than his convenience; and *if* the Bible be a revelation, it is even so with that.

VIII. I may here note another analogy of a similar practical character, between the Word (if the Bible be such) and the Works of God. For as the philosopher is apt to complain that the Bible is not systematic enough for him, so the man of imagination is sometimes repelled by its frequent homeliness, its unpoetic *realism*, and complains that it is not all so "perfect in beauty" as the human mind might conceive it would have been. The useful, and therefore the homely, is no doubt there in close relations with the beautiful, and often mars or impairs the effect of it. But so it is in Nature, and with the same result. In either case it is what the poetical mind naturally resents, and in the products of art laudably endeavours to prevent. It is the function of that wonderful faculty of imagination which God has given us, to idealise Nature, and give it a homogeneity, a symmetry, an ethereal grace, which Nature never has. It is the province of poetry, as Bacon says, " to give some shadow of satisfaction to the mind of man in those points wherein the nature of things doth deny it—the world being in proportion inferior to the soul ; by reason whereof there is, agreeable to the spirit of man, a more ample greatness, a more exact goodness, and a more absolute variety than can be found in the nature of things."[1]

Poetry, therefore, in consistency with this partial design of art, eliminates from its pictures of reality all that is mean, vulgar, homely, and presents to us objects not as they *are*, but as they may be *conceived* to be—in unsullied beauty ; just as the painter refuses to put into his scenes anything that merely suggests the idea of what is simply repulsive, and incapable of being exhibited with a picturesque effect. The poet's aim, in like manner, is to select such objects, images, and expressions as shall be pleasing, or at all events give an excess of pleasurable over painful emotions. He is as sedulous to clear everything that is disgusting from his description as the painter from his canvas. This is his design, and his efforts terminate there ; but far different is it in that world of realities from which, by selection and elimination, his beautiful, but ideal scenes are drawn. There the production of the beautiful is but one of

[1] Advancement of Learning. Book 2.

the many indissolubly connected designs which Nature has in view. We feel offended with the poet Cowper for even introducing into his beautiful description of a "garden" the mention of the "dunghill," though without it the garden would lose its charms; and are still more displeased by his attempting to give an affected disguise to it, but really a double emphasis, by the unpoetic periphrasis of the "stercoraceous heap." But Nature is not, and cannot afford to be so squeamish. She is intent upon more serious things than poetry and painting; she is profuse in giving us the beautiful, so long and so far as it may be compatible with all the objects of her vast system, but will not postpone the *useful* to it. Adorning the world with as much beauty as is compatible with other and more practical good, she has no horror of "stercoraceous heaps," or anything else that is conducive to her manifold ends. The purposes of benevolence and manifest utility come first, however they may mar a picture or cloud the ideal. And therefore it is that we so seldom see landscapes to which the artist cannot take exceptions, and which he could not in fact improve, if the mere purpose were to produce a scene of faultless beauty. True it is that there are thousands of scenes in Nature infinitely more replete with grandeur and loveliness than any that the artist can at all adequately represent on his canvas; but few in which, looking at the beautiful and picturesque alone, he could not suggest something superfluous or defective. He will exclude objects which simply suggest the idea of what disgusts us, however really there; and if he paints the scene, will annihilate or transmute them.

The peculiarities referred to in these two last sections,—apparent defects of method and apparent violations of taste,—must characterise the Scripture (or any true revelation), if it is to answer the manifold and diverse purposes of such a book to the entire race of man;—to be the universal counsellor of all ages, of every land, of every race; of men of all conditions, old and young, prince and peasant, the learned and the ignorant, and these in every degree of moral excellence or moral degradation; to say nothing of being its own interpreter, commentatory, and evidence. Like the universe, it is a system indeed, but a system too vast, too complex, prosecuting too many ends simultaneously, to be amenable to the philosopher's trim analyses or the poet's idea of beauty. Though it may contain, in many parts, wisdom, sublimity, beauty, eloquence, and pathos, which will more than compare with anything of the kind in merely human literature, it has too many purposes to serve, is too deeply steeped in the real and the actual, too intent on practical utility, to permit of its pursuing exclusively or pervadingly any such logical or poetic ideal. The sick, the poor, the ignorant, the vicious, the miserable, will claim its care as much as philosophers and poets; and more, since they are more numerous. For these reasons (to say nothing further of the scope which such a various structure affords to the intellectual activity of men, in exploring its characteristics and analysing its contents), that unsystematic form given to a revelation may well be justified. At any rate, the traits in question are in analogy with the mode in which, for apparently similar reasons, the natural phenomena of the universe are presented to us.

IX. If the contents of the Bible are exhibited unsystematically, like the objects and phenomena of the natural world, the proportions in which the different elements in each exist for *us*, present another analogy. As what is essential to life is cheap and common, like the air and sunshine, and what is necessary for subsistence is for the most part easy of acquisition ; so it has often been remarked that in the Scripture, what is of primary moment, is insisted on and illustrated with proportionate fulness and iteration, and is equally accessible to the learned and the ignorant.

Things that are of chief importance are made plain, and exhibited in every diversity of light. It is for the most part only things that are of little practical moment, of curiosity rather than utility, or which seem *designed* to exercise our modesty and humility, or to stimulate our curiosity or industry, that are left obscure.   Their *rationale,*—the complete solution of the mysteries which environ them, are not essential to salvation.

X. In a previous lecture I said a few words on the probable *complexity* which would characterise any volume, designed to be a guide and light to all men in every condition of life, and for all purposes of moral instruction and education, *if* it be indeed a revelation.   That complexity, seemingly inevitable on any hypothesis, would seem still further increased in the case of the Bible by expedients to attain at once these manifold *primary* ends, and certain *secondary* ends simultaneously with them.   I illustrated this by referring to the historic form which it has assumed, and which, in addition to manifold advantages as a vehicle for instruction, secures important contributions to the internal evidence.   Similar remarks apply to certain expedients and peculiarities of language and style adapted to secure the integrity of its text ; to aid its interpretation ; and, not least, to impress upon it a character which facilitates its easy translation.   This complexity is still further increased by the interfusion, with all its elements, of various marks and evidences of its truth ; a πάρεργον, or "byework," indeed, but apparently more or less contemplated in the entire fabric of Scripture.   Let it have, then, as much simplicity as is consistent with these multifarious ends, as much beauty as is consistent with the higher purposes of perspicuity and utility, such a structure is yet necessarily very complex.   Now this is just what so often strikes us in the analogies of nature ; where we are filled with wonder that so many ends should all be attained by the same set of instruments, with so little sacrifice and with such approximate perfection.[1]   Every species of creature

---

[1] There are few things that strike a reflecting mind as more wonderful than that set of operations, all of them of primary importance in the vital economy, which are performed by the conjoint action of the tongue, mouth,

affords illustration of it.   But perhaps it is seen most conspicuously in man himself; on the wonders of whose organisation,
material and mental,—on the mechanism, anatomy, physiology,
chemistry of whose body, on the nature and faculties of whose
mind, and on the laws of reciprocal interaction between them,
—a thousand volumes have been written, and a thousand more
will not exhaust the theme.   In the entire phenomena of this
"abridgment of the universe" (as he has been called), we have
an object of the greatest conceivable, or rather of utterly inconceivable complexity (corresponding to the variety of purposes
which are all to be fulfilled), in the small compass of a few
solid feet, and with the least possible sacrifice of higher to lower
ends.   We are filled with amazement that such diversified and
important purposes should be conjointly attained.

XI. When that genuine Christian philosopher, Robert Boyle,
composed his admirable essay on the "Style of the Holy
Scriptures," he replied at length to some *a priori* objections
which would scarcely be insisted upon now even by the
sceptic, at least since the appearance of Butler's Analogy;—as,

palate, and throat.   Functions essential to the life of the body, and by
which that of the soul is expressed, are performed by these few organs,—
the organs themselves in such close proximity, and working in and by each
other with such marvellous intricacy, that the wonder is that the functions
should be performed at all, much more with such ease.   It is true, indeed,
that we cannot perform them all quite simultaneously ; but with how inconceivable facility do the organs by which these all-important processes of
respiration, mastication, deglutition, articulation, are effected,—by which
tastes are perceived, sounds produced, thought expressed,—I say with how
inconceivable facility do these organs commence and cease, alternate,
modify, suspend, resume their various functions !   "In a city feast, for
example," says Paley, in his lively style of illustration, "what deglutition,
what anhelation ! yet does this little cartilage, the epiglottis, so effectually
interpose its office, so securely guard the entrance of the windpipe, that
whilst morsel after morsel, draught after draught, are coursing one another
over it, an accident of a crumb or a drop slipping into this passage (which,
nevertheless, must be opened for the breath every second of time) excites in
the company, not only alarm by its danger, but surprise by its novelty.
Not two guests are choked in a century."

for example, that the Bible left many "mysteries and difficulties" unsolved on its pages, and that many parts demand deep study and prolonged investigation to master them, even when they do at length yield to persevering effort. Such traits, it must be conceded, are not *evidences* for the truth of any revelation ; but, so far from being *objections*, they are rather of the nature of necessary conditions of it. Though they would prove the truth of no professed revelation, their absence would be a great presumption against the claims of any. For :—

1. A revelation without mystery is not even conceivable. A revelation, if it deserves the name, must make known some new truths ; and every augmentation of knowledge, even of a lower kind, is attended,—not accidentally, but necessarily,— with the revelation also of our ignorance. The horizon widens, but the indistinctness is still upon it ; and the larger that horizon is, the larger becomes the periphery of haze that surrounds it. Thus it is in natural science, and must be as long as man is a progressive being; that is, until (if that be conceivable, which to men in general it certainly is not) "he shall know all mysteries and all knowledge." If that ever come to pass, then, constituted as man is, he will probably have consummated his misery just as he has arrived at perfection ! For he will still have as strong appetite for knowledge as ever, but nothing wherewith to satisfy it.

But this is not likely to be the case ; and until it is, every new truth he learns reveals to him his ignorance, and he seeks to know more. Thus, when the law of gravitation was discovered, and explained so many phenomena, men asked (as they do still), "What is this property with which all matter is endowed? What is the *rationale* of it? What is the 'law' of this 'law'? How is it inherent in matter? Is it inseparable from its very nature?" And hitherto all speculation on this subject has been in vain, and probably will ever be. It is the same with the law of chemical affinities ; it explains some mysteries and discloses others.   It is thus with every new law, which is either but the ultimate fact of the moment, and ceases to be so the next year or the next generation; or, if the point thus reached be absolutely immovable, it is so, not because there is nothing more to know, but because we have reached in that direction the limit of our faculties,—a limit as insurmountable as the barrier which separates us from the planetary worlds. We have sufficient proof, indeed, that such limit is not soon attained, and may often fancy we have reached it when we have not. Still, whether attained or not, there is always the horizon of mist, sometimes immovable, sometimes capable of being rolled back. Only a few years ago almost everybody believed the ocean depths to be devoid of life : we are now led to see that a whole world of future science has been concealed from our ignorance, and we wait for further exploration. Only a century ago, geology opened a new hunting - field for the intellect of man, and it is hard to say how far our adventurous Nimrod will be carried. A few years ago he was chasing the megatherium and ichthyosaurus : he has disposed of that small game, and, mounted on his hippogriff, is pushing his incursions into the uttermost deserts of time and space. But with every excursion he finds, if not clear knowledge, most absolute proof of an ever-widening frontier of darkness.—A few years ago men seldom made expeditions much beyond the planetary system; now they are busy with the problems of sidereal astronomy, and every new fact discloses that "man is but of yesterday and knows nothing."

Now if this be so when men tell us of " earthly things," can it be otherwise if God tell us of " heavenly things "? *These,* too, must have their relations and connections with other and unknown truths,—truths at least as deeply veiled from us as the ultimate truths of secular science. And especially may we expect such mystery, if the revelation not only refuses, as Scripture does, to tell us anything that merely tends to gratify curiosity, —but seems to give us incidental glimpses of some truths, as involved in the course of revealing to us *other* truths of more immediate importance to us; so that we only see them by gleams and sidelights, as we might catch a glimpse of an object behind a curtain, as it fluttered in the wind.

2. But, again; if a professed revelation were given without *mystery* and *difficulty*, it would be in such startling contrast with all the analogies of the previous revelation in nature, that it would rather be an obstacle to receiving it than not.   Here, as just shown, we cannot move in any direction without soon finding that we are stopped by a present limit, and, if we go far enough, by a permanent one;—one that we cannot hope to surmount, because our very faculties fail us.   This is notoriously the case with certain great mysteries,—as, for example, the essence of matter or of mind, the laws of their union or interaction, the origin of evil, and the problem of the consistency of the Divine Government with freedom of the human will,—on all which men have been guessing, speculating, and reasoning, from time immemorial, without coming to any satisfactory solution.

If there were no difficulties or mysteries in a professed revelation, parallel with those which are so abundant in the world, the contrast would probably rather startle than conciliate us.

XII. Though I do not here contend for the actual occurrence of miracles or prophecy, I think it may be said, not only that they form a species of evidence, which, if there be a revelation at all, is in conformity with the only conditions on which man, from the constitution of his intellect, could be rationally expected to receive it, but is also in analogy with the tendencies of his nature in general.   A sense of the supernatural,—an expectation of its manifestation, somehow and at some time,—would seem among the most characteristic phenomena of human nature, and has been attested generally by the facts of man's history; and, not least, by the eager credulity with which he has listened even to the most idle legends which have been invented to gratify it.   In short, it would seem that a belief in the supernatural is founded in some of the deepest and most ineradicable instincts. " This love and belief of the supernatural," says Dr. Mozley, " has flourished successively upon heathen, upon Christian, and upon scientific material ; because in truth it is neither heathen, nor Christian, nor scientific, but *human*.   Springing out of the common stock of humanity, which is the same in all ages, it adapts itself to the belief, the speculations, and the knowledge of its own day." [1]

Somewhat similar remarks apply to prophecy.   The yearning of the heart of man for some glimpses into futurity is so natural. that it has ever prompted him to practise, in all ages and countries, a hundred arts of divination.   It would seem a tendency of our nature, which, like the belief in the supernatural, is ineradicable. [2]

The unequivocal tendency to believe in miraculous interposition, and the equally unequivocal desire to penetrate the future, would seem to indicate an origin in the *principles* of our nature ; and if so, the provision for them in the alleged phenomena of the Bible is in " analogy " with that nature.

But I may go a step further than this statement of *general* analogy.   There is a special point of the argument worth considering.   I do not enter now into the question whether the miracles recorded in Scripture are *facts;* if not, the Bible is false by its own verdict, for it appeals to them : but appeal it *must*, if its evidence is to be in unison with the constitution of human nature.   Every revelation made to *one* man,—or to a few men in order to be communicated to the world at large,— containing things confessedly undiscoverable by human reason, and demanding to be received on the testimony of the first witnesses, must thus appeal.   If a professed emissary from the skies tells me only what my own instinct or reason had anticipated, I tell him I do not need him, and that he may go.   If

<hr>

[1] Miracles, p. 163.   *Third Edition.*

[2] See some pertinent observations on this subject in Davison on Prophecy. pp. 213, 214.   *Sixth Edition.*

again he tells me only things which, indeed, I had not suspected, but which when known are seen to be involved in the premises which nature has furnished (though I had not discovered them), I tell him that his professed revelations may have been discoveries made by himself, or by others; and that for such truths no revelation is necessary. But if he demands my assent to propositions, which by the very terms of them are palpably beyond all human discovery, for which neither he nor I have any natural data,—as, for example, the resurrection of the body, the *certainty* of the soul's immortality, the incarnation of Christ, His atonement for the sins of men,—then he is bound to make good his claims on my faith by evidence as preternatural as his communications. I ask him, " Who told you all this? Why am I to believe you?" It is in vain to say, " I had it in a dream of the night, or in a vision by day." " Dreams and visions, they must remain," I reply : " to you they may be, to me they can be, nothing more. You must give me evidence miraculous as your message." So reasonable, so *natural* is this course, that even a man utterly sceptical as to the possibility of miracle and prophecy, would have little difficulty in assenting to its hypothetical propriety. He would reasonably argue, that if a revelation of the kind described was to be given at all, it must be thus corroborated.

It was in analogy with *nature*, therefore, that the Jews asked of Christ—" What dost thou work?" and He, by working miracles, admitted their claim ; and more expressly still when He said, " If I had not done among them miracles which none other man did, they had not had sin,"—that is, in rejecting His message. It was natural, in like manner, for the followers of Mahomet to ask *him* for miracles ; and if nothing else had stamped his professed revelation as destitute of trustworthy evidence of its celestial origin, it would be sufficient to point to the fact that he evaded this only sufficient test.

It is accordingly in *analogy* with this that men proceed in analogous circumstances of ordinary life. When their belief or action is demanded by unknown persons, and on momentous matters, the intrinsic truth of which is not evident, and may seem *a priori* incredible, no reasoning nor seeming honesty nor vehemence of asseveration on the part of the messengers, can or ought to satisfy.   Men ask and must have the indubitable σημεια of a right to demand their credence ;—the letters, the sign-manual, or other accredited proofs that the messengers speak with authority.   Such peculiar "signs" alone will suffice ; and these, in the supposed case of a Revelation, can be nothing less than miracle and prophecy.[1]

To any one, therefore, who demands implicit assent and obedience to things absolutely undiscoverable to human reason, man, if he be reasonable, will say, "Show me that you have the authority of Him whose emissary you say you are.   When the Lord of Nature and of Time, He who can control causes and predict the future, confirms your message, I shall believe you, and not till then."

I have said that I am not now arguing for the truth either of miracles or prophecy, but merely that the appeal to them is in analogy with the constitution of human nature.   The claim to have furnished such evidence, no more proves a revelation to

---

[1] A slight, but curious illustration of my meaning, showing the naturally extreme circumspection with which men demand evidence, when an error either way may be fatal, may be cited from the life of Sir Francis Drake. Returning from a distant expedition, with a part of his men and some native Indians, we are told that "when within five leagues of their vessels, Drake consented to halt, his men being spent with travel ; but being very anxious to ascertain the condition of the men who had remained with the vessels, he sent one of the natives to the ships, with a gold toothpick as a *token*.   The officer in charge knew it, but would not consent to obey the instructions which the Indian brought him, the General having expressly ordered him *not to credit any messenger*, unless he brought with him his handwriting.   At length he perceived that Drake had scratched his name upon it with the point of his knife, on which he immediately sent a pinnace to meet them ; and on the 23rd of February the entire company were reunited, and Drake, with his usual piety, celebrated their meeting by thanksgiving to God."—Barrow's *Life of Sir Francis Drake*.   Chap. ii.

be *true*, than the existence of mysteries does, for they may both characterise a false revelation ; but the absence of such claims would be a presumption *against* a revelation, and out of analogy with the constitution of that human mind which is summoned to submit to them.

My space forbids me to pursue this topic of " Analogy " further.   I must content myself with referring the reader to some further examples in Bishop Hampden's admirable work on the " Philosophical Evidence of Christianity," and begging him to bear in mind that *all* the analogies insisted on by Butler are also to be taken into the account ; for they are available on this, the positive side of the argument, though they derive th..r chief force from being a reply to specific objections.

This lecture may be considered as complementary of the two first.   If these show that the Bible is not in conformity with what might have been expected to proceed from man, analogy shows that it has, at all events, certain conformities with what has incontestably proceeded from God.

It will be seen, from the train of reasoning generally pursued in these lectures, that I infer no more than that the Bible, in its substance, had a *superhuman* origin.

It is possible to contend that this does not show it to be *Divine ;* nay, it is possible to imagine some sceptical Quixote suggesting that even if it had a preternatural origin, it may have been a *malevolent* one.   But as such an objector is hardly conceivable, we may wait till he appears before indulging in the equal Quixotry of confuting him.   Unless one of those old Pharisees, who imputed the miracles of Incarnate Benevolence and Mercy to the agency of Beelzebub, could rise from the dead, I do not know that such an objector could be found ; and even then he would be answered by our Lord's own argument, " That a kingdom divided against itself is brought to desolation —and that a house divided against itself cannot stand."

If it be once granted that the Bible, on the whole, is not the work of man, few will hesitate to whom to assign it.

At the same time, it is incumbent on me to mark distinctly the limits of the thesis I contend for.

It is not necessary for me to affirm that the Bible, as we have it,—or even if we had it (as we *cannot* have it) in the very autographs of its original writers,—is absolutely free from errors. To show that these questions do not affect the conclusions I am concerned with, I would offer a few brief observations.

As apologists for Christianity justly affirm that the sum of the general evidence for it cannot be neutralized by minute errors, referrible either to accidental corruptions of the text, or even to less than infallible accuracy in the writers, so I may say the same of the reasoning I have endeavoured to develop. No difficulties in minute points of chronology or history, no various readings, no mistakes as to numbers, nay, nor even such errors of detail (if they can be *proved* such) as have been charged on the original writers, will invalidate the conclusions for which I contend. All the *facts* I have dwelt upon remain, and point still in one direction.

The evidence for the general conclusion cannot be equated with these specific objections. They may require, more or less, a limitation of our faith; they may affect in a certain degree the sum of our deductions from the book or our theories of its inspiration;—whether that was plenary or partial, continuous or intermittent. But they will still leave its substance untouched, and the great doctrines it unfolds and the great duties it enjoins, just as they were.

If, for example, all the alleged historic contradictions which, with any tolerable plausibility of argument, have been charged upon the Bible, were admitted to be such, and withdrawn from its pages as errors which had got there we knew not how, none of the paradoxes which the supposition of the human origin of the Bible involves would be at all diminished, nor any argument founded on them refuted. Similarly, if all the passages in which it is contended that fact or doctrine is affected by

corruptions of the text or discrepancies in the manuscripts,'
were given up on all sides,—so various and copious are the
statements of Scripture, that their surrender would make
scarcely any appreciable difference in the determination of the
points for or against which they may have been cited.

These things cannot affect any of the facts on which I have
argued that the Bible, *as a whole*, is not such a book as man
would have compiled if he could, or could if he would.

Now, let a man only grant that the Bible is really such a
book, and it is certain that he will not lightly tamper with its
contents ; his veneration will make him very careful how he rejects any portion of it ; he will exact the severest proofs that
what he is summoned to reject is *demonstrable* error, before he
casts it away.   The excrescences which the accidents of time
may have produced, he will remove with a cautious hand, lest
his critical scalpel should go too deep.   Alleged errors of the
original writers themselves he will approach (to use the language
of Burke on another subject) as he would " the wounds of a
father," with "awful reverence and filial tenderness ;" but if
they can be *proved*, he will, as an honest man, feel no temptation to harbour them.   He will be simply careful to ascertain
that they *are* errors which are charged upon the writers ; and,
except for the most coercive reasons, will rather modestly distrust his own wisdom than theirs.

Nor need we hesitate to affirm that whoever acts with this
reverential caution, and rejects only what has been *demonstrated*
to be contradiction or error, will find, when he has subtracted
every *iota* to which he can attach that character, that his Bible
is much the same, both in bulk and weight, that it was before.

' " Make your thirty thousand various readings as many more," says
Bentley, " if numbers of copies can ever reach that sum : all the better to
a knowing and considerate reader, who is thereby more richly furnished to
select what he sees genuine.   But even put them into the hands of a knave
or a fool, and yet with the most sinistrous and absurd choice, he shall not
extinguish the light of any one chapter, nor so disguise Christianity but that
every feature of it will be still the same."—*Remarks on Free thinking*, § 31.

But it can no more be his duty to reject the whole, on account of such errors, than of the theist to reject the conclusion that there is a Divine artificer of the world, because there are many things in it he cannot comprehend, and some phenomena which seem even at variance both with wisdom and goodness. The theist leaves these, and, notably, all the phenomena of evil, in all their insolubility. Feeling, as Butler puts it, that the whole system of things, though plainly a *system*, is utterly beyond his comprehension, he waits for further light and the slow evolution of the vast *plan de Dieu.* As I have elsewhere said, " his faith is exercised indeed ; but he feels that to ignore the evidence of his reason for his *general* conclusion, would be to sacrifice faith and reason too ; to make his ignorance the rule and measure of his knowledge, or, rather, to abandon what he knows, because there are other things which he knows not." [1]

That there are errors in the Bible, as we have it, is incontrovertible. Not only are there errors, but there *must* have been, even on the principles of those who hold the most rigid theories of inspiration. For even *they* do not deny that the book of God was, like every book of man, committed to human custody under all the ordinary laws on which the preservation or corruption both of the one and the other must depend. To all the casualties which can affect the integrity of the latter, the former is equally liable, qualified only by that exceptional reverence which it has in fact inspired in those who transcribed and transmitted it ; by the facilities for revising the text which the greater number of copies (produced by the same exceptional estimate of its value) would supply, and by certain artifices in its construction, which, as pointed out in a former part of these lectures, subserve, and seem intended to subserve, a like purpose. But, apart from such deductions, whatever imperfections, arising from the ordinary causes above referred to, are found in any human author whatever, may, nay, *must* be

<hr>

[1] *Reason and Faith*, pp. 32, 42.

found in the Bible.   Every species of error that could flow from inadvertence or negligence of the transcribers, from ignorance or presumption in editors, from lapse of memory or illusion of eyesight, and which so largely deform profane literature—substitutions of one word for another, slight omissions, *lacunæ*, mistakes in numbers, and so on — may be equally expected here.   Whatever difficulties from these causes may perplex the critic who edits or interprets Plato's dialogues or Livy's history (and none need be told how manifold and often baffling they are), must also be found in the Bible,—aggravated in some degree by the far greater antiquity of a large portion of the book, and by the greater number of various readings which the incomparably more frequent transcription has occasioned.[1]   If we find in these authors, as we do find, passages which, from such causes, are obscure, or ambiguous, or palpably corrupt, or unintelligible, or contradictory—passages on which infinite ingenuity of conjecture, and all the resources of learning, often exhaust themselves in vain—we must expect to find the same or similar passages in the Scriptures.   That these difficulties must be very considerable in number, if not in weight, considering that the book has been transmitted through such long periods, and so often transcribed by ignorant or incompetent copyists, can hardly be doubted.   If it be asked, "Then what trust can we have that the very substance may not be touched by this class of error?" the answer is, "The same warranty

[1] This last source of difficulty is, however, probably more than compensated by the aid which the various readings afford in the revision and recovery of the text.—The manuscripts which exist in whole or in part of the New Testament are so much more numerous than those of any other ancient book, even the most popular, that that circumstance would lead one to conjecture that the preponderance of the impressions of the printed volume over every other printed book (to which reference has been made in a previous page), was as great, in *proportion*, in the manuscript copies. The immense efforts made, and yet in vain, to destroy the copies of the New Testament during the fierce persecution under Diocletian, confirms the suspicion of an exceptional activity of transcription, as there was afterwards of the press.

that we have in the case of any other book, and no more." The laws on which the transmission of the Bible depend are at least as certain as those on which the transmission of any other book depends. Now we find, in point of fact, that the limits of error are always very moderate, and leave the essence, even of writings far less carefully guarded than those of the Scriptures, untouched. All the reasons therefore which satisfy us that we have the substance of Plato's or Livy's genuine thoughts (let what deductions we will be made for the injuries of time and negligence), may satisfy us (and much more fully, if we weigh and number the passages which are incurably corrupt, doubtful, or contradictory in the several cases) that we possess the genuine substance of the Bible; that the life is untouched, though the skin be razed here and there; that the tree is sound, though some twigs and leaves may have been carried away in the storm.

I have sometimes thought that the amount of error in the Bible, from these causes, may be somewhat greater than the comparison of manuscripts will disclose, and may even embrace some of those cases for which it is supposed nothing but ignorance or mistake, on the part of the original writers, will account. It may be suspected that in some, at least, of the difficulties which exercise and baffle our ingenuity or provoke injurious surmises, our embarrassment may originate in the unguarded substitution or omission of a word or clause. Considering what errors have thus ept into the text, we can hardly be quite sure that, though the testimony of the manuscripts is of course our best, and indeed our only safe guide in ascertaining it, many minute errors do not still exist, of which the manuscripts give us no sufficient indication, or in some cases none at all.

Such a suspicion is sometimes forced upon one in the examination of those *parallelisms* which, as said elsewhere, seem to have been, in part, intended as a device for conserving the text. In some of them we see that the alteration of a syllable or even a letter will at once restore the parallelism which the received reading obviously violates. I would be the last, indeed, to plead for any other emendations of the text than those which manuscript authority justifies ; for it would be better to let intractable passages remain so, than sanction the freaks of conjectural criticism at one time so liberally indulged in. Still it is impossible not to suspect that in many cases, where the substitution of a single resembling word, or even the insertion of a single resembling letter, will remove all obscurity or solve a difficulty, that the copyist, not indeed intentionally, but from inadvertence, has been unfaithful to his text.

I think it is perfectly competent to the Christian apologist to proceed one step further. Supposing there are some difficulties or discrepancies incapable of being solved by the theory of some casual corruption of the text,—difficulties which would be found on the face of the autographs themselves, if we could inspect them, and finally shown to be insoluble,—it is impossible that even *that* can neutralize the positive evidence of so many kinds for the substantial truth of the Bible. In all argumentative fairness we should merely have to surrender so much *proven* error,—no matter how it originated. It is accordingly asked by many in the present day, " What would it matter if the sacred writers, on immaterial points, and wholly foreign to their functions as religious teachers, now and then spoke in ignorance or forgetfulness, or in compliance with the current notions of their times, or under natural prejudices of education ? What would it matter if it were *proved*, as it has been surmised, that Stephen by a *lapsus linguæ* said ' Sychem,' when he was thinking of another place, and that the New Testament has *truthfully* recorded his blunder ? "

This theory is altogether consistent with the admission of the substantial truth of the Bible, and is in fact untenable by none, but such as claim for it that it is absolutely " perfect chrysolite," inspired in every particle, if not verbally, yet plenarily, from the first verse of Genesis to the last verse of the Apocalypse.

Without professing or pretending that this is demonstrated to be the true explanation of the difficulties in question, I know of no reasons why the theory should invalidate, in any degree, the evidence on which the claims of the Bible to our belief, reverence, and obedience, essentially depends. It could make no difference to the honest mind. It would eliminate only those errors that are *demonstrated* to be such, and which must therefore be rejected, however we may account for them. But it could no more destroy the huge accumulation of proof for the Bible in general, than some minute errors detected in any memoir or history could destroy the evidence on which its general trustworthiness is affirmed. And in the case of the Bible,—if the whole of those passages in which it can be at all pretended that error has been *demonstrated*, were subducted from it, the sum of all its more important contents would remain just what it was.

Without affirming or denying this theory, it must be admitted that, if true, it is by no means without analogy in the constitution of nature and the dispensations of Providence. How often does God permit His most excellent gifts to be in some degree marred by the hands through which they are administered! How often does He allow the slips and weaknesses of the wisest and best to tarnish their worth or diminish their usefulness; not indeed to the frustration of the great objects for which they are equipped and sent into the world, or of the benefits they were destined to confer upon it; but so far as to evince that there is a baser element in even the most precious things of earth, of ignorance and infirmity even in the noblest forms of humanity. It is thus conceivable that, as the sun has its *maculæ*, so may even inspired genius; that even "the water of life" may have some tang of the conduit through which it reaches us; and the "heavenly treasures" bear marks of the "earthen vessels" in which they have been deposited. If it be so, it is no more than in analogy with nature, while it would be by no means inconsistent with some of the purposes of revelation.   To ascertain the limits of our ignorance and know-ledge, of error and truth, would impose a perpetual exercise of caution and candour, patience and docility; and if the trait in question answered no other purpose, it would at least (as Bishop Butler says of the designed *obscurity* which rests on the evidence of religion in general) admirably serve as an instru-ment of "probation," and in some respects serve that end better than if there were no such difficulties at all.

To him, then, who admits the substantive truth of the Bible, founded on the aggregate of all its evidences—the amount of *demonstrable* error in it, measured by the contradictions and discrepancies actually *proven*, will give little difficulty.   It little matters to him what theory may be formed as to their origin; he will simply ignore them.   They will be as if obliterated from the book; but they will not disturb the general conclusions, any more than some minute discrepancies among witnesses, of which neither bench nor bar can suggest any explanation, will arrest the verdict of a jury founded on the convergence of all the principal lines of evidence.

But before surrendering any such fragments, such a man will justly demand rigorous *proof* that they are to be surrendered. He will not hastily reckon that all the passages on which error is confidently charged,—especially some of those relating to primeval history, and involving most dark and difficult problems of a cosmical, ethnological, and chronological nature, and which science too often proclaims to be utterly incredible,—are of this description.   They may often be left *sub lite* till both the interpretation of Scripture and the discoveries of science shall have advanced much nearer to incontrovertible conclusions. The theologian, on his side, has still a good deal to do for the full elucidation of the Bible; and science on hers must not only proceed much farther than she has done, but hush her own clamorous discordances, and be quite sure that her theories of to-day will not (as often in the past) be corrected or even ex-ploded by the theories of to-morrow.   Till then she cannot be allowed that magisterial tone which, in spite of her very self, of all the prescient warnings of her great prophet in the " Novum Organum," and the still visible ruins of so many futile theories, she is so fond of employing; till then, she cannot be allowed to speak *ex cathedrâ.*

As to those more extensive excisions which demand the surrender of all that is supernatural in the Bible (however interfused with all its elements, and as incapable of being rent from it without destroying it, as the system of bones or arteries from the human body without destroying *that*), the advocate of the Bible will justly require, before even listening to such a demand, that science shall not affirm, but *demonstrate*, the impossibility or incredibility of miracles. When she has done that, I for one acknowledge that it will be time to shut the book as a hopeless riddle of fable or falsehood, or both,—which it will be hardly worth while to open again.

Mean time he who admits, in any degree, the reasoning in these lectures—namely, that the Bible is not to be accounted for by merely human forces, ought not to feel much difficulty in this last matter; for if he concedes a revelation at all, in which are discovered truths and facts undiscoverable by human faculties, and conveyed in modes and forms for which human nature will not account—he has already admitted a *miracle*—a fact as much in the face of that "invariable order" of nature, and those "immutable series of antecedents and consequents" on which the objector to miracles insists, as any that can be conceived. The only difference is that the miracle here has been wrought in the sphere of mind, and not in that of matter, —a difference which, to a man who knows what the objection to all miracles logically involves, will not affect the question.[1]

---

[1] On some of the difficulties referred to above, a few pages will be found in the Appendix, No. VIII.

APPENDIX.

APPENDIX.

No. I., p. 26.

WHILE the morality of the Old Testament is substantially the same with that of the New, both being summed up in those " two commandments " which, as Christ says, embody all that " Moses and the prophets" taught, and which contain, by implication, all the principal developments of the Gospel, it cannot be denied that the ethics of the New Testament modify in certain points the code of the Old ; not, indeed, by relaxing any moral precepts, but by enlarging them beyond the scope of what *equity* strictly demands, and making that a part of Christian morality which nature had not made so. This, it seems to me, is implied in that " new commandment " which Christ gave to His disciples. He forbade to Christians much which Jew or Gentile might blamelessly have felt and done ; for neither would have done what was *wrong* in exacting, within the limits of equity, retribution for injuries—provided the claim was urged strictly within those limits, and without malignity of feeling. Exact reparation for injuries wantonly inflicted, when enforced only on these conditions, cannot be censured as injustice. But the Gospel code takes man *out* of himself ; lifts him into a loftier plane of morals ; tells him to refrain from much which it would be natural, and, by other codes, not wrong to do : in many cases, to waive the rights he might press, and endure wrong, rather than requite or resent it.

And this is what our Saviour plainly means when He says, "It has been said by them of old time, An eye for an eye, a tooth for a tooth " (this is truly part of the Mosaic law, and no *gloss*), " But *I* say unto you, Love your enemies—Do good to them that hate you, and pray for them that despitefully use you and persecute you." It is as though He had said, " I abolish the *lex talionis*, though it is a part of your law, and is in itself bare justice ; but I show you a more excellent way."

I confess I am very much perplexed to know how this more

elevated morality, not only *above* nature but *against* it, should have proceeded from the heart of man ; and as little can I conceive it coming from the Jews as from any body, since it was in contradiction to a law they deemed to be Divine, and which sanctioned, as they thought, a very different practice.[1]

To the observation that the moral precepts of Christianity seem against the grain of human nature, it may be thought, on a superficial glance, sufficient reply to say that the practices adopted under many systems of false religion,—for example, the frightful self-torture and austerities so often enjoined and submitted to,- are as much against it. The brief but conclusive answer is,—that the facts in question are *not* contrary to human nature, but as abundant

[1] It seems to me that in the distinctions here suggested we must find the answer to many of the difficulties in what are called the " imprecatory " Psalms. I am aware that some of these difficulties admit of grammatical answers, and are solved by a more just translation ; but not all. Of these, it is often said, " What an unchristian spirit they display ! " forgetting that David was not a Christian. A Christian *would* be wrong in cherishing a desire for even just retribution on those who had most deeply wronged him. Whether David was so, would depend on whether malignity prompted his feelings and language. But we must put ourselves in *his* situation, before we can justly weigh, far less harshly press, his expressions. They were wrung from one who had been driven from home and friends, and the "house of God ; " chased "like a partridge on the mountains ; " his life sought, his blood thirsted for, by those to whom he had been a signal benefactor. Even so, they would still be inconsistent with the code of the gospel, though (Christians as we profess to be) it is impossible not to recognise the same spirit in the satisfaction often expressed at the condign punishment of some abnormal iniquity. To understand David aright, we must remember how Englishmen feel and speak during the agony of an Indian mutiny, or when they are stung by some atrocity of Greek brigandage. The feelings are felt to be natural and—*just ,*—so David's were ; but they are not the gospel. On this point there are some admirable remarks, full of philosophic discrimination, in Isaac Taylor's Lectures on Hebrew Poetry. " We fail to realise circumstances and states of mind such as are here" (in some of the Psalms) " brought into view. To do so, we, in these easy times, must travel far away from the secure and tranquil meadow-lands of ordinary life. But there have been tens of thousands in ages past, who have trodden the rugged heavenward road, and found it to be a way, not only very thorny and flinty to the feet, but beset with terrors ; for spiteful and remorseless men have couched beside this narrow way, and have rendered it terrible to the pilgrims. A path of anguish and of many fears it has been. In our drowsy repetition of these Psalms, cushioned as we are upon the soft luxuries of modern life, we fail to understand these outcries from the martyr's field, —
    ' Arise, thou Judge of the earth,—
    Recompense a reward to the proud.'
Let only such times return upon us as have been of more frequency than these times of ease in the history of the Church, and we should quickly know how to understand a Psalm such as the 94th. Christian men and women, when they are called in like manner to suffer, are required to pay respect to a rule of suffering which is many centuries later than the times of David ; but which, although it is a higher rule, does not bring under blame the natural and the religious emotions that were proper to the earlier dispensation."

experience shows, quite in analogy with it. Fanaticism will submit to any course of discipline and suffering that promises to realise the dreams of spiritual ambition, or lay the spectres of a guilty conscience ; but it is a *selfish* impulse that exacts the obedience, whether it be for the expiation of guilt, or the attainment of superhuman sanctity, or in the hope of reabsorption into the Deity. But though it is easy to account for such cases, I know not how to account, on the mere principles of human nature, for such a general principle as this—" Love your enemies ; do good to them that hate you, and pray for them who despitefully use you and persecute you." This fruit is not grown on the crabbed stock of a selfish superstition.

APPENDIX.

No. II., p. 28.

IF the miracles were falsely *imputed* to the historic Christ with His acquiescence, it occurs to ask the following questions :—

1. Did He pretend to work them, though He never did ?

If so, then in spite of all M. Rénan's sophistical attempts to justify Him in such *tracasserie*, His conduct is at utter variance with the impressions of that intellectual and moral greatness the world has ever accorded to Him. He was equally weak and wicked. He was weak, because, though plenty of miracles can be palmed on credulous ignorance in behalf of systems already firmly established,—to appeal to them in order to establish a new religion, and in the face of inveterate prejudice guarding an ancient religion, is so far from being a likely thing for a wise man to attempt, that as Davison[1] justly says, there are but two religions in which the attempt would seem ever to have been made ; that is, the *Jewish* and the *Christian !*

Mahomet, it is well known, declined this test, which his astuteness doubtless saw would be fatal (as it has often been found to be) when a hostile and therefore vigilant world is to be the judge. Accordingly we find that Mahomet tells us of many wondrous things acted behind the scenes,—as of his monstrous night journey on

---

[1] *Lectures on Prophecy.* Paley also well says : " To hear some men talk, one would suppose the setting up of a religion by miracles to be a thing of every day's experience ; whereas the whole current of history is against it. Hath any founder of a new sect amongst Christians pretended to miraculous powers, and succeeded by his pretensions? . . . The French prophets, in the beginning of the present (18th) century, ventured to allege miraculous evidence, and immediately ruined their cause by their temerity."—*Evidences,* p. 133.

horseback, from Mecca to the seventh heaven,—but he does not bring such things on the public stage.

But the above supposition reflects still more on the goodness than on the wisdom of Christ. If He attempted this cheat, it is impossible that He can have been possessed of those qualities which have ravished the world's admiration, and which seem to beam out upon us from His whole history. To invest Him with such contradictory attributes, is indeed to make Him a paradox in human nature !

It is hardly worth while to ask how it came to pass that He cheated *prejudiced* and *hostile* multitudes into a belief that He had performed miracles when He had not. If He did, their character as human beings is almost as inexplicable as His own. I am content to say, that if Christ pretended to work miracles, and did *not*, His conduct is wholly inexplicable on the principles of human nature, supposing the portrait to be that of a real personage ; for he has undoubtedly impressed the world,—even those who have been most hostile to His higher claims,—with strong convictions both of His intellectual and moral greatness. But I need say the less on this point, as it is now almost universally conceded that Jesus Christ was wholly incapable of any such conduct ; and, indeed, not a few writers against Christianity taunt its advocates with perpetually trying to prove—what they *now* say nobody denies that it is not a forgery, and that Christ is no impostor ;— though, in fact, this was long the favourite theory of scepticism, and is even now partially resorted to by Rénan and Strauss, who, in the difficult task of accounting for everything by myth, feel that it may be as well not wholly to reject it. They forget that, if it be not rejected wholly, it may as well be accepted altogether ; for as the subject of the great controversy says, "He who is unfaithful in the least, is unfaithful also in much ;" and if Christ cheated the world at all, it is impossible to say how far.

2. Shall we next, then, suppose that the miracles were never wrought by Christ, and that He never falsely pretended to work them, but that He *fancied* He had wrought them before the gaze of the world, and that the world *fancied* it too? How shall we reconcile this weakness, or rather madness, of fanaticism, with the qualities which belong to the historic Personage described to us? —with His self-possession, His calmness, His singular prudence, His entire freedom through all His discourses and conduct from every trait of an ill-balanced mind? And, further, how shall we

account for multitudes of men simultaneously fancying the same thing? Surely, it is to suppose an inconceivable subversion of human nature, not only in Christ Himself, but in all that came in contact with Him!—But on this point, again, it is not necessary to say more. The *naturalism* (one would imagine the name was given in irony) which once conjectured that the miraculous phenomena of the gospel might be resolved into misunderstood natural phenomena, and that a *number* of people simultaneously mistook lanterns for stars, thunder for articulate speech, women in white, or even men in armour, for angels,—is not the *naturalism* of human nature.

The author of "Ecce Homo" regards it as indubitable that Christ must have been *accredited* with the performance of miracles; and if that able writer has not made it so clear as could be wished whether, in his opinion, those miracles were real or not, logically his argument can lead to no other conclusion than that they were real. He believes that Christ's disciples and followers fully acquiesced in thus accrediting Him; and that nothing less than their plenary honesty in this, will account for all that influence He exerted over them. If so, and their belief was the effect of deception or delusion on His part, all the anomalies in His character reappear; His fraud or His fanaticism stands out in glaring contrast with all those traits of intellectual and moral greatness which the world has attributed to Him, and which even the majority of those who reject His claims have not been slow to concede. Such are some of the paradoxes in which the mere ascription of the miracles to Christ, if He was a real personage, and knew anything about that ascription, involves us.

APPENDIX.

No. III., p. 39.

THE paradox in the text is not at all diminished, rather in many respects increased, by the fond theories adopted by many critics of modern times, who assure the Jews of what their halting patriotism failed to find out for themselves,—that their annals are fabulous, the inventions of a late age, and successfully palmed on the nation as their true history!

Every one can see, indeed, what it is that has led to the projection of these theories; namely, the necessity (as the rationalist supposes) of getting quit, at any cost of contradiction or absurdity, of the preternatural events in the history,—of miracles and prophecy. Apart from such exigency, which demands a later and fabulous origin of the documents which record them, there is not one in ten thousand who would not feel that there was abundantly greater reason to acquiesce in their authenticity and genuineness than to accept any such hypothesis; for the obstacles are enormous.

Its advocates are at infinite variance among themselves; the periods they assign for the imagined origin of the books differ by many centuries, and are in any case determined by the merest conjecture, which wanders through all epochs, from the time of the Judges to that of Malachi, " seeking rest and finding none." On the other hand, every such hypothesis is in defiance of the vehement and consentient testimony of the Jewish nation in every age; of the astonishing proofs they have given of the care and honesty with which they have preserved what they so revere ; and in the absence of any, the faintest, indication that their nation possessed any tradition of the persons by whom, or the time when, these libellous annals were substituted for the true, and, disgraceful as they are, adopted without a protest or a suspicion by the people ! The very names of those who operated so gigantic a fraud, and inflicted at the same time such a stab on national vanity, have been suffered to drop into oblivion : while the victims, who could not but be aware when these pretended chronicles of an older time were *first* attempted to be palmed upon them, clutched the ignominious records to their hearts, affirmed that they contained God's own account of their nation ; and not only clung to their shame, but lied, and lied universally, that the stigma might abide for ever !

If the Bible be not what it professes to be, the conduct of the Jews abounds with paradoxes. On the other hand, supposing it to relate a true history of the Jewish people, they vanish. It is possible to conceive that the successive generations of Israelites, being conscious that the conduct charged upon their ancestors and themselves was truly charged, would accept the recital, and submit in silence to the unmeasured reproaches cast upon them,—though even this would demand the indisputable notoriety of the facts. It is impossible, indeed, to point out any entire community which at a late period of its existence has accepted mythical fabrications as its genuine history ; certainly it would never do so unless they enormously flattered its vanity, nor even then without provoking suspicion and protest in many quarters. But is it imaginable that it would do this, with absolute unanimity and in absolute silence, when stigma and invective marked every page? Only those who have carefully read the Pentateuch, the Historical books, and the Prophets, with express view of ascertaining the extent of this element, can have any adequate idea of the space occupied by invective, rebuke, and reproaches addressed to the nation, though mingled, it is true, with the most inimitable touches of pathetic remonstrance on their wilfulness, wickedness, and folly.

APPENDIX.
No. IV., p. 117.

THE *impossibility* of prophecy (as of miracles) is a pure dogma, or prejudice rather, of pseudo-science, unworthy of *true* science, and as much a generalisation beyond the data,—as much a precipitate "anticipation" of facts,—as any that Bacon has exposed and denounced in his "Novum Organum." It is a position which a theist, in any proper sense, can hardly be imagined to maintain ; nor probably has there ever been one who would venture thus to limit the Divine omnipotence and omniscience. There would be this additional absurdity in it, that it would deny to God what many modern *savans* believe will one day be possible to man. We are assured that, in virtue of advancing science, man is at length to endue himself with the power of *pre-vision*, whether God ever gives it to him or not. To say, then, that God cannot speak to us by prophecy, is to say, either that He is not so well acquainted with the relations of all possible events,—with the whole chain of antecedents and consequents,—as man will one day be ; or, that having that knowledge, He cannot impart it, though man (when he has thus equipped himself) certainly can !

On the other hand, to say that prophecy is absolutely *incredible*, not because God *cannot*, but because he certainly *will* not give it, is little better ; for in the first place it is impossible to imagine how we are to ascertain this ; and secondly, it is not very compatible with the above speculation of man's possibly becoming a seer himself. For if that shall ever be the case, it must still be because God, who gifted him with such powers, *wills* it ; and if so, one would surmise it to be not improbable that God might, in some cases, anticipate a gift which it seems He wills man should one day possess ; and confer, for special purposes, on some favoured persons, what He designs that certain sages and *savans*, with more liberal hands, shall hereafter bestow on the world at large !

It must be admitted, however, that the argument from prophecy, let it be ever so strong, may, by a little stratagem of criticism, be often plausibly eluded. Prophecy, however expressed, may always be alleged to be too *plain* or too *obscure :* if too plain, it was written after the event, and is history and not prophecy ; if obscure, its reference is uncertain, and we cannot be sure that it is prophecy.

This solvent immediately discharges all colour from much of the prophetical matter to which it is applied. Is there any obscurity about the prophecy? Then it is *not* clear that it refers to the events of which it is interpreted. Is it perfectly clear, so that no one has any doubt that it *does* refer to them? Then, *ipso facto*, it is proved to be no prophecy at all, but history. So that, in short, we may say the ingenuity of man infallibly arms him against almost any impressions that prophecy, let it be ever so true, can make upon him, if he but act courageously on these principles.

It might, indeed, appear reasonable to say, that if the world is to be governed on the ordinary principles on which God at present governs it ; if events are to be brought about by moral agencies and moral forces, that is, by rational creatures acting upon motives ; then, unless men are to be tempted to tamper with the Divine plans,— to accelerate or retard (as they imagine) the events they deem predicted,—it is hardly conceivable that prophecy should not have such a degree of obscurity resting upon it, be here enveloped in such twilight, lie there so deep in shadow, that it shall be always possible to feel, or to affect, doubts about its application, till the events which fulfil it make it plain.

I see not, however, how either of the principles above mentioned.—one depending on the allegation that documents are *later* than the facts they record, the other on the allegation that they are not *decipherable*,—will suffice to explain those " coincidences " between Scripture and the world's history to which reference has been made in the text, and to many others like them, in which none can pretend that the facts preceded the documents, or that their interpretation is ambiguous. I only mentioned them in that place, as amongst the many eccentric traits, τά παράδοξα, of the Bible ; for that is all my present theme required. But I apprehend it will be difficult to give any explanation of them which will not involve true prophecy.

It may be as well to remark that difficulties in relation to some portions of prophecy must result from the *historic* form of any such revelation as the Bible professes to be. Slowly developing through many ages, the earliest utterances will be covered with the "hoar of antiquity" before the last are spoken. Of many historic facts, therefore, cursorily related, it may be difficult to recover the true account. Nay, it is conceivable that the prophecies (supposing them, for argument's sake, to be such) of the decay and extinction of some kingdoms,—for example, of Edom and Moab,—may be so true, that there are no longer adequate relics to verify them ; and that though (as Davison says) they may have done their work at the time they were fulfilled, and inspired confidence in other prophecies then unfulfilled, may, so far from being evidence to *us*, be simply problems for our diligence and research; perhaps even difficulties to our faith, and tending, amongst other things, to make the conditions of that faith much more nearly equal in different ages than is often imagined.

APPENDIX.

No. V., p. 133.

THE wildest hypotheses have been formed as to the character and history of Melchizedek, founded on the expression, " Without father, without mother, without beginning of days, or end of life." They have arisen, as it seems to me, simply from forgetting that in any " type" it is only *analogical* resemblance that is pretended. Indeed, anything more would destroy the type. If the " type" and the " antitype" had not only similarity of attributes, but identity, there would no longer be between them mere resemblance, and the image would vanish. From the words quoted above, it has been imagined that Melchizedek must have been literally " without father and without mother ;" whence it has been argued, though there is not a syllable in the brief record to favour so strange an hypothesis, that he must have been a superhuman or celestial personage ; or the Messiah Himself, anticipating His own incarnation ,—one of those transient manifestations which are much more rationally associated with the character and attributes of that " Angel of the Covenant " who plays so conspicuous a part in the transactions of the Pentateuch.

The theories in question are as superfluous as irrational, if we duly consider what a type not only is, but to be truly such, must be : always founded on partial and often remote and accidental resemblances, though still sufficient to suggest the relation between the type and the thing typified.

Not only is this the case with the types of Scripture ; in fact every poetical comparison between objects which have only a certain "analogical resemblance" (and may differ by a thousand contrasts) demonstrates the same thing. Whether the analogy be between animate and inanimate objects, or between animals and men, or between material objects and abstract qualities ; in all, it is very partial and often very fanciful. Thus the peculiarity in question, so far from applying to Scripture imagery alone, is equally applicable to poetry generally ; and whatever peculiarities may be technically predicated of a "type" of Scripture beyond a mere image, its fundamental principle is illustrated by a universal law of human thought and language. When a hero is compared to a "lion," or a "ship" to a "bird," or a "nest" to a "house," everybody perfectly understands in how infinite ways these conceptions differ from one another—how shadowy is the resemblance between them ; and, moreover, that that resemblance is not founded on any essential identity, even of the qualities in which they are compared but on the analogical resemblance of those qualities, on the λόγων ὁμοιότης, the "equality of ratios," as Aristotle aptly expresses it ; and accordingly every metaphor, founded on analogical resemblance, can always be expanded in the terms of a geometrical proportion. Thus, when we call "youth the morning of life," or "virtue the enamel of the soul," we mean that what the morning is to the day, so is youth to life ; or that as enamel is to that which it encases and preserves, so is virtue to the soul. The courage of the hero, conscious of danger, and "looking before and after" while he braves it, is no more the courage of the lion, than the innocence of Christ is the innocence of the "lamb ;" though superficial appearances, as in other cases of resemblance, justify the simile, and give vividness to the correspondent conception. If these obvious facts with regard to the nature of "types," and indeed of poetical imagery in general, had been remembered by those who commented on the seventh chapter of the Epistle to the Hebrews, it would have spared the world much strange speculation. It would have been seen that the manner in which Melchizedek appears on the stage of history, emerging like a phantom out of darkness for a moment, and vanishing into darkness again ; springing from no known progenitors, and having no known relation to posterity ; independent in his priesthood of any priestly lineage; deriving his functions from no predecessor, and consigning them to no successor; were sufficiently striking, though only analogical resemblances, to constitute him a type of the great High Priest with whom he is compared. They are as intelligible as a thousand other resemblances on which similar imagery, both in ordinary allegory and in the types of Scripture, is rationally founded. This is said in explanation of what appears to me the natural exegesis of the apostle's language. The fact of the singular *correspondence* among the scattered allusions to Melchizedek, which occur between the book of Genesis and the Epistle to the Hebrews, is quite independent of it, and is the point on which I have insisted in the text.

APPENDIX.

No. VI., p. 136.

I MUCH regret that my limited space did not permit me to treat the "Unity" of the Bible at greater length. Those who wish for further information may consult the excellent lectures of Dr. W. L. Alexander, "On the Connection and Harmony of the Old and New Testaments," and the works to which he has made reference. The little book of Lord Hatherley on the "Continuity" of the Bible contains some excellent observations on the same subject; and the like may be said of a section in a little tractate entitled "Divine Footprints in the Bible." The book is designed, the author modestly tells us, for "youth;" and it needs only a more cautious statement of some points, and greater expansion and illustration in others, to make it a valuable "manual" for those for whom it is designed.

Many in our day, as well as some in former times, would endeavour to extricate Christianity from certain difficulties by cutting the ligaments between it and Judaism. They would displace it from what they regard its precarious foundations in the Old Testament. I am profoundly convinced that this cannot be done without leaving both in ruins. Much stress has been laid on an admission of Paley, which is in itself a very reasonable one, but which has been pressed in a way which, liberal as he was in his theology, he would have been far from approving. He states, with his usual admirable succinctness and precision, his main reasons for his belief in the superhuman origin of the Jewish dispensation.

" I conceive it," he says, "to be very difficult to assign any other cause for the commencement or existence of that institution : especially for the singular circumstance of the Jews adhering to the unity of God, when every other people slid into polytheism ; for their being men in religion, children in everything else ; behind other nations in the arts of peace and war, superior to the most improved in their sentiments and doctrines relating to the Deity. Undoubtedly, also, our Saviour recognises the prophetic character of many of their ancient writings. So far, therefore, we are bound, as Christians, to go." He then proceeds to say : " But to make Christianity answerable with its life for the circumstantial truth of each passage of the Old Testament, the genuineness of every book, the information, fidelity, and judgment of every writer in it, is to bring, I will not say great, but unnecessary difficulties, into the whole system." Now I conceive every rational man would concede as much as this, and even more ; for he would not " make Christianity answer with its life for the circumstantial truth of each passage" in the New Testament, any more than of each passage in the Old. But this is very different from fancying that the Old Testament generally may be given up without affecting the position of the New. It were well if youthful theologians would ponder the following words (expressly intended for them) of Herder. In spite of his free spirit of criticism, he writes of the Old Testament thus :—
" Der Grund der Theologie ist die Bibel, und der Grund des N. T. ist das alte. Unmöglich verstehn wir jenes recht, wenn wir dieses nicht verstehen : denn Christenthum ist aus dem Judenthum hervorgegangen. der Genius der Sprache ist in beiderlei Büchern derselbe ; und den Genius der Sprache können wir nie besser, d.i. nie wahrer, tiefer, vielseitiger, angenehmer studiren, als in Poesie, und zwar so viel möglich in den ältesten Poesien derselben. Es ist falsch und verführend, wenn man jungen Theologen das N. T. mit Ausschliessung des alten anpreiset ; ohne dieses ist jenes auf eine gelehrte Weise nicht einmal verständlich. Dazu ist in ihm, dem A. T., eine so reiche Abwechslung von Geschichten, Bildern, Charakteren, Scenen : in ihm sehen wir die vielfarbige Dämmerung, der schönen Sonne aufgang ; im N. T. steht sie am höchsten Himmel, und jederman weiss, welche Tageszeit dem sinnlichen auge die erquickendste, die stärkendste ist. Studire man also das A. T. auch nur als ein menschliches Buch voll alter Poesien, mit Lust und Liebe, so wird uns das Neue in seiner Reinheit, seinem hohen Glanz, seiner überirdischen schönheit von selbst aufgehn. Sammle

man den Reichthum jenes in sich und man wird auch in diesem kein leerer geschmakloser oder gar entweihender Schwässer worden."—*Herder.* Preface to his *Geist der Ebräischen Poesie.*

APPENDIX.
No. VII., p. 212.

IT is no slight testimony to the adaptation and comprehensiveness of the religious contents of the Bible, that so many millions have declared that all the moods and necessities of their moral and spiritual life are exhaustively expressed there. As there is scarcely any condition in human life but may find its parallel in the scenes of the Scripture history, so may it be truly said that all the phenomena of religious experience are there described with incomparable force. The devout mind finds every shade of emotion,—of penitence, faith, hope, devout aspiration, — and every variation of spiritual consciousness, already expressed to his hand, in words better than his own, and as if by one who knew man better than man knows himself. His whole nature is reflected, as it were, in that faithful mirror. This is especially the case in the Psalms, Gospels, and Epistles, which have made so many say that they found in the Bible the vivid expression of what, till they read it there, was hardly known to themselves, or could be uttered only in faltering accents and with a stammering tongue.

Accordingly, they have felt that the strongest evidence of the truth of the Bible is to be found in its own pages, and that its moral and religious elements are to them no less than demonstration. The consciousness that its representations find an echo in their own hearts; that the doctrines it propounds are exquisitely adapted to meet the conditions of that nature which it thus reveals, and yet so out of the range of all ordinary human speculation, and so little likely to suggest themselves ; that, above all, an unfeigned faith in those doctrines has transformed their whole life, made them emulous of all goodness, and filled their hearts with joy and peace ; —the consciousness, I say, of all this, has been to them the "evidence of evidences." To such men, it seems the climax of absurdity that the Scriptures should be false.[1]

[1] This subject has been very powerfully dealt with by Dr. Chalmers in his " Evidences." Vol. II. bk. iii. ch. 3, pp. 99–169. *Experimental Evidence.*-- It is true that this evidence cannot be directly appealed to in arguing with a man who rejects Christianity. The argument, while he is in such a condition,

APPENDIX.

No. VIII., p. 323.

§ 1. PERHAPS the difficulty which in this age has been as much insisted on as any, is the Scriptural account of " Creation " in the first chapter of Genesis. Some indeed maintain that the phenomena with which geology chiefly has to do are not involved with the first chapter of Genesis ; that the first verse simply ascribes the original of all things to the will of God ; and then passing by (with characteristic silence about all subjects of mere curiosity, whether connected with distant worlds or primeval time) the immense interval occupied by those changes which chiefly challenge the study of geologists, proceeds to describe the phenomena which were immediately antecedent to the appearance of man, and preparatory to it. According to these commentators, the account of Moses does not properly come into collision with geology. The unnumbered centuries which the geologist demands for the processes by which he contends the world was constituted, are given him *ad libitum*. On the other hand, it is fair to say that many geologists maintain that if this theory were adopted, similar difficulties would still encounter us in the interpretation of this chapter.

Now without venturing into this controversy, or pretending to say whether the chapter professes to relate only the changes wrought at one epoch of the world's history, and introductory to the creation of man, or embraces phenomena far anterior to it, may it not be possible to say something for the chapter independently of either hypothesis ? Is it not possible that both those who contend

must take lower ground.   Yet even *he* may be reasonably asked to attach some weight to the immense "cloud of witnesses" that depose on its behalf ; the multitudinous examples of a transformed life it has furnished ; and the moral changes, the revolutions in sentiment and practice, which, after making all deductions, it has wrought in modern as compared with ancient civilization. Some exceedingly powerful remarks will be found on this point in Mozley's " Bampton Lectures."   Lecture 7.

And though the argument from *experimental* evidence cannot in strictness be used with a man who rejects the Bible altogether,—for the controversy would be, as Frederick the Great said of a war between Prussia and England, like "a fight between a dog and a fish,"—yet even one who rejects the Bible may, if he faithfully consult his own consciousness, at least judge of the fidelity or falsehood of its own draft of our moral nature.   On the other hand, the impossibility of giving the full impression of this species of evidence to him who lacks it, is no argument against Christianity, because its own express test of its truth is that man shall make a practical trial of it.   Those who will not, can as little disprove the testimony of those who will, as he who will not use a physician's prescription can disprove the allegations of its efficacy on the part of those who do.

for the literal accuracy of the description, and those who would gauge that accuracy by the standard of geological research, may be in the wrong? Is it not conceivable that any statement whatever on such a subject, under similar circumstances, would be liable to similar criticism?

I would illustrate my meaning thus. There has been much controversy as to whether this chapter is poetry or history, and champions have appeared for either opinion. That it is very little like ordinary poetry in manner, and as little like ordinary history in its matter, is obvious. But is it not conceivable that it may, in any ordinary sense, be neither the one nor the other? May there not be *another* art, which may give juster conceptions of the possible significance of the chapter than either history or poetry? I mean the art of painting, in which objects are represented, not indeed according to their real dimensions or in their true relative positions, and yet not untruthfully; in which they are delineated in the same *plane*, though they are not in it, and in which foreshortening and perspective make strange work with the actual proportions and appearances of objects? This necessarily follows from the very attempt to give us any idea of a landscape on the same plane. Yet none call the representation *false*. On the contrary, we say it is sufficiently true, to convey to us a very vivid conception of the real scene. A still better illustration, perhaps, might be taken from the same art, in those panoramas which are sometimes exhibited, in which some hundreds of miles of scenery are represented in as many feet of canvas, with the unrolling of which the spectator seems to traverse many degrees of latitude and longitude, and sees all their scenery in an hour or two. It is not a *false* representation which thus cheats the eye of the spectator. It is simply an inadequate one; quite inadequate, no doubt, but such as is alone possible for the spectator to receive; a view adjusted *ad modum recipientis*. But it gives a true approximate conception. That it can go no further results from the nature of things, and the limitations under which the communication is made.

Now let us suppose, for the sake of argument (and it will hardly be thought a very extravagant postulate), that, by way of preface to a volume of Revelation, it was desirable not only to inform man that all things originated in God's will, that all in heaven and on earth was the effect of His creative energy and wisdom, but to give him some general conception—such as it was possible for him to receive—of the gradual development and succession of the principal phenomena by which this mundane system arose. What but such description as would be analogous to a pictorial delineation, with all its dislocation of real relations, would be *possible* to such a creature as man, and within the limits of a mere superscription to the book—which was of course to consist mainly of widely different matter? All the phenomena, in the nature of things, are supposed to have preceded the appearance of man ; he could not be a spectator of them ; he could only be addressed through the medium of his imagination—by the presentation of some mental picture of what "eye had never seen." If the true processes, which all reasoning shows to have been carried on by a very gradual development, and, according to many geologists, during thousands or millions of years, had been fully described, the " records of creation," instead of forming a brief preface to the book, would have been as long in the telling as in the doing ; the compilation would have been as slow as the earth's stratification ; so voluminous, that the "world itself could hardly contain the books that would have been written." Or if the story did not proceed as leisurely as the processes it described, it must, at least, have been as voluminous as the books by which science (though indeed it has hardly yet mastered the alphabet of Nature's mysteries) has so slowly spelt out the hieroglyphics of creation ; or rather, as voluminous as the records of science will be when it has finally deciphered them. But, in that case, the " Preface " to the book of Revelation would have been a thousand times as big as the Revelation itself ; if, indeed, the volumes of the " Transactions " of Science shall ever terminate, and the world last long enough to bring its researches to a close.

In the mean time, such a commentary, voluminous as it would be, would have been of no conceivable use. It would have been quite unintelligible for many successive generations of men, and even then Methusaleh's life would not have been long enough to master it.

What imaginable course, then, could be taken but that of giving man a brief and general, though most imperfect, conception of the apparent procession of phenomena ; to exhibit the wondrous scene as in a picture, in which objects are necessarily distorted, and their real distances and dimensions disguised. In whatever way we imagine a representation given to man, of phenomena which he never saw nor could have seen,—whether in mental vision or graphic language,—it is impossible to conceive it given otherwise than with these limitations.

Of the Mosaic cosmogony, these two facts may, at all events, be without hesitation affirmed. First, that it deviates far less from the conclusions approximately reached by the most careful inductions of modern geology, than any other ancient cosmogony ;—so that, comparing it with them, and supposing it only one of the guesses of a rude primeval philosophy, it is difficult to understand how the writer of Genesis should have been so superior to all other ancient speculators. Secondly, that there is not one of these cosmogonies that approaches it in the combined simplicity and sublimity of description, and unexampled compression of style, to be found in the first chapter of Genesis.

One cannot but lay great stress on the former point. The ancient cosmogonies, Egyptian, Greek, Hindoo, Chinese, commit themselves so hopelessly by outrages on all physical science, and abound in such monstrous fables, that they are the subject of universal derision. How is it that in the Hebrew cosmogony (without pretending to conceal the difficulties of a literal interpretation) the reader is struck both with its approximation to many of the results of modern science, and its utter divergence from all ancient speculation? If Moses did not know as much as modern world-builders, still, how is it that he is so superior to all the ancient ?

Nor is it a point unworthy of remark that the Bible has very little that *can* come into conflict with modern science. This is the effect of its characteristic abstinence from what is not closely connected with its great object. The point has been well argued by Dr. J. H. Gladstone, in his recent lecture, entitled "Points of Supposed Collision between Scripture and Natural Science." He shows that in the ordinary systems propounded in quasi-sacred records (whether independent of the Bible or grafted on it), the tendency to play the philosopher—always so pleasant to human nature—has tempted the authors to betray themselves by their egregious attempts at explaining physical phenomena. " It seems to me," says he, " a question worthy of consideration, How did it come to pass that these (the Jewish) writers did not profess to explain the phenomena of the universe? So completely is this the case, that it is rarely possible to ascertain their own views. . . . But in order fairly to understand the significance of the fact that these writers avoid scientific explanations, it is necessary to turn to other professed revelations, or to the commentators on the Bible itself. It is well known that the Phœnicians, Babylonians,

Persians, Indians, Greeks, Chinese, and other nations, had wonderful cosmogonies, in which a mundane egg generally appears ; and that the Puranas give a large amount of such information, as that India is surrounded by seven oceans, composed respectively of salt water, sugar-cane juice, wine, clarified butter, curds, milk, and fresh water. The books that grew up alongside the sacred Scriptures are still more to the point."[1]

§ 2. The few statements that the Pentateuch makes on ethnological and some related subjects, are of strikingly different character from those which we find usually put forth by nations in their cradle. There is nothing in them that savours of the pride of race ; they are singularly cosmopolitan. Moses does not pretend that the Hebrews, like the Greeks, were *Autochthones*, or that their race, like the Hindoo or Egyptian, flourished some millions of years before other nations began. He affirms that " all men are of one blood," and that their " speech " was originally one—very singular declarations to make in the face of so many apparently conflicting facts. They have been accepted, however, to a great extent, by modern science, though just now again questioned ;—perhaps, after further research, to be accepted again. But however this may be, one cannot but wonder how Moses came to think so differently from all the rest of the ancient world.[2]

It similarly surprises us, that if he spoke from conjecture in that early age, in ignorance of the extent of the world, and of the species of creatures it might contain,—he should so confidently have promised man the dominion of the earth—that he should people and subdue it ;[3] and that no great physical disturbance should ever interfere with that " law " (of the stability of which he seems to have had as clear an idea as any modern could desire) which guaranteed the perpetual recurrence of " day and night, summer and winter, seed-time and harvest." Experience has confirmed these things, but at that early date they were somewhat bold speculations.

Whether some points in dispute between the Bible and science, and still *sub lite*, are to be added to or subtracted from the difficulties of the Scriptures ; whether they are to be accounted errors which require to be met by one or other of the theories referred to in the

[1] Lectures on " Faith and Free Thought," p. 165.
[2] This is well illustrated in " Aids to Faith," Essay 6 ; in Birk's " Bible and Modern Thought," ch. 14 ; and by Dr. Gladstone in the lecture just cited.
[3] This point is well put in Dr. Redford's Lectures, entitled, " Holy Scriptures Verified," pp. 66–85, 140–146.

text, or,—by being shown to be in harmony with more advanced knowledge,—shall be transferred to the side of proofs, must be left at present to conjecture. Such are some of the questions connected with those prehistoric problems which the present generation is so eagerly discussing ; for example, as to the primeval condition of the human species ; its antiquity ; the ethnological relation of its various races ; the order and date of their diffusion ; the origin of language ; and whether all languages are related to one another by radical affinities, and spring from one source. On some of these questions, perhaps, we shall never get much light ; on others we require far more than we have (both from Scripture and science) to justify a definite conclusion. Nor is it unreasonable to ask, both of the believer in the Bible and its opponents, to exercise patience, for it is quite as necessary to one as to the other. For if the first, in his unwise presumption, and haste to defend himself, has often snatched up a weapon which has broken in his hand, the last has quite as often greedily listened to any whisper of a discovery which promised discomfiture to the Bible, even though in a few brief years it has been dismissed, by science itself, with contempt. He has waited for no rigorous verification, but caught at the too welcome conclusion at once. Both parties, in truth, have reason to exercise much indulgence towards one another ; for, as the history of science and of theology shows, both, though for different reasons, one from love of tradition and the other from love of novelty, have anticipated the conclusions which should have waited for a calm and patient weighing of evidence.

Perhaps those who read these admonitions to patience may smile at the possible alternative above stated ; namely, that some of those difficulties of science which are still *sub judice* may be solved in a manner which, instead of *adding* to the difficulties of Scripture, will prove strong confirmations of its truth. I grant this is conjecture : nevertheless it is founded on many analogies in the past history of science. The first immature speculations in almost every branch of modern science have been presumed to be of ominous aspect on the Bible. But many of the objections science has raised, science itself has in a few years dispelled.

§ 3. There are those who find great moral difficulties in the Bible, and it may be deemed uncandid not to say at least a few words about them. The whole book, in accordance with what I have represented as one of its *pervading* characteristics—to vindicate the claims of God and His moral government over us—is so perspicuous and so earnest in its assertion of all duty, and its protests against all "ungodliness and unrighteousness of men,"—it is throughout so irradiated by the light of the Divine purity,—that it is impossible any doubt can exist as to its *general* tendency.

Accordingly, the objections are to certain special portions or details, which, if they be *demonstrably* of immoral character or tendency, are *ipso facto* condemned by the whole tenour and substance of the book : if they are not, their purport ought to be determined by its universal spirit. Nevertheless, it is not difficult to give a specific reply to the greater number. I have only space for a few.

Sometimes it is inferred that, because the Bible relates evil deeds without express condemnation, it must sanction them, or at least deem them venial. To this it is sufficient to reply that, as on the one hand it is one of the most marked characteristics of Scripture to state bare facts dramatically, without comment and without reflection,—leaving the reader to draw his own conclusion,—so its perpetual and emphatic assertion of the claims of the Divine law and of human duty leaves him in no doubt as to the inference which, in such cases, he ought to draw.

In some cases, actions in the Old Testament are, no doubt, represented as pardonable or justifiable, which, judged by the Christian standard, would not be so. But they are unfairly measured by *that* standard, -which to a certain extent is an innovation on all moral codes, and condemns many acts of strictly retributive justice which the instinct of a natural sense of equity would not. But to this I have already referred in the first article of this Appendix.

Sometimes objection is taken to what is called God's " partiality " towards certain "favourites," in spite of enormous delinquencies, and criticism has especially fastened on Jacob and David as examples. This accusation, again, might be left to be answered by the general character of the book,—which perpetually assures us that, whatever *appearances* there may be to the contrary, "God is no respecter of persons," and that He will, in due time, prove it. Mean time I cannot but express my astonishment that these two instances should ever have been pleaded as affording even *primâ facie* evidence to the contrary. For if ever sin was seen to be a " hard bargain,"—if ever it was seen in its punishment,—it is in the history of those two men. The whole sequel of their lives was tinged, and in a great degree embittered, by it. Rebecca never

saw again that darling son for whom she had brought the guilt of
perjury on her soul and his : Jacob himself was driven into exile
from his father's house for twenty years ; and during nearly all that
time he was the hireling and the victim of his rapacious kinsman,
who " deceived" him by just such trickery as he himself had practised on his father ;—palming upon him Leah for Rachel, and
" changing his wages ten times." After twenty years he returned,
but in abject dread of his injured brother, at whose approach he
was thrown into that ecstasy of sorrow and terror which ushered in
his solitary night-vigil by the brook Jabbok. To this add all the
mournful episode of Joseph's exile, Dinah's dishonour, and his
other domestic trials, and who can think his sin " unvisited " ?

As to David, it was declared to him, at the very moment he was
told that his repentance was accepted, that his iniquity was marked,
and would be remembered before God ; that though he thought he
had wrapt his crime in secrecy, it should be blazoned to the world
with every note of shame and ignominy. So the oracle ran ; and
left David for long years to expect when and how this dreaded bolt
would fall,—perhaps not the least part of his punishment. At last
it fell, and hardly could he have imagined how dreadful the stroke
would be. His favourite son Absalom rises in rebellion against
him, drives him from his throne and apital, involves his people in
the horrors of civil war ; and, in pursuit of his detestable policy,
visits on his father, and "in the face of the sun," the dishonour, and
worse than the dishonour, which David had brought into the house
of Uriah. If such chastisement in the case of Jacob and David be
instances of the Divine *partiality* and *favouritism*, who of us but
must pray, " Oh, God, in Thy great mercy, deliver us from being at
last accounted among Thine enemies " ?

It is true that on deep repentance and forsaking of their sin, God
did forgive even such transgressors. But is there any heart so hard
as to wish it otherwise ? Shall our " eye be evil," because God " is
good "? Is it not precisely what the book says God *will* do, and
is " delighted" in every such case to do? Is it not our highest felicity to know it ? If any one says, " No ; such men ought never to
have been forgiven, nor received into favour more ;"—but no, I
cannot suppose any that is but a man will say *that.*

Another difficulty has been found in the slaughter of the Canaanites. Now, appalling as such a fact is, and incomprehensible
as it must *a priori* be, yet, so far as the moral government of God
is concerned, it is no more appalling in the effects, nor quite so

incomprehensible in character, as those things which we are compelled to say He does or permits to be done in His ordinary administration of the world. The devastations of pestilence, earthquake, famine,—involving guilt and innocence, age and infancy, in the same indiscriminate ruin,—are just as awful, and equally mysterious, however firmly we may believe that God will at length vindicate all His proceedings : while they are hardly so incomprehensible, because we are assured that in the case of the Canaanites the visitation was *judicial;* that their iniquity had been long borne with, and that "its measure was now full;" that such was the grossness of all unutterable crimes with which they were tainted, that, as in the case of Sodom and Gomorrah, something little short of extirpation was the only remedy.

The reader may doubt, if he will, whether this be the *true* history of the transaction ; but in founding a *moral* objection on the Bible *account* of it, it is utterly unreasonable to forget that this is the scriptural account, and, as far as the book is concerned, the one cannot be separated from the other. Nor must we forget, as a confirmation, that the Israelites were forbidden to carry on ordinary war in the same ruthless fashion : in other cases they were enjoined to resort to the usual expedients which temper its inevitable horrors. In this case alone they were to recollect they were not so much warriors as executioners.

But though we cannot deny, if we open our eyes to the facts of God's administration of the world, that the destruction of these doomed nations is parallel to many of the appalling calamities with which, in His providence, He visits it ; it may be thought that, though *God* may be competent to do such things, it *cannot* be competent to Him to commission men to do them. But if it be competent to Him to do them ; if He can do them, and rightly do them, and vindicate His doing of them, is it quite so certain that in no case will He make men His agents? Or how is it more incomprehensible than His employing (as He perpetually does, though without any express commission) one nation to be the scourge of another? The difficulty, therefore, in this and every like case, is not so much a difficulty of Scripture, as a difficulty of the Divine Government in general ; and we shall be able fully to solve the one when we have solved the other, but not till then. So long as a man believes in a God at all, the objection is fully met by the "analogies in the constitution and course of nature ;" and if he will be consistent in urging it, he must abandon not only the Bible, but his theism.

A difficulty again has been found in the enjoined sacrifice of Isaac as "a test of faith." In my judgment, infinitely greater difficulties have been made in attempts to get rid of it by some of the utterly incredible versions of the history suggested by modern criticism ;—one of which is, that so far from Abraham's "faith" being "staggered," or there being any occasion for "staggering," he acted in blind but willing obedience to it ; only it was a pagan "faith," from which ("friend of God" though he was) he had never been redeemed ;—the faith in the acceptableness to God of human sacrifices ! I must say that to me this interpretation of the history is abundantly more difficult to digest than the ordinary one, even when taken in all its literality.

If it be said to be morally impossible that God should have exacted this proof of the patriarch's faith ; that though God could blamelessly (as no doubt He can, for He does it continually) have taken away an only and darling son "at a stroke," yet He could not command a parent to take that life away as a test of obedience, even though He never *intended* the sacrifice to be made, one cannot help asking on what principle this is affirmed? If God can *rightfully* do such a thing, and does it continually for reasons unknown to us, are we certain that He could not, for like unknown reasons, enjoin Abraham to be the agent, although He never intended the command to be acted upon ? If it be said that God had given Abraham a certain *moral* nature, which made it impossible that he should do (even though God enjoined it) what God might *blamelessly* do, we must take heed lest we stultify the argument which argues the *character* of God from the analogous moral qualities found in ourselves. If there be those analogies, then, though we may justly believe that there are still many things which, not having God's unlimited wisdom and authority, we may not do, while He may, it will not be so easy to believe that, in spite of these moral analogies, there are many things which, while God can blamelessly do them, man may *not*, even when God commands them !

Mean time, we must not forget that not only did God never intend the sacrifice to be made, but the Scripture shows that Abraham himself was convinced that, even if he obeyed the command to the letter, his Isaac would still be restored to him He believed that even in that case God in some strange way would restore him from the grave. This is represented as the very triumph of his faith, and a mighty faith undoubtedly it was. "By faith Abraham" (says the Epistle to the Hebrews), " when he was tried, offered up Isaac ; accounting that God was able to raise him up, even from the dead ; from whence also he had received him in a figure ;"—that is, as the child of miracle and " of promise," both of which confirmed his faith that (whatever might be present appearances) " in Isaac " still would all the Divine pledges given to him be fulfilled.

Some have said, " Well, human nature will not and cannot believe in the reality of this history, on account of the moral paradox it involves." But then the question must be asked—*What* human nature ? Is it human nature, born only yesterday, and still developed only in a few individuals ?—for until quite recently the generality of readers, and the generality of them even now, have felt no difficulty in receiving the history. If it be said they must all be supposed to be morally obtuse, can we believe the great majority of mankind to have been so in reference to so fundamental a principle of morality ? Have myriads of the most enlightened and virtuous minds in successive generations, and among them, the Apostles James and Paul, both of whom applaud the act of the patriarch as an act of heroic virtue, been utterly in the dark ?

Until the modern objectors can prove that their moral instincts, and not those of the founders of Christianity and the generality of mankind, are right in this matter, it is a simple begging of the question to say, as has been so often done of late, that this portion of the Bible presents an insuperable moral difficulty.

§ 4. A well-known sceptic as to miracles, but a truly candid man, and of first-rate scientific reputation, confessed to a friend of mine that he saw no reason in the nature of things,—none in our intuitions or in our deductions from them,—why miracles should be regarded as either impossible or incredible. He said he imagined that the physicist was prone to think so, because from the habit of contemplating phenomena in which uniformity of antecedents and consequents obtained, he could not refrain from coming to the assumption that nothing that was at variance with that limited, though constant experience, was possible. This frank confession, I apprehend, exactly represents the truth of the case. The dogma in question is a hasty generalisation from very partial data ; nay, in the last resort, from the data of *individual* experience ; for, if a miracle be incredible except verified by experience, each man would be justified in disbelieving them unless *his* experience had also verified them. But though this candid opponent gave a true account of the matter, the " prejudication " and " anticipation " of the "possible" or " credible " from so inadequate data, is no less a violation of true science than any of those which Bacon has so severely judged as amongst the errors of the vulgar philosophy. The impossibility or incredibility of miracles is one thing ; their impossibility or incredibility to minds that have superinduced that belief on themselves by certain habits of thought, is quite another.

The impugners of miracles will never be able to do justice either to their adversaries or themselves until they bear in mind : First, That what is required to prove their point is, not a precarious generalisation from a limited experience, but a demonstration of the impossibility or incredibility of miracles, founded either on such intuitions as all universal or necessary truth is based upon, or on logical deductions from them. This is constantly asked for, but as constantly declined ; and consequently the debate goes on. Secondly, That the question really is not, as they are too apt to represent it to themselves, whether it is more probable and credible that the ordinary sequences of phenomena should take place or be broken,—whether, for example, it is more probable or credible that a dead man should remain in his grave, or return to life ?— for there is no question about this ; but whether, if the exceptional events called miracles be not impossible or incredible, sufficient reasons may not be assigned (in the communication and authentication of a Divine revelation) which fairly meet their antecedent improbability ? Admitting that miracles are not impossible or incredible, then, as Paley has admirably shown, the improbability of their occurrence is no greater than that of God's vouchsafing to give us a revelation. Whatever reasons make the last credible, will make the other credible also. Admirably has Paley argued this point in the Introduction to his " Evidences."[1] Thirdly, The opponents of miracles must also bear in mind, that if a revelation

---

[1] " Mr Hume states the case of miracles to be *a contest of opposite probabilities,* that is to say, *a question whether it be more improbable that the miracle should be true or the testimony false ;* and this, I think, a fair account of the controversy. But herein I remark a want of argumentative justice, that, in describing the improbability of miracles, he suppresses all those circumstances of extenuation which result from our knowledge of the existence, power, and disposition of the Deity ; His concern in the creation ; the end answered by the miracle, the importance of that end, and its subserviency to the plan pursued in the work of nature. As Mr. Hume has represented the question, miracles are alike incredible to him who is previously assured of the constant agency of a Divine Being, and to him who believes that no such Being exists in the universe. They are equally incredible, whether related to have been wrought upon occasions the most deserving, and for purposes the most beneficial, or for no assignable end whatever, or for an end confessedly trifling or pernicious. This surely cannot be a correct statement."—Paley's *Evidences,* p. 5.

be given at all, then, unless it be made known specifically to each individual mind,—which, however, since a revelation is itself miraculous, would be but the multiplication, and not the suppression of miracles,—it passes the wit of man to imagine how it could be unexceptionably made known to those who had not personally received it, except by such means as miracles. But on this I have briefly spoken in the text.

The credibility of "miracles" has no doubt been much debated in the present day, and perhaps a larger number of persons than at any former period have been disposed to adopt the negative side of the question. Yet I must profess my conviction that their scepticism is not due to the force of any novel arguments. When thoroughly examined, the general objections are found to be identical with those which were currently used long ago. Nor is there anything in the discoveries of modern science which really affects the ancient conditions of the controversy ; perhaps it may be even said that much which is held as unquestionably true by a certain school of *savans* should in candour lead them (whether they admit the possibility of miracles or not) to concede that the chief argument usually urged against miracles ought not to be listened to, simply because it is abundantly contradicted by their own scientific hypotheses. For what, after all, is the *palmary* argument (now as of old against miracles? Is it not that they are inconsistent with that experience which teaches us to expect similarity of antecedents and consequents in the phenomena of nature, within the limits of variation authentically made known by that same experience ? and that no such variation as would be *transcendental* to such experience is to be admitted. Now, this is to be taken as universally and immutably true, or it is not. If it is, then there is really nothing for it but to adopt some theory similar to some of the exploded dreams of ancient Atheism ; and to hold not only that all idea of *creation* is chimerical, but that of a gradual *development* of the universe, such as modern science contends for ; that is,—of organic and inorganic natures, under conditions and by a series of metamorphoses altogether transcendental to experience. Nevertheless, this is a favourite speculation, in the hasty prosecution of which science has often been betrayed into oblivion alike of the maxims of Bacon and the practice of Newton. But if we are to go strictly by experience, we can admit nothing but a constant succession of phenomena, such as we now see, within those limits of variation of which that same experience can take cognizance.

If the above axiom is *not* to be taken absolutely : if we are to believe, either in any *origin* of things at all, or in a series of transformations of which a tadpole may have been one term and man another ; then there have been immense periods of the unknown past in which phenomena were occurring which utterly elude our conception ; of which we have, and can have, no historic trace ; and which are beyond and beside all our experience.   If so, then let men dispute as they will, they without doubt concede that which carries with it the refutation of that cardinal maxim on which the possibility of miracles is usually denied, or the probability of their occurrence asserted to be incredible.   For, let it ever be remembered that the validity of the above argument against miracles really depends on the *unlimited application* of the principle it involves, and has nothing to do with the question of *time*.   If a man were raised from the dead, even though a thousand years be supposed to be occupied in the process, it would be no less a miracle than if he had been raised in a moment, because the *fact* would contravene all our experience.   Similarly, the wondrous metamorphoses asserted to have taken place by processes which transcend the sphere of all experience, are by that very fact incredible, if miracles on the like account be so.   They are not less miracles in the sense of contradicting the axiom in question, than a miracle technically so called. It is granted that such phenomena as are implied in the conception either of " creation," or of a gradual " evolution " of the universe from two or three " primordial germs " (though how these are got without " creation," no man can say), differ from what are technically called miracles ; but not in that *one* point which makes them all alike incredible, if miracles be so.   An event, contradictory of all present experience, which demands a thousand or a million years to bring it about, may be different from an event equally contradictory of present experience, which is instantaneously wrought ; but they differ not at all in this,—that if either has occurred, it refutes the fallacious *criterion* on which the impossibility of all miracles is made to depend.   As far as *that* goes, both stand on the same level, and if the one be incredible, so will the other be. If the possibility of miracles is to be disproved, it must be by some other principle than one which will serve equally to show that the process by which the world was either " created " or " developed," or *originated* in what way soever (for all the modes contravene all our experience), is incredible likewise.   The only escape from the rigorous application of *experience*, within the limits of variation itself

prescribes, will be one of those rejected theories which once main
tained that day and night have eternally succeeded one another ;
that generations of men have been infinite, and that neither the
dead nor the living came first ; and that that ancient problem,
"which was first, the hen or the egg ?" has no meaning, for that
neither was before the other, and both from everlasting !

Neither will that *principle* of the mind, on which all the obstinate
prejudice against miracles is supposed to be justified, bear the
weight attached to it,—I mean the *expectation* (as Butler calls it)
"that things will continue as they have been, unless we have
reason to conclude that they will be otherwise." That such a "law
of expectation" does operate upon us, must be conceded ; and,
indeed, unless some such law had been impressed on the human
mind, it is impossible that such a creature as man, in such a world
as this, could have existed to any purpose at all. We could not
have anticipated that even the near events of the future would
be like the past ; and memory, and the experience it garners for
us, would have been of no use. But *what* this law is, *whence* it
springs, and how far it rightfully extends in its anticipations of the
future, it has infinitely perplexed metaphysicians to explain. Some
say it is itself the result of experience. If so, it palpably cannot
transcend experience ; it can neither guess at the unlimited past
nor anticipate the unlimited future. And, indeed, that its limits
are very restricted, whatever its origin, seems sufficiently proved by
the caution with which men in general apply it. "The morrow,"
say they, "will be as this day." Yes ; but you cannot get one in
a million (who yet, if the principle as urged against miracles were
correct, *ought* to affirm it with undoubting dogmatism) to affirm
that the experience of the morrow will be that of an eternal succession of to-morrows, or that the experience of yesterday was that of
an eternal precession of yesterdays ; that the sun, for example,
which set last night, has so set from everlasting ; or that, as he
will rise to-morrow, so he will rise *in secula seculorum.*

Others affirm that the said principle is not a result of experience,
but an anticipation of it. Even so, it seems to be of limited application. It is not of the nature of the intuitions on which we base
the knowledge of what is called necessary truths ; for that would be
inconsistent with the ready way in which the mind strengthens or
relaxes its hold on the principle, according as the future is near or
remote. No man believes that two parallel lines, if they be but
produced far enough, will meet ; nor that there is probably some

world in which two intersecting right lines will, if produced far enough, intersect again, or in which the three angles of a triangle are greater or less than two right angles. Some, therefore, are disposed to think that this general tendency to anticipate that the future will resemble the past, is arbitrarily inserted in our mental constitution as a necessary condition of our activity (since without it all experience would be in vain), but requiring to be itself corrected and limited by experience. If so, we need not wonder that though in general a safe and true guide, in relation to the near and constantly recurring phenomena of daily life, it hesitates to extend its inference either to the unlimited future or the unlimited past. Anyhow, it has no such predominance as either to prevent the ready belief of supernatural events by the great bulk of mankind, or to induce them to apply the principle in question without limit to the past or the future.[1]

It is in vain to say, as has sometimes been said, that in whatever direction, in whatever department of nature, the scientific eye now glances, it sees no miracle, and that all is subordinated to "law.' This is no refutation of the assertion that there have been miracles,

---

[1] This principle, the nature, origin, and legitimate operation of which are metaphysically so obscure, which looks at all events so much like an instinct arbitrarily inserted for a special purpose, and which men dare not apply without limit to past or future, resembles an intuition of a necessary truth as little as can well be imagined, and certainly seems an unstable foundation for the weighty inferences suspended upon it. The characteristics of this tendency of our nature, and the insecurity of the reasoning founded upon it in disproof of miracles, have been admirably treated by Dr. Mozley in his " Bampton Lectures."

On one point, by-the-bye, he seems to me to have conceded too much to his opponents. While contending, and justly, that the idea of successive " creations," or the introduction *per saltum* of new species, involves similar conceptions with miracles, he seems to concede that if a *savant* adopts that *fluent* theory of unlimited transformation, by which (for aught we know) anything may by gradual change be evolved out of anything ; by which antecedents lead, by absolutely continuous steps, to utterly unknown and indeed unimaginable consequents, the said *savant* escapes the above difficulty. On the contrary, it seems to me that our author might have said that the difficulty is then at its *maximum ;* that if a miracle be that which contradicts our experience, the world of perpetual flux is the world of " miracles " *par excellence.* Dr. Mozley, indeed, justly argues that the *fixity* of the present (and of all historical ages) must be accounted " miraculous," if the theory of universal *flux* (resembling that of Heraclitus, with which Socrates and Theodorus make themselves so merry in the Theætetus) be true. But it is equally clear that if the criterion of the incredibility of miracle be founded on the unchangeable relations of antecedents and consequents, that ductile state of the world which such a theory as the above involves must be conceived as a perpetual miracle. None can tell what consequents will follow from what antecedents: so far from the "law of expectation " being in operation, no one can say what we may expect, or rather what we may *not* expect ; the experience of the moment could only justify us in saying that nothing *is*, but everything is *becoming* something else.

which, having fulfilled their object, have ceased and will not recur. To argue against miracles from their cessation, is like arguing that volcanoes, long extinct, were never active. No one contends that the miraculous is now to be expected, any more than the repetition of those primeval processes which (whether people contend for the hypothesis of "creation" or of "development") must have taken place at some time, however unknown to experience now.

The usual uniformity of antecedents and consequents in natural phenomena is freely conceded ; and, indeed, always has been felt to be the general "law," even in ages, and among nations, in which the belief in the miraculous has been most excessive and irrational. Uniformity, as the *law*, has been the universal belief ; the "miraculous" having been held to be the exception to the rule,—occasional and temporary deviation from the law. I am aware, of course, that the contrary has been sedulously inculcated by many modern sceptics, who would fain persuade us that it is only within the last few generations that any just conception of "law," as presiding over the phenomena of nature, has been attained by the human intellect ; that, till our modern *savans* taught them better, men's general belief was that every effect depended on a variable and capricious will. "It is necessary to bear in mind," says M. Rénan, "that all antiquity, *except* the great scientific schools of Greece, and their Roman pupils, believed in miracles ; that Jesus not only believed in them, but had not the *least idea of a natural order regulated by laws.*" [1]

It is, of course, only to point the argument against Judaism and Christianity, that he admits that some *approximation* to the idea of "law" was found in the philosophic schools of Greece and Rome, though Christ and the Jews had no notion of it ! Now to say nothing of the fact that belief in miraculous phenomena,—of their occasional intrusion into the sphere of ordinary experience,—was equally shared by Greeks, Romans, and Jews, it may be easily shown that among none of them was such belief inconsistent with a clear recognition of prevailing "law,"—a conviction that the "miraculous" has been the exception in every age and nation of the world. This is equally proved, whether we look at the matter *a priori*, or by the light of history ; whether we reason from that very principle by which the existence of the preternatural is denied, or from the history, philosophy, proverbs, or any nation, ancient or modern.

[1] "Vie de Jésus," p. 257.

For, first, *If* that principle on which the impugner of miracles relies, be true ; if, by the very constitution of the human intellect, it is impelled to believe that nature is uniform in her operations, and that what we have seen to-day we may expect to-morrow and always, it could not but be that the general idea of "law" would be developed in all men,—however it might be (as it doubtless has been) qualified by the belief of the exceptional "miraculous." If it be said this is doubtless true, but that this is not the idea of "law" contended for ; that what is meant is such a "law" as never has been or will be departed from,—that is, a law which is exclusive of all "miracles,"—then, whether such a "law" is to be predicated or not, is still the very question, and to assert it is simply to beg that question. But that the bulk of men have arrived at the idea and conviction of the *general* law of uniformity, is beyond a doubt ; and, indeed, if it were *not* so, we must admit that the asserted necessary "law" of the human mind, which uniformly prompts to this belief, has failed,—which would be something as unaccountable as a miracle itself! It is as though it was contended that the faculty of vision or the appetite of hunger was a principle of human nature in general, and yet that whole communities of men for many ages showed no trace of either, and that it is vain to look for more than partial traces of them before these last ages.

Secondly. If we look at history,—the proverbs, the maxims, the conduct of mankind,—we see the same thing, as we might well expect to do ; for except for the general operation of that same principle which leads to the conception of this "law," there could have been no calculation of the future and no rule of action at all ; there could have been no assurance that the events of the morrow would resemble those of to-day. It would be easy to adduce a thousand citations from ancient writers of Greece and Rome, to show that their general idea of the stability of nature, in spite of the influence of their superstitions—superstitions quite as rife as were ever imputed to the ancient Hebrews or to mediæval Christianity—was as decided as our own. That the writers of the Old and New Testaments very distinctly participated in the same conviction, is plain from numberless passages, of which it will suffice to cite two or three : "As long as the earth endureth, seed-time and harvest, summer and winter, day and night, shall not cease ;" "He appointeth the moon for seasons, and the sun knoweth his going down ;" "Do men gather grapes of thorns or figs of thistles? a good tree cannot bring forth bad fruit, neither doth a corrupt tree bring forth good fruit;" "Thou hast established the earth, and it abideth;" "They continue for ever according to thine ordinances, for all are Thy servants."

In short, man's asserted ignorance of "law" in past ages would have been utterly inconsistent with that "law" in *himself,*—the tendency to believe in the uniformity of nature, which is yet supposed so strong as to teach him that miracles are even impossible!

But if the world in all ages has admitted the fact of nature's *general* uniformity, it has not believed in it so as to exclude the "preternatural,"—though contending that it is *exceptional.* It has known nothing, on the one hand, of universal caprice in the phenomena of nature,—as some modern speculators affirm; and as little, on the other, of absolute scepticism about miracles. Whether those who utterly exclude the preternatural be not as unreasonable as those who too readily admit it, whether there may not be a *juste milieu* in this matter, evidence must determine. The fact of men's undoubting assent to the general law of uniformity, combined with the facility with which they have also given assent to the occasional "miraculous" and the impossibility of getting them to assert that the uniformity of phenomena has been or will be an eternal uniformity, indicate that there *is* such a moderate position, and form a presumption that it is the true one.

It may be worth while to notice a certain modern objection to miracles, plausible, but assuredly shallow, since it subsists only by abuse of terms. By a studied, but most arbitrary, antinomy of "law and will," some sceptics urge, that to suppose God working miracles, is to suppose that He acts by a "will" that is opposed to "law;" in other words, that His will, as ours is apt to be, is arbitrary and capricious. But this, in truth, is a most whimsical restriction, resulting from the most gross anthropomorphism. No such antinomy between "law" and "will" is imaginable by him who has worthy conceptions of the Deity. In the first place, if the universe be under the dominion of perfect wisdom, it is quite consistent with *that,* to suppose general uniformity of administration to be the law; but not so, to suppose that that administration can never vary, no matter what changes be supposed in the system administered. To illustrate by a familiar example: God has given "will" to us His creatures; and the very action of *that,* if abnormal, may involve variations from what would have been the normal rule of His administration, had our will been obedient to

His. If "law" that *ought* to have prevailed, has by *truly* capricious "wills like ours" been infringed, it may be the part of a wise and benevolent Governor to adjust His administration to that fact; to vindicate the laws thus broken, and correct the evils thus introduced into the universe; and, for aught we know, Revelation and Miracle may be instruments to that end. There is no caprice in will thus exercised; the caprice would rather be, if it did not so act. A "capricious" governor would be one who did *not* vary his administration as circumstances required, however true it may be (as it will always be) that a wise government will be administered in a course of general law. But, secondly, there is another fallacy involved in this objection. It loses sight of the fact that to *infinite* wisdom there is, strictly speaking, no such thing as "law" and "exception" to it. These are relative to *our* conceptions. To infinite wisdom the same perfection of reason reigns in the minutest details,—in apparent deviations from general law as in the most conspicuous uniformities. Everything ordinary, or as to us it may seem exceptional, will, as Butler says, be administered according to "general rules of wisdom," and will be equally comprehended in the Divine plan.

To affirm that "will" and "caprice" are inseparable, is futile. Will, founded on the perfection of knowledge, wisdom, and power, is the most stable thing in the universe; and what the author just quoted says of "Goodness," may well be said also of *that.*[1]

[1] A sufficient justification of miracles is found in the authentication of a Divine revelation; but even independently of that, a man must be very confident to affirm that they *might* not be at some times desirable and expedient, if God is not to be absolutely forgotten by His creatures. The principle which enjoins us to believe in the absolute and immutable uniformity of the material machinery of the universe, is not, it is true, inconsistent with theism. But it has an unquestionable power of concealing God from us, or inducing the belief that He, too, is in bondage to fate. Man, indeed, is a creature whom it is hard to satisfy. If all things "continue as they were," he is apt to say that God exists not at all, or, if He does, takes no interest in the universe. If miracles were frequent, and the stable order of things often interrupted, it is all but certain he would soon say that "chance" alone governs it.

UNWIN BROTHERS, THE GRESHAM PRESS, CHILWORTH AND LONDON.